SIMPLE COURAGE

SIMPLE COURAGE

A TRUE STORY OF PERIL ON THE SEA

FRANK DELANEY

R A N D O M   H O U S E
L A R G E   P R I N T

Frontispiece photograph of Captain Kurt Carlsen, from the
Leigh Bishop Collection, reprinted with permission.
Photographs of **Flying Enterprise** on pages TK and TK
reprinted by permission of Bettmann/Corbis. Photograph of
Flying Enterprise on page TK reprinted by permission of
AP/Wide World Photos.

ISBN-13: 978-0-7393-2662-6
ISBN-10: 0-7393-2662-7

**The Library of Congress has Cataloged the Original
Edition of this work as follows:**
Delaney, Frank
Simple courage: a true story of peril on the sea / Frank
Delaney.
p. cm.
ISBN: 1-4000-6524-0
1. Carlsen, Kurt. 2. **Flying Enterprise** (Ship).
3. Shipwrecks—North Atlantic Ocean. I. Title.
G530.C297D45 2006
910.9163'37—dc22
2006041766

www.randomlargeprint.com

FIRST LARGE PRINT EDITION

10 9 8 7 6 5 4 3 2 1

This Large Print edition published in accord with the
standards of the N.A.V.H.

Dedicated to the Carlsen women:
Sonia Carlsen Fedak
Karen Carlsen Mueller
and their mother,
the late Agnes Carlsen (1911–2005)

PROLOGUE

THE BEAUFORT SCALE TAKES THE weather's blood pressure. At the bottom of the scale, Beaufort Force 0 indicates a sea as calm as glass; and at the top, Force 12 defines a hurricane—which takes its name from **hurakán,** the Caribbean Indians' term for "an evil spirit of the sea."

Admiral Sir Francis Beaufort, an Irish officer in the British Royal Navy, launched his thirteen classifications in 1838 and, in his original construction, the scale estimated the wind's speed for ships under sail. Almost as soon as he published it, the meteorological scientists of the day began to debate and refine it; over decades, they made many adjustments, including breaking Force 12 into the five categories by which hurricanes are assessed today.

Eventually, the London Meteorological Office took it further. To give a rounder picture, its officials addressed the scale in joint sea and land terms, and they couched it in accessible images. For example, the Force 0 of Beaufort's mirror-calm sea has, on land, an air so still that "smoke rises vertically." Next, in a Force 1 at sea, we get ripples "but without foam crests," while on land we have "light air. Direction of wind shown by smoke drift."

These comparatives rise gently through the levels and grow impressive when the wind strengthens. A long way past the "small wavelets" and "leaves rustle" of Force 2, we reach the "strong breeze" of a Beaufort Force 6, at which point "large waves begin to form." On land, this translates to "whistling heard in telegraph wires; umbrellas used with difficulty." Force 7 is called "Near Gale. Sea heaps up with white foam from breaking waves." Onshore, as the British meteorologists delicately put it, this level of gusting makes "inconvenience felt when walking against the wind."

Now begins the true ramping up: Force 8, "Gale Force"; Force 9, or "Severe Gale"; and Force 10, "Storm Force," which introduces "very high waves with long over-hanging crests." The English Meteorological Office observers say that a Force 10 is seldom experienced inland; but if it is, expect to see "trees uprooted."

After that, if you're out anywhere under the sky, everything becomes a matter of luck. A Force 11, "Violent Storm," brings with it "exceptionally high waves—small and medium-size ships might be for a time lost to view" and, on land, "widespread damage."

Finally, we have Admiral Beaufort's Force 12: "Sea completely white with driving spray; visibility very seriously affected." On land: "Hurricane."

Mariners, naturally, think of these categories with more feeling. When Force 10 is reached, the waves climb, the crests roll over and hang like ornamental scrolls, and the wind whips the water into foam. This is the moment when the sea seems to turn completely white and the swell seem sluggish, almost torpid—until it finds something to hit.

And this is when visibility begins to shrink. Culled from the spume that looks like milk spillage on the surface of the ocean, a stinging, obscuring spray begins to fill the air. At Force 12, this thick white curtain blots out what little vision you had until then, and the sea under your hull seems like a heaving carpet of liquid snow. And you gasp in a Force 12, because the wind hits your face at anything between fifty and a hundred miles an hour. Merely to breathe, you have to turn your face away, into the lee of your shoulder, and make a pocket around your mouth with your hands.

If you're on the North Atlantic Ocean in

such a gale, and if the temperature is heading below the freezing point, and if, much earlier, as the wind was building, you supposed the flecks of foam and the lengthening spindrift no more than pretty whitecaps—think again.

As the wind climbs, do not stare at the ocean; it has now turned a lethal white that will feel like pins in your eyes. The view that you had gazed on earlier when it was green on gray or blue on blue, and calm or heaving gently or even thumping in a swell—this has become a foaming, pulsating ice field. But the sight is so compelling, so liquid, so fast and savage, and, in the daytime, has a light so beautiful and preternatural, that you'd almost risk the stabbing blindness just to glance at it.

In which case you will expose yourself to further danger. The gale can pick up a knob of that white foam, freeze it, and skim it over the waves. It might as well be a steel arrowhead; the salt compressed in that glassy shard of ice will flay your skin to the cheekbone as though a savage had aimed it straight at your face.

Any seafarer out in such conditions knows to wrap up, turn away, and—only if essential—negotiate the decks of his vessel with the care of a tightrope walker. Otherwise: Stay inside. Those who have a right to be out there, the gulls and the whales and the other marine species—it's their home. Man is the one who is mortally out of his element.

IN LATE DECEMBER 1951, the upper reaches of the Beaufort scale took control of Captain Kurt Carlsen and his ship as though they were the playthings of the winds. He was thirty-seven years old, and his cargo vessel, **Flying Enterprise,** had fallen foul of a hurricane in the North Atlantic. She listed grievously, far over on her port side. Dense green waves lashed her tilting decks, and a thick veil of that opaque white spray hung in the air, cloaking visibility and deepening the darkness. With her masts bent and her radio antennae in shreds, the black freighter rolled in pain like a dying beast.

Now Carlsen had to deny this biblical tempest any further gains—he had to save the lives of his ten passengers and forty crew. One of his lifeboats had been shattered—it swung loose and useless like a broken limb; the other hung too close under the listing hull to be launched safely. He sent out a Mayday, and a variegated fleet of ships, from all around his part of the ocean, changed course and steamed toward him to help.

When they arrived, Carlsen then gave the

order that no master ever wants to give: "Abandon ship." The crew led the ten frightened passengers out of the cabin block of **Flying Enterprise** onto a deck that tilted at an angle of sixty degrees, on a ship dipping so low that her masts—what remained of them—sometimes touched the sea, a broken, out-of-control vessel that might go down in a sucking vortex at any moment.

The passengers—four men, five women, and a boy—slipped and slid, here and there; nobody could walk across those slanting decks without tumbling down far and fast. Instead, each movement required a lurch as far as the next handhold: the stays of a hatch cover, the nearest stanchion, a length of pipe. As the passengers grabbed, they held on so fast that they seemed stuck to these metal fitments.

And they needed to cling; otherwise the surges that kept pounding over the ship would swipe them off like debris. Not one of these people, passengers or crew, not even the captain himself, had ever been subjected to anything so relentless and fierce as the weather of those chilling December days. Earlier, Carlsen had addressed the passengers. In an unpanicked voice, he'd told them that they had fallen into great peril and that their best hope lay in embracing further danger—they would have to jump into the roaring waves. Mutely, they had prepared to do what they were told.

Now that their moment had come, Carlsen selected as the first to jump overboard a German woman in her early fifties named Elsa Müller. She would fulfill the sailor's traditional injunction for "women and children first." Her example would inspire: Who could dare refuse to follow this modest wife and mother?

Frau Müller reached the ship's rail, gripped it, and, hand over hand, inched her way along to where the captain stood, under the lifeboat he couldn't deploy. She wore only a nightdress under her coat; all her other clothes had been ruined by the storm when it burst into her cabin. The bitterly cold ocean swept over her bare legs again and again.

On the deck above, her family watched, fearing for her life. Curt Müller, a man of deep Christian faith, had been questioned more than once by the Gestapo and so had a working knowledge of fear. Beside him stood the Müllers' nineteen-year-old daughter, Leanne, and twelve-year-old son, Lothar.

Captain Carlsen, calm and matter-of-fact, handed Frau Müller one end of a rope. The other end ran down to the surface of the water, where it disappeared into the swell. Carlsen, fluent in German, told Frau Müller that a lifeboat, from a rescue ship standing nearby, waited on the other end of this line, that the boat had already come in, had thrown the rope aboard the ship, and would presently come back for her.

From where she stood at the rail, this quiet, obedient woman saw no rescuers, but Elsa Müller understood how to make a leap of faith; she had, after all, embarked on this voyage to create a new life in the New World—with the Mormons in Salt Lake City. Every possession that the family owned in the world was stowed in the flooded holds below: twelve pieces of modest luggage. And she had now placed her life in the hands of this young sea captain with the level voice and strong Danish accent.

Carlsen helped Elsa Müller clamber onto the rail, where she sat looking out at the terrifying sea. The rope trailed from her hand—and still no boat materialized through the spray. The captain delayed and delayed her jump, waiting until **Flying Enterprise** came up again briefly from the almost horizontal pitch to which she had rolled. Then, through the spray, Carlsen saw the lifeboat, tapped Elsa Müller's shoulder, and called out a blessing.

PART ONE

1.

IN THE NATIONAL ARCHIVES OF THE United States in Washington, D.C., lies a dense report—several inches high of typed papers—on top of which rests a separate, summarizing document ten pages long. This is "the record of the Marine Board convened to investigate subject casualty, together with its Findings of Fact, Opinions and Recommendations." Dated February 26, 1952, and signed by "P. A. Ovenden, Chief of the Merchant Vessel Inspection Division in the United States Coast Guard," this official prose contains no hint of the magic energy that conceives a legend.

Mr. Ovenden's conclusions, sent by the Coast Guard to the chief of Merchant Marine Safety, begin by observing that a welded freighter named S.S. **Flying Enterprise** "departed from Hamburg, Germany for New York on 21 December 1951, loaded, among other things, with 762.6 tons of pig iron in No. 2 lower hold and 508 tons of pig iron in No. 4 hold."

Flying Enterprise, a freighter in the class known as "C1-B," was built in the Wilmington yards at Los Angeles by the Consolidated Steel Corporation and released from the shipbuilder's yard to the War Shipping Administration on March 18, 1944. (The man who stamped her brass registration plate made an error in the date, and his original "1943" is overstamped with "1944.") She had the registration number 245133 and the combined signal and radio call sign KWFZ. After the war she went, in January 1946, to the U.S. Maritime Administration, where she was named **Cape Kumukaki.**

On April 25, 1947, **Cape Kumukaki** became one of twelve vessels in the Isbrandtsen Line, out of New York, owned by a buccaneering Scandinavian, Hans Isbrandtsen, who, to echo the old sailing clippers, used the prefix **Flying** for all his cargo ships. He had accumulated his fleet largely by purchasing, at bargain prices from the U.S. Navy, those ships no longer required for the transport of wartime supplies. For this, his competitors in the bare-knuckle freight shipping business disliked him—largely because he had stolen a march on them.

His son, Jakob Isbrandtsen, thinks today that **Flying Enterprise** "must have been one of the last of the C1-B class. They weren't great freighters; they were too small and too slow."

Yet they were not, in a landsman's terms, insignificant ships. Here are **Flying Enterprise**'s vital statistics, which become crucial to her poignant history. She had three decks and two masts; her length, stem to stern, was 396 feet, her breadth 60 feet, her depth just short of 26 feet; she had 4,000 horsepower, weighed 6,711 tons, had a range of 15,000 miles without refueling, and had a cruising speed of 14 knots (equivalent on land to 16 miles per hour, a knot equaling 2,027 yards per hour).

You will not find anywhere in her papers the astounding fact that S.S. **Flying Enterprise** once became the most famous ship in the world—a renown that lingers, especially among career sailors. And among men who, inside themselves, can still be boys: for us, this cargo ship, longer than a football field and painted jet-black, became and remained part of our inner lives. In the typeface named Cheltenham, the white name ISBRANDTSEN stood ten feet high along her sides, with FLYING ENTERPRISE inscribed smaller on her bows; for two weeks these thrilling words dominated the conversation of the planet.

She was that most romantic of sea creatures, a tramp steamer, and after departing New York on November 24, she called to Philadelphia, Baltimore, and Norfolk, Virginia. Now, almost ready for the homebound leg of her twenty-seventh voyage, she sat patiently, being loaded in Hamburg on the shortest day of the year.

I WAS NINE YEARS OLD in December 1951; and, if a shade too shrewd for Santa Claus, I believed in everything else: miracles, the power of magnets, haunted houses, the truth of all stories, time travel. As do all wary children, I watched everything—my parents, my seven older siblings, the sky above my head. On good days I believed that every time I ran anywhere, the globe of the world spun faster under the pressure of my feet. On bad days I looked for ways of escape.

Soon, this American ship in a German harbor, and a sea captain whose name had a hero's ring to it, would take and maintain a grip on my romantic but uneasy world. In the way of only the most inspiring stories, **Flying Enterprise** and Carlsen, her skipper, would, in effect, bear me to the eventual safety of great example. In the process, I developed a permanent near obsession with this man and his ship and the legend that grew up around them.

Although my family lived solidly inland, I

already had a strong awareness of the sea's wonder. Limerick, the city of my mother's birth, has a port on the river Shannon, Ireland's largest waterway, which runs on down to the Atlantic on the southwestern coast. The Shannon estuary favors big ships—or at least they seemed big to me when my grandfather first took me down to see them at Arthur's Quay.

He was known to all in that small city—Stephen O'Sullivan, six feet four, benign as a sultan and with what he told me was "grass" growing under his nose, a bushy mustache. None of the menace that I already felt in life, and the daily fear that I already knew, came from him. This big, warmhearted man ate breakfasts that were world-famous in our family: steak and eggs, bacon, sausages, blood pudding, fried bread, fried potatoes, mushrooms if he could get them—his plate looked like a market food stall. He himself cooked this huge dawn feast, to the accompaniment of bawdy songs, which, to my mother's consternation, I picked up.

Mischief clung to him. Steve Sullivan drove trains but refused to handle the honored carriages bearing Queen Victoria around our province of Munster. "Let her drive it herself—it'll do her good," he said. Of humble origins, he married a woman of substance, but all his life he refused her trappings—the furs, the cruises, the haughty friends. He smoked a pipe hour upon hour, with the most rancid tobacco ever rubbed—a cut plug that stank, as he said, "like a hoor's boot."

On our walk to Arthur's Quay that day (I was about five years old), he told me to watch out for "a gent on a bollard." This was an old sailor who pulled a stunt for passersby: he would pare his own plug of tobacco with a hunting knife and then slam the blade vertically into his thigh, halfway above the right knee. There it stood, the white bone handle projecting from the unbloodied blue of his canvas trousers.

That day we went down, the cork-legged sailor never showed. I went back many times on my own, but I never found him. Am I and my imagination the richer for not having seen him? In any case, my grandfather overturned my disappointment by leading me along the line of moored ships at the quay. I had never seen a ship before and we stopped at each and every one. Big, black, tawdry vessels they were, and the white paint had rusted on their housings, but I gazed up at them wide-eyed.

Each ship had a "load line," better known as a "Plimsoll line"—a legal, Egyptian-looking hieroglyphic running down the side into the water; my grandfather told me that a freighter must carry this to indicate how heavily she was permitted to load. To the small boy's inevitable "Why?" he told me that ship owners used to overload the holds with useless cargo so that the vessel would sink and they could claim the insurance, like people who had what he called "a good fire." And he then explained the term "a good fire." My mother, when I told her, grunted a knowing concern at my grandfather's mischievous ethics.

AFTER SHE LEFT AMERICA, **Flying Enterprise** "discharged and loaded cargo" (according to the Coast Guard report) "at several north European ports"; this included five tons of carpets loaded at Antwerp on December 10. In Rotterdam five days later, she picked up her pig iron freight, plus 447 tons of rags, 486 tons of coffee, six tons of onions and gherkins in brine, and seventeen tons of animal hair, listed as "bristles."

At the port of Bremen, she loaded thirty-nine tons of peat moss, a dozen Volkswagen cars, a few tons of birdcages—and a cargo of antiques, with eight early Chippendale chairs, a collection of Worcester china miniature pitchers, a gilded convex mirror decorated with the insignia of the British Order of the Garter, and a needleworked fireplace screen dated 1740.

These glorious pieces, in addition to Louis XIV furniture, a small orchestra's worth of priceless antique musical instruments, a handful of Old Masters, and some rare Belgian porcelain, were being shipped, port by port, to New York antiques dealers on Third Avenue and East Forty-seventh Street. Not detailed item by item, they came aboard under catchall terms such as "general" or "special" cargo.

By the time she was ready to sail from Hamburg, **Flying Enterprise** had also taken on such oddities as several hundred typewriters, as well as zirconium or zirconite powder, one application of which included the making of fuel for the U.S. nuclear submarine program. She also loaded thirty tons of the volatile chemical naphthalene, which is a coal tar product smelling of mothballs, used in the making of plastics and dyes; they stowed it on deck so as not to contaminate the foodstuffs in the holds.

Far from fully loaded (always disappointing to a ship owner), she was due to reach New York on January 3.

2.

THAT DOCKSIDE WALK WITH MY grandfather in limerick stays in my mind like a song. Like a shell held to my ear, or any of the commonplace magic that adults weave for children, it gave me a flavor of ships and the sea as piquant as the first taste of coffee or coconut. Pointing out the great hairy ropes angled down to the quayside, he told me that rats ran up along these mooring lines and into the ships; in the tropics, he said, the monkeys climbed them. He showed me the anchor and told me the word meant a crooked angle, a hook that caught in things.

When I worried about the rust marks on the white trim, he said that all sailors had to swear an oath to paint their ships constantly and that on some vessels, such as the great ocean liners, no sooner had the men finished than they had to start all over again, because the salt of the sea grew rust so quickly.

"It's how they learn patience," he said. "That's why they don't mind long days at sea when nothing happens. Sailors are very patient men."

He knew the Limerick stevedores—slightly confusing, given that everyone on the docks called him Steve. Then he told me, with huge authority, that they were all named after him, because he was the "Steve" who first showed them how to load the cargo down into the holds, and that he was famous because he could shove more cargo down a hatch faster than anybody else. I believed every word; I needed this whiff of adventure. The atmosphere of our household too often crackled with the bewildering terror of my father's hair-trigger rage, and even at that age I had begun to grasp the hope of the horizon. These ships, my grandfather said, sailed the world. And he spun the names of glorious ports as though they were foreign coins: Tangier, Hyderabad, Marseilles, Famagusta, Montevideo, Valparaíso, Cairo, Casablanca, Venice.

Their holds contained bales of silk, barrels of port, casks of brandy and wine, carved elephants of ebony with tusks of real ivory, huge crates of chocolate ingots that would later be trimmed down into chocolate bars, slabs of gold for the priests to melt down and make into chalices, bales of tobacco from which his own plug was cut personally, dancing shoes for men, corsets for, he said, "comfortable ladies," boxes of sheet music for the piano players of Ireland, and brooches of jade and necklaces of jet for their singers and sweethearts.

It never occurred to me to ask what customers existed for such exotica in Limerick (corsets excepted), because his talk boomed like a South Seas conch. And presently, my lessons in school supported his wondrous version of freight. The poem "Cargoes," by John Masefield, appeared on our English syllabus and Masefield's ships carried "diamonds, emeralds, amethysts, topazes, and cinnamon, and gold moidores." No reason, therefore, why these shabby old dames in their rusty black couldn't also bring back to the docks of Limerick "apes and peacocks, sandalwood, cedarwood, and sweet white wine."

Thus, in the afternoon of a child is a man's lifelong pathway of fancy and possibility opened up, like the moment when a plowman cuts a headland in a rich field. After that afternoon walk and its ships and ropes and anchors, and all the fancies of a beneficent and merry grandfather, **Flying Enterprise** with her valiant skipper, with the mysteries of their 1951 Christmas voyage (mysteries that I have

now at last solved to my own satisfaction)—
she made steam shipping at least as glamorous
as schooners and square-riggers and she had an
easy passage into my heart.

3.

FLYING ENTERPRISE HAD FIVE HOLDS,
each of whose hatch covers was the area of an
average living room floor. Every hold went
down three levels; if you fell from the bright
open deck to the darkness of the keel, you'd
have dropped off a three-story house.

Hamburg has long, gray wharves; they seem
to stretch for miles. As the last freight came on
board there that December afternoon, Carlsen
reckoned his ship little more than a third full,
with individual loads distributed here and
there in the holds, many of them according to
their shape and nature. The Volkswagen cars,
for instance, had arrived in Bremen un-
crated—they were, in effect, "parked" on the
second level in the No. 3 hold, close to midships, along with twenty-nine tons of steel
pipes.

Then, with sailing a matter of hours away, a

large cargo of U.S. mail came into Hamburg.
Mainly from American servicemen still in the
German postwar garrisons, there were seventeen hundred or so mailbags weighing close to
five hundred tons. The chief mate directed the
Port of Hamburg's dockhands and his own
crewmen to load this pile amidships too, in
No. 3 hold, which had a strong room for the
fifty sacks of registered mail.

Other valuable cargo had already come
aboard—consignments that have contributed
substantially to the half century of questions
hanging over **Flying Enterprise.** They included registered and unregistered packets
containing international currencies, unspecified amounts in liquid stock certificates, and
more than a thousand watches. These valuables
arrived from Switzerland and Belgium, addressed for New York, and when the nature of
this freight was later identified, conspiracy theorists seized upon this detail (among others) as
a possible explanation of Kurt Carlsen's "inexplicable" behavior.

Her cargo as a whole, both in form and con-
tent, plays centrally to all considerations of
Flying Enterprise. The boatswain, Arthur
Janssens, from Washington Heights in New
York City, had already challenged the way the
ship was loading on this voyage. Back in Rot-

terdam, he had questioned the decision to put the pig iron in Holds 2 and 4. The ship, as everyone knew, was sturdiest in front of the engine room, where she had been built strongest to accommodate the plant, the generators, the huge boilers—in other words, right amidships at Hold 3.

Now, with all the U.S. mail going into Hold 3, the boatswain raised the stowage issue again, and used the word "misbalance." The first mate referred the question to the captain, who overruled the boatswain; Carlsen cited orders from the owners of the shipping line and support from their Hamburg agent.

If Janssens had prevailed, they would have had to redistribute some of the pig iron from Holds 2 and 4 into Hold 3, and as they did not have the time to do that (or the money; dock labor is costly), the boatswain's arguments faded—for the moment—on the cold quayside air.

Did he have a valid point? In the final stowage plan of **Flying Enterprise,** she can be perceived densest with heavy cargo at the upper two levels, the "tween decks," of Holds 2 and 4. Both holds also had open space, fore and aft, on their lower levels. Not ideal, this combination of weight and empty air; no freight skipper likes it. It means, obviously, that his ship is not employed as profitably as she could be. It also means that, **in extremis,** there's room for loosely stowed cargo to shunt about, especially in rough weather.

THE WORD "STOW" derives from an ancient European word for **place**—it crops up still as a suffix in England: Bridestow in Devon, Felixstowe in Suffolk. I know this because my grandfather's induction also brought to me a fascination with the language of the sea.

He said the word **mate** came from **meat,** from the person who sat beside you at the table, from the meat that he ate with you. (Even though lacking—or not caring for—the finer points of etymology, he wasn't all wrong.) The word **inundate,** he told me, comes from **unda,** the Greek word for **wave.** A fathom, he showed me, stretching wide in his black three-piece suit and silver watch chain, is the measure of the arms across the body from fingertip to fingertip, because **fathom** or a word like it (**fadom**) was the old northern European word for **embrace.** The "boatswain"—he said "bo'sun"—was the boy who looked after the ship's ropes. Sadly, I later discovered that the term **stevedore** came not from my grandfather's name, as he blithely avowed, but from a Mediterranean word, **stivador**—one who stives or stows.

By twilight that Friday afternoon, **Flying Enterprise** had stowed all she was going to get on this trip. To an expert underwriter, the freighter might have seemed a touch canted at the dock: her bow was eight feet higher than her stern. But such tipping, though never ideal, represented no great abnormality.

Frank Bartak, the chief mate, came from Maple Heights, Ohio. He answered to the captain for the loading of the ship; a captain is not a crew member—he is the ship owner's representative aboard. Bartak professed complete confidence in his stowage. He had drawn up the cargo plan, which he then, under orders, "before leaving Hamburg, or with the Hamburg pilot before the ship left the Elbow [sic] river," sent by mail to the Isbrandtsen office in New York.

The New York Coast Guard inquiry questioned Bartak closely about his work methods. (His testimony—and the evidence of several witnesses—was recorded verbatim by the stenographers at the inquiry.) The chief mate seemed to have total recall of how he had handled his cargo in each port. "You see, you have to conform your loading to the routine you have in Rotterdam. They have these motor trucks and they ride in, and if he has one big lot he stows it, he makes it fast, and we will stow it fore and aft athwartships."

Bartak was describing the swiftness and efficiency of the Dutch port workers, who lowered big electric trucks down the hatches, dropped the cargo on their flatbeds, and then ran the trucks all over the holds, where Bartak had the stevedores and his own crewmen distribute it. The holds in these freighters were as big as a school gymnasium.

Many of the Coast Guard's questions focused on the Rotterdam stowage—on how differently, in two of the five holds, the ship had loaded her cargo of pig iron. It consisted of heavy ingots. Some were four-inch-thick oblong slabs measuring eighteen inches long by six inches wide, as big as a tall old Bible. And some of the ingots were oval with a domed top and flat bottom. All, in crew opinion, weighed about five pounds apiece.

The inquiry board questioned Bartak insistently on the way in which the stevedores had actually distributed the iron. (Janssens, the boatswain, hadn't yet given his evidence, in which he said that he had raised the same query.) Although each quantity had been correctly placed at the appropriate level of the appropriate deck, and sensibly spaced along the length of the ship in Holds 2 and 4, their positioning within each hold differed.

Hold 4's 508 tons of iron was spread out evenly and flat; it lay in equal and regular piles, and this received general approval. In Hold 2, however, the iron pigs made something of a rectangular pyramid; the 762 tons stood up like a ziggurat directly beneath the hatch of Hold 2.

Then they spread out what was left in lower, flatter piles that tapered out across the floor of the hold to the side of the ship. Lying flat, and no more than one, two, or three pigs high, this distribution represented no problem, because it couldn't fall over. The tall pile beside it, though, had no more stability than a tower of bricks. Bartak defended this "pyramiding."

"It wasn't very high," he argued. "I was down there in the hold." But it was, he agreed, tall enough to be noticeable—"six, six and a half feet high." A difficult load to manage, "it was dropped in the middle—while loading—with grapples, and pushed in the wings." The handlers, waiting below, had already spread the smaller, flatter piles out across the floor of the hold—but they left the bulk of this pile standing upright, more or less as the cranes lowered it.

To "soften" the iron pyramid, the peat moss

bales and some of the coffee sacks were piled aganst the ingots. Before leaving Rotterdam for Bremen and Hamburg, the chief mate also, in a customary procedure, made his crew, assisted by locally hired carpenters, fence it all in with wooden spars, or "cribs," to keep that portion of the cargo from shifting—as if anything of any devising could have controlled anything on that ship in the days that were to come.

Bartak was the one person aboard **Flying Enterprise** who had a complete grasp of how the ship was loaded. If they could have scanned his mind, the board of inquiry would have seen an exposed side view of the ship showing the piles of these little chunks of pig iron on the floors of two holds, one consignment flat and spread out wide, the other in a tall, peaked, and somewhat irregular stack. And they'd have seen the piles of burlap sacks of coffee here, there, and everywhere, and the ungainly consignments of peat moss and grass seed swaddling but not quite sandbagging that zigzag pyramid.

The chief mate used the same loading method on all the decks below. Where a cargo needed packing, anything soft went to cushion the harder materials, to keep them from moving or crashing into other freight. Effectively, he used cargo to protect cargo, so that his ship could do her job and bring home the bacon. In the classic tradition of stowage, cargo becomes its own dunnage.

The word **dunnage** (which may or may not come from a corruption of the word **thin** in its meaning of **insubstantial**) embraces any materials planted under or beside cargo items to keep them dry—or, as in this case, wedged among other freight items so that nothing turns into a loose cannon. Typical dunnage in a general-freight ship has adhered to the more or less universal guidelines of marine commerce, and dunnage by itself has enough weight to be reckoned a factor in assessing a ship's loaded tonnage.

During loading, a sharp-witted mate will keep dunnage in mind all the time, and he should know what the regulations require for the stowing of certain freights (and if he doesn't, his master will). Some foodstuffs, for example, such as rice and tea, traditionally called for bamboo housing. Where a cargo has known fragility or possible mobility, no matter how well packaged, the mate uses soft dunnage; on **Flying Enterprise** they deployed the sacks of coffee and several tons of grass seed.

The cleanliness of dunnage also has great importance. When scorpions, tropical beetles, snakes, or baby crocodiles turn up unexpectedly in places where they don't belong, sailors know that they probably came aboard in the dunnage, which can include sawdust; coconuts; all kinds of wood, including rattan; wads of old sacking—anything that will pack around objects with comfort. Dunnage, in short, amounts to a kind of ad hoc bubble wrap dating back centuries. **Flying Enterprise** had a varied cargo, and therefore her stowage required much—and mixed—dunnage.

THOSE WHO OWN, insure, and handle ships assume that the loading will be expert—as well as economical in terms of labor costs. They hope that her cargo will be housed in her holds prudently and securely, fenced and firm and shored against shifting, her dunnage deployed astutely. They assume that everything possible will be done to ensure the safe passage of everyone and everything on board.

At the same time, they acknowledge openly that they carry out all this work more in hope than in confidence—because they know that no matter how expert they are, no matter how hard they work, they do not have the last say. And they do not have the last say because every ship in the world is entirely subject to two greater forces. This pair of Greater Authorities will undo the best cargo plans ever drawn, will scorn the tightest, sweetest dunnage ever packed, will splinter the neatest cribs, will overrule the best deckhands, the best stevedores, the best longshoremen, the best mates, the best masters in the world.

That is why, throughout generations of marine commerce, the names of these two overriding powers have appeared in the last phrase of every freight-shipping contract. Cargo vessels depart from the dockside "Subject to the Will of God and the Perils of the Sea."

4.

AFTER MY GRANDFATHER'S MAGICAL captivating introduction to the sea by way of cargo ships and ports, I couldn't get enough ocean lore—ghost ships and tall ships, harpoons, whalers, rafts, mermaids and messages in bottles. I learned how to tie knots: a black knot, a bowknot, a hitch knot. My grandfather claimed, "It's the one thing women can't do and it annoys them; they can't tie a knot."

Like so many boys of that age, I dabbled in Morse code and learned the most exciting dialogue in the theater of the sea: SOS, three dots, three dashes, three dots. I long believed that it meant "Save Our Souls" or, possibly, "Save Our Ship." It meant neither; the Germans chose it for emergencies because the particular Morse sequence proved easy to memorize—a regrettably prosaic derivation. Robert Louis Stevenson, Herman Melville, Joseph Conrad, and myriad other seafaring writers created their own oceans in my mind. Tantalizing ghost ships sailed across my nights, the **Flying Dutchman,** the **Mary Celeste,** empty and chilling, steered, very possibly, by the Ancient Mariner, circled on high by his accursed bird. And, real and alive, and therefore almost most wondrous of all, an old lady in the next parish had made it to the lifeboats of the **Titanic.**

She constituted one of my two most direct encounters with the ocean's drama; the other arrived by air. From time to time, on the prevailing west wind, an egregious seagull landed in the fields near our house, obviously a long way from his base. He alighted on a tuft of grass as though it were the crest of his own personal wave and sat there unperturbed.

He troubled me; with his harsh yellow bill and glittering eye he glanced at me like a little white-suited mugger. And he brought with him an acrid lick of reality; the gull had flown inland, said the people, to escape a storm at sea. On those rare and uneasy days when I saw him in our fields, forty miles at least from the Atlantic—those were the times when my mother recited her family prayer: "Heaven help the sailors on a night like this."

FLYING ENTERPRISE COMPLETED her loading early in the afternoon on Friday, December 21. With just over four thousand barrels of fuel aboard and nearly four hundred barrels of fresh water, she caught the Hamburg evening tide. Fog came in—no surprise in the north of Germany. The helmsman, with Captain Carlsen standing beside him at the wheel, eased the ship's black nose out into a thick gray blanket. Hamburg has a winding port, which enables ships to "feel" their weight before setting out on the long ocean haul.

By the time the Elbe flows into Hamburg, she has traveled over seven hundred miles from the Giant Mountains on Poland's borders. This river has always worked for her living, a trade route of large ships, with every cargo imaginable. The hospitable and deep central draft, navigable from the North Sea deltas back down to Prague, makes her one of Europe's most effective waterways. Beyond Hamburg the river first tapers into a long, winding estuary and then widens out like a fan.

Throughout that first night, Captain Carlsen stayed on the bridge as the Elbe's banks crept by in the fog. The spiked mines of the war still bobbed in the sea-lanes of Europe, and even though the keepers of the river had swept a course, they had not succeeded in creating a straight one—but they had marked all remaining ordnance with warning buoys. For the next thirty hours Carlsen never took his eyes off this course; he wanted to make sure that he navigated every one of those lethal porcupines. And so, early on Saturday, December 22, we find **Flying Enterprise,** muffled and all but invisible, leaving the soft jaws of the Elbe, gliding slowly into the North Sea, about to change course from northwest to southwest, looking for the moment when she can at last turn her face west toward New York.

"From Hamburg to the English Channel the vessel encountered continuous heavy fog and the master deemed it impractical to hold boat drills," said the U.S. Coast Guard report. Understandably so; in that visibility, the crew would scarcely have been able to find the ten passengers had they ventured on deck.

These "civilians" had boarded on the morning of sailing. A cargo ship was allowed up to a dozen fares—thirteen and she'd have been reclassified as a passenger ship. Though obviously less suave than a liner, **Flying Enterprise**—and many freighters of the day—offered a reasonable travel deal. Carlsen's voyagers, European emigrants, all had relatives or friends waiting to accept them into the New World.

The ship's "Manifest of Inbound Passengers (Aliens)" lists them with their luggage. Curt and Elsa Müller and their two children, Leanne and Lothar, all registered as "German." Leonore Von Klenau, a thirty-nine-year-old photographer, was listed as "Danish" and had "3 cases, 2 trunks and 3 parcels." Rolf Kastenholz, a twenty-seven-year-old German accountant, hoped to meet his father for the first time in twenty years and had "2 trunks, 1 suitcase." Nina Dannheiser, aged fifty-six and also German, stowed "10 suitcases, 3 parcels"; she also carried a small, fluffy white dog.

The "stateless" Nikolai Bunjakowski, age fifty-four, had "8 collis" (a now archaic word for a package or bundle). Seventy-year-old Frederic Niederbrüning had "1 trunk, 1 case, 2 collis." And Maria Duttenhofer, age forty-five and German, had "3 trunks, 2 suitcases and 2 collis"; she was listed as "single," as were all the others except Mr. Niederbrüning and the

Müller parents; Mrs. Dannheiser and Mrs. Duttenhofer were widows. All of their possessions except their most immediate cabin essentials were listed as "general" in the cargo manifest and stowed below. And all found their cabins roomier and more comfortable than the word **freighter** might connote.

THAT FIRST SATURDAY, the watch changed as usual, in its universal way, every four hours. By then, all ten passengers had succumbed to some of the weather's dank torpor, and the Müllers and Mrs. Dannheiser and Mrs. Duttenhofer and most of the others left their cabins only—and not always—to go to the saloon at mealtimes.

Sensible travelers facing a long sea voyage prepare mentally. After the first romantic thrill of embarkation, the unprepared passenger feels, to begin with, massive boredom—nothing to do, nowhere to go. Until landfall, the limits never change: that distant, permanent line of horizon defines all. An experienced or prepared passenger sets a schedule for every day at sea, plots the number of hours spent reading, eating, walking on deck, looking out to sea, and does not rely on the other passengers for diversion. Many fear to socialize aboard, lest seasickness become a humiliating fact.

Now and again, an incident out on the water will call every passenger to the side in excitement: a passing ship, a school of creatures showing off their arcs and prancings, a gossipy piece of flotsam—cords from a torn old net, a bottle, a spar of wood, loose wheels of weed. Seabirds will drift over, and if there's a thunderstorm, lightning will likely find the ship, because to its vicious fingers—indeed, to all of the sea's wanderers—you are, for that moment, the nearest solid point in a constantly shifting world. And at sea, many people sleep better than they can ever imagine, with an unforgettable quality of soft, safe oblivion.

ON SUNDAY, DECEMBER 23, the fog began to lift, and showed **Flying Enterprise** the English Channel, twenty-one miles wide, frantic with history and ships. The busiest sea west of China, this strip of water gets as frazzled as a city street; craft warnings crowd the frequencies.

Every veteran sailor knows to respect the Channel, and to fear the weather in her approaches. Sure enough, early on Monday morning, as though to prove the Channel's love of chicanery, the fog came in again. Carlsen, who had grown up within the moods of northern Europe, knew how to deal with this; he also knew that these waters, though fully swept for mines, had a notorious reputation for collisions, and he slowed down, half speed ahead, followed by dead stop.

Then a wind came in from the northwest, a wind so disrespectful that the weather forecasters immediately began to track its threat. It saw the fog off—and saw it off fast.

Notwithstanding, "Captain Carlsen of the **Flying Enterprise,**" as the world was about to know him, began to relax. He left the bridge at last, went to his quarters, and took a little time off. When he awoke, he radioed his wife, Agnes, and his two daughters, Sonia and Karen, in Woodbridge, New Jersey, to wish them the compliments of Christmas. He said he would see them after he docked, in ten days' time. No, he would not.

5.

H ENRIK KURT CARLSEN BEGAN HIS seafaring on sailing ships. As a boy of fourteen, he got apprenticed to the square-riggers still trading grain out of Denmark in the 1920s. First a cook's assistant and then general deck-hand, he soon had to learn how to mend a sail.

When the salt spray drenched those old masts, the canvas got stiffer than a body in rigor mortis. Fingers broke, fingernails ripped, wrists sprained: nobody had hands like a sail-maker—that weathered, rough skin, those yellow welts deep as the cleats on the sole of a boot. By the age of thirty-seven, and long a skipper of steam, Carlsen had softer, almost cultured hands—but he still had calluses so thick and ridged that his fingerprints would have been difficult to take.

He never lost his sewing skills, however. While he was commanding a different Is-brandtsen ship across the Indian Ocean, one of his crew slashed off a shipmate's ear. Carlsen, using the ship's medical kit, sewed it back on, giving the man a proud lifetime badge: the restored lug stuck out at a jaunty angle. On another voyage, in another fight, a crazed sailor handed the third engineer twelve ghastly stab wounds. Again Carlsen's needlework saved the day, and for the rest of his life the third engineer proudly bared the railroads of stitches on his chest. Nor had the strength in Carlsen's hands diminished. Even though others now did the rough work on board his ships, in the **Flying Enterprise** crisis he took a thick steel cable in his hands and hauled it in.

He had the physical characteristics of the south Scandinavian islanders: thick, Viking-blond hair, blue eyes, excellent skin, and a stocky frame, height about five feet six inches. And he had the bandy walk known as "sea legs." Photographs of Carlsen show a serious man who smiled a lot. Generally he had a grave personality, with the dry and dark humor that marks the Danes. Imbued with the gift of focus, he looked straight ahead and stared down the tunnel of any task facing him. Men who get pitched against abnormal physical odds or who take on fierce challenges seem to share a concentration found on the borders of autism; they home in on the job at hand and use every cell in their bodies to clinch the thing.

However, some—not all—such men can adjust themselves from the extremes of that focus and, by use of personality, return to the ordinary world. Carlsen's strongly accented speech may have added force and a little mystery to the impression of authority, but he also had the gift of getting himself liked—all his life he could grin like a boy.

"He had what I call a real Danish personality; he had humor but he could leave humor aside and become very serious," recalled Jakob Isbrandtsen, who took Carlsen along as a crew member in a 1960s transatlantic yacht race: "Never once did he question my presence as the skipper of the boat."

On that voyage, Carlsen had extra value as a crewman on account of his communications skills. The amateur-radio boom had come into its own during his lifetime at sea; he embraced it totally and became an expert "ham"—a perfect pastime for a man of tight rein, this intimate yet distant medium. And he used it well. On one level it simply brought him friendship—all over the world. In Hamburg, for instance, just before he weighed anchor in December 1951, a local ham, knowing that W2ZXM/MM had come into port, called to see him at the dockside. Their visit would have a noticeable and quirky reverberation in the events that followed.

He also used shortwave in his personal life.

Ben Stevenson, Carlsen's oldest surviving friend, lives in Colonia, New Jersey, his memory still fresh at the age of ninety-four. Early in their friendship, Carlsen asked Mr. Stevenson, who had nothing to do with the sea and ships, if they could speak by radio every day. In the course of these conversations, from everywhere on the globe to New Jersey, Carlsen would ask Ben to forward a message to the pregnant wife of a sailor, or the ailing mother of a passenger. Above all, by means of Ben patching the short-wave calls ingeniously through to the family telephone, Carlsen spoke to his own wife and daughters every day, no matter how far away he was. And when his greatest crisis arrived, his fellow radio hams all over the world tracked his fortunes.

He came from the village of Bagsvaerd, near Copenhagen. This used to be feudal country, terraced with small houses of rural folk who worked the land. These people were natural Calvinists; they adhered to creeds that set limits to sensuality and leisure, because they believed work and its products crucial to life and to answering a great practical question: How can such a small country, with such minute holdings of land, make its living? They answered by setting standards. For example, Danish farming became famous for its milking parlors of pristine hygiene. From their curds and whey, they didn't make mere cheese; they spun gold.

With a father who did local odd jobs, no silver spoons had appeared at his birth. After schooling, Carlsen could go in one of three basic directions. He could work for local farmers, who were numerous and industrious. But ever since the eighteenth-century divisions of land in Denmark, the farms had been too small to provide significant labor income, and most farmwork would at best prove merely seasonal. He could also move to a city and toil in the black mills of industry. But Carlsen had formed open-air tastes in childhood. So even though Bagsvaerd lies inland (if "inland" can ever apply to Denmark), he therefore took the third main option: he went to sea.

His father liked to tell a story of Kurt Carlsen at age thirteen, walking along the dock at Elsinore, near Hamlet's castle, looking up at the moored ships. A sailor on watch asked the boy to take over for a few moments, and thus was Kurt Carlsen hooked. Not that he needed such direct initiation; many of those Danish village boys dreamed of mastering an oceangoing vessel. A sea captain had a lofty status in that society, and still does. When Carlsen received his master's ticket, he became a local hero, even though it soon took him away from Denmark—to the United States, under whose flag he would sail for most of his life.

After his apprenticeship, Carlsen joined the Danish navy and got his AB docket before he was eighteen—young for an able seaman. Six months later he enlisted as a cadet in the Danish Merchant Marine Academy in Copenhagen, a training school with one of the most demanding sets of academic standards on the northern European seaboard. Cadets seeking the highest qualification of master mariner needed to speak and read fluently in at least two international languages, have a first-class grasp of the finer principles of navigation, understand and prove competent to operate all steamship machinery, and become at least familiar with some of the Law of the Sea.

Out of this education and out of further experience on ships, Carlsen was awarded a Danish master's license in October 1936, at the age of twenty-two, and an American master's license in May 1947, at the age of thirty-three—young tickets in any seas. By then, his seamanship had the soundest and most comprehensive foundations. He excelled in radio communications; he knew how sail powered a ship; and he had triumphed as a student of steam. In practical terms, he knew how to do almost every job aboard. From the moment he received his Danish ticket he won commissions and began to sail the world.

When discussing Carlsen's character, those who knew this even-tempered man with iron in his frame, this serious man with the dazzling smile, those who worked alongside him, who sailed with him, who lived with and loved him—they all seem to reach for the same phrase book. They begin with such words as "determined" and "forceful" and then they hesitate. Each one knows that Carlsen had those properties in abundance—but each also knows that such words cannot tell the full story.

Ben Stevenson recalled to me Carlsen's steadfastness in his sense of authority, his strictness in leadership. Once, the Stevensons joined Carlsen's ship at Puerto Rico, on the last leg of a voyage. When they came aboard, Carlsen said to them, "Here, we are not equals. I am the master and you have to do as I say. That is how it is on a ship and I hope you never have to discover why."

Captain Charles Weeks, who now teaches shipping in Bangor, Maine, sailed with Carlsen for two years as a second mate. "He wasn't a martinet," Captain Weeks said. "I never heard him raise his voice. But when he gave an order, you knew he had given an order and you knew that he expected it to be carried out."

Those standards, duty and aspiration to duty, ruled Carlsen's life. He was known to hold fierce opinions of sailors who malingered; entries in his logs show him tracking down a crewman's "illness" until a doctor proved or dismissed it. And his American-born daughters describe how he tartly corrected their grammar—in his strong Danish accent.

Finally, every question about him—to family members, to shipmates, to friends, to anyone who knew him—produces the same general answer: "What you saw was what you got"—as though Freud and Jung would have excavated Carlsen in vain for buried strata. In the events that defined him for the world, he did indeed turn out to be what he seemed.

CARLSEN SPECIALIZED IN finding or improvising good solutions—he took stock of a situation and used his instincts to back up his experience. As a prime example of how the two worked together in him, consider his old motorbike, manufactured twelve years earlier, a Zündapp (much beloved of the panzer regiment outriders). No matter who hooted at it,

Carlsen sang this bike's praises. He took it with him on his voyages because it got him around a port fast and easily; he couldn't bear to wait on the dockside for a cab to take him to a consulate. And if his radio batteries failed, he could power his shortwave off the bike engine. (He also owned a much more impressive Harley-Davidson.)

All who recall him remark on his steady, level way of looking people in the eye. Not short on asperity, this was not a man given to false emotion. Though a tender family man, he could be rough as stone tearing a strip off a lazy crewman—or standing up to a ship's owner. He was a friendly parent and a warm neighbor, but some of his crewmen had difficulty in liking him. He never allowed them behind his own barriers of command; he maintained a firm, almost fierce distance. Thus, as with all men capable of heroism, he had a birthmark of paradox.

Carlsen was a man who would always have done his duty—but would resent anyone who told him to. A human being who respected the working seaman deeply, he once crossed a longshoremen's picket line because he had an obligation to his employer. He had a deep, and in time utterly demonstrated, love for his wife and children, yet he spent most of his life away from them. He seemed an ordinary man, yet he possessed remarkable psychological strength.

Men who crewed with Carlsen often heard him say, "When you have lived all your life at sea you can't have fear for the seas. You have a profound respect for the elements, you learn to respect them because you know what they can do. But you can't fear them. If you do, then you can't go to sea."

In forty-three Atlantic crossings during twenty-three years, in voyages through the Indian Ocean, the Pacific, along awkward estuaries, by difficult coasts, threatened by uncertain shorelines, he had seen the water and the weather rage. As with so many mariners, his blood and bones told him that the sea lacked, in the words of Joseph Conrad, any "respect for decency."

6.

ON CHRISTMAS EVE, AFTER HE HAD finished speaking to his wife and children, Carlsen returned to the bridge. The sea had come up with the wind that blew away the fog.

"In the English Channel, heavy weather was first encountered on 24 December," says the Coast Guard report. It came from the southwest, "generally Beaufort force 6 or 7, probably reaching 8 at times. Becoming westerly force 5 or 6 near midnight on the passage of a cold front. Weather—mainly fair or cloudy at first with drizzle and rain spreading from the west later. Cloud breaking about 2100 GMT and then fair conditions with an occasional shower."

Plowing the waters not far from Carlsen that day, a British cargo ship, S.S. **War Hawk,** made the following entry in her deck log: "Day overcast with squalls about 11 A.M. . . . Heavy and rough confused seas from W'ly to NW'ly. Winds increasing to force 7. Vessel rolling and pitching heavily at times. All deck and cargo hatches secure."

On Carlsen's ship, Force 6 proved highest that day, the comparatively milder weather described as "fair or cloudy with occasional showers, sometimes with hail or thunder." Yet by early evening, when **Flying Enterprise**'s passengers and crew tried to celebrate with the traditional turkey dinner, they had to give up. The heaving seas made the stewards lurch; the festive lights dipped and swayed. No one sat at the captain's table that night because he ate his

Christmas dinner on the bridge. In a short time, all the passengers ceased any attempts at festivity and returned to their bunks, either seasick or simply wishing to anchor themselves, to stop being flung about in this rising gale.

By daybreak on December 26, legions of European weather forecasters were issuing strenuous warnings, so graphic that no private vessel would have dared put out to or remain at sea; toward sundown, David Greene, **Flying Enterprise**'s radio officer, was picking up SOS messages. Carlsen had by now left the Western Approaches, where the English Channel meets the North Atlantic, and had headed out into the ocean.

The area facing him has a reputation for foul weather. In 1979, during the biennial Fastnet Rock yachting race, which traverses the same part of the sea, an unpredicted system of violent weather killed fifteen sailors and sank five boats. Not more than a quarter of those who started the race managed to finish, and it remains one of the most emotive tragedies in international sport sailing.

Steaming through here, Carlsen took **Flying Enterprise**'s speed gradually down to four knots throughout the daylight hours. At around three in the afternoon, with a dusk hastened by dense cloud, he decided to heave to, not just because of the weather but because he wished to reduce as much as possible the discomfort of his passengers, some of whom were less than young. (Like all men in their thirties, he considered the mid-fifties "elderly.") As night fell, the hell that had been threatening finally broke loose. The wind climbed to Force 12, the top of Admiral Beaufort's scale.

No matter how slow her speed may seem, a ship makes pleasingly good time at sea because she never stops. Even a loaded freighter, cruising at fourteen knots, is covering those fourteen knots every hour of every twenty-four hours. For all his enforced heaving to, and all his passenger considerations, by the evening of December 26 Carlsen had cleared Land's End, England's southwesternmost tip, by almost four hundred miles. At dusk, he entered his sixth night at sea, close to the halfway stage. He had sufficient experience to expect reasonably that the gale would blow itself out; for the moment he would depend upon seamanship.

In the radio shack, David Greene was still eavesdropping. Every weather office in western Europe said that early gusts had reached ninety-five miles an hour. The ether's gossip warned of a full-blown, flat-out phenomenon; this might turn as bad as any storm in the living memory of this untranquil sea.

Sure enough, it soon blew along every coast of England. It smashed small craft at their moorings, flooded the streets of towns, and carried roofs up into the night sky. Piers and seaside buildings on England's south coast were ripped out and rode away like makeshift rafts on the massive waves. Houses a mile inland were lashed with spray and found salt encrusted on their windowpanes. At Southampton the master of the famous Cunard luxury liner **Queen Mary** reported the worst conditions he had seen since 1914; concerns were voiced as to whether Winston Churchill, about to embark for New York, should sail.

Along the flat reaches of Romney Marsh, at the village of Dymchurch, near the port of Hastings, the army had to be called in. The sea breached defensive walls first built by the Roman Empire—and then lunged at the pleasant clapboard facades of the houses. (Two days earlier Carlsen had steamed past this pretty but unprotected little curved bay.)

Much farther west, at Falmouth, in Cornwall, gusts hit the land at 103 miles an hour. On the nearby Scilly Isles, a Swedish cargo ship, smaller and lighter than **Flying Enterprise,** lost power and simply drifted, shepherded by a Belgian ship that had hoped—but failed—to help. Around the corner, still heading west, in the Celtic Sea between south Wales and the southeast of Ireland, **Buccaneer,** a steamer registered in Panama, lost her screw and was being towed by a French tug, trying to reach the port of Barry in south Wales.

Several hundred miles due north of there, up in Scotland, the gale blew a steady ninety-nine miles an hour on the beautiful Hebrides, east of which, at Ardmore Point, as naked a headland as the Atlantic has ever stripped, the sea dumped a trawler on a sandy beach—"high and dry," her owner said. Over on the southwest coast of Ireland, a Spanish fishing ship, **Argentina,** foundered and went down with a loss of fifteen lives.

The fierce weather struck everywhere. Soon it built into a major news story; **The New York Times** observed that a storm in Europe had created "a cauldron that boiled from Scandinavia to the Iberian peninsula." My mother can't have been praying too hard; heaven wasn't helping the sailors that night. Dozens of ships foundered all along Europe's western seaboard. Off La Coruña, on the north coast of Spain, nineteen people vanished when the sea cut open the Norwegian oil tanker **Oesthav.** It could have been worse—from her severed front half, more than thirty people were taken off the tanker by another Scandinavian vessel.

At Biarritz, a Dutch vessel, **Gemma,** crashed aground outside the harbor, and her eight-man crew died. A German freighter went down in the North Sea with twenty-two dead.

An old, romantic trade description calls tugs, those tough guys of the sea, "the ocean's strong helpers." They weren't able to help much or many that night; in the ever-treacherous Bay of Biscay, the powerful **Zwarte Zee** out of Rotterdam drifted at the gale's whim, wounded in a crash with a Danish freighter. And in Hull, in the east of England, the waves swept two men from a tug's deck.

American meteorological records suggest that the great North Atlantic storm of 1951 did not originate in the English Channel on or around the time Carlsen was coming through. Its system seems to have risen on the eastern seaboard of the United States as perhaps the tail of a very late hurricane, dipped a little south, changed direction, and then moved across the ocean toward northwest Europe. At the same time, a different system was building in the south of the Bay of Biscay, down toward the Galician coast of northern Spain, and it may have come up and squeezed through the Channel, then out into the Atlantic.

On December 17, four days before **Flying Enterprise** left Hamburg, a German freighter,

Adolf Leonhardt, left Norfolk, Virginia, headed for Bremerhaven. The next day, she was overtaken by the American end of the storm and found herself in a Force 11; she raised the first alert about this fierce weather. She steamed on within the punishing winds and a week later, sandwiched between both weather systems, called for help because she had lost her rudder. A tug out of the Frisian Islands, north of the Netherlands, got to her on New Year's Day.

WEDNESDAY, DECEMBER 26, inched on, with **Flying Enterprise** deliberately stationary—"hove to"—for much of the time. During the night, the weather deteriorated astoundingly. The gale warnings on all sea and land frequencies intensified in their urgency as the wind rose.

On Thursday morning, in the hour before dawn, Carlsen stood shaving in his cabin. Under his feet, he could feel his ship rolling and laboring. Suddenly, he was pitched sideways by a terrific lurch; this was followed by a series of severe, flat thumps—**boom!boom!boom! boom!**—beneath his feet, as if the ship had been picked up and dropped on her keel two,

three, four times. Next, he heard a short series
of loud explosions.

Everyone on board heard them. Some crewmen said the noise sounded like an artillery
round or a "gunshell" after a "sudden plunge,
plunge, plunge," a "snapping" sound, "gunshots," a short fusillade of loud and sharp
"cracks." The chief mate, Frank Bartak,
thought it "like the report out of a gun."

John Edward Crowder, from Florida, held a
license of "Second Assistant Engineer, steam,
any horsepower." He was on duty in the engine
room at the time of the crack, and he testified
that "the ship was going through heavy seas
and was suddenly thrown from the water and
took a heavy pound. Was the heaviest pound I
ever seen. It was so severe it knocked myself,
the fireman, the oiler to the floor plates." The
pounding came from the waves slamming repeatedly on the underside of the keel, an effect
known to every ship in a storm. Crowder also
said, "This heavy pound—it was accompanied
by this snapping sound."

Flying Enterprise's older hands knew
straightaway what had happened. The weather
during the night had kept Arthur Janssens
awake, and at about six o'clock in the morning
the boatswain rose, went out to the mate's

room, looked around, and then went back to bed but didn't sleep. Less than an hour later, lying in his bunk, he suddenly felt the ship go up; she seemed to suspend herself.

At the inquiry, Janssens testified, "I says, 'She's hung like this' and then I heard a crack. So I says, 'She's gone. She's cracked.' So I opened my porthole, looked through the porthole, looked on deck and saw that the ship was cracked."

As the "gunfire" noises echoed across the sky, **Flying Enterprise** was thrust on her side as though kicked by a giant boot. The passengers fell from their bunks to the floors of their cabins, with their possessions flying all over them, and they thought that the ship was exploding. **Flying Enterprise** wallowed massively again. Janssens put on his coat, Bartak jumped from his bunk, and Carlsen ran for the bridge.

7.

IN THE THICK SPRAY OF THE STORM, with water flying everywhere, Carlsen could see nothing. Bartak went out on deck—and found as bad a development as a mate could report to a master. The "gunfire" had indeed been the sound of metal cracking; **Flying Enterprise** had snapped open amidships.

This appalling development preoccupied the U.S. Coast Guard: "After a night of pitching and rolling, without pounding, the vessel, at about 0630 on 27 December, riding high up on a heavy sea, suffered fractures. The cracking was heard in all parts of the ship. Examination determined that there were two main fractures."

Imagine the freighter as a long piece of wood. Now visualize a great savage ogre, hacking down on her with a tomahawk, twice, three, four times—but not quite slicing through. Or, reaching down and plucking the ship out of the water, the giant grabs the bow and stern in his huge grip and tries to bend the ship, in order to break her in half. She yields a little by cracking in the middle but she doesn't break and, like a child in a tantrum with a toy, he tosses her back in the water, on her side.

Flying Enterprise's metal plates split to the waterline. The fissure opened widest just behind the hatch of Hold 3, right at the ship's main superstructure, which houses the ship's "buildings": the wheelhouse, the accommodation block. From each of the front corners of the housing, a wide split ran across the plating

on both sides of the deck and tapered in thin
slivers down the ship's sides.

Not surprisingly, the metal opened where
the greatest weight pressed. To a layman, the
skin of a freighter such as **Flying Enterprise**
might seem inappropriately thin, especially
considering the trials of the ocean. The steel
plates on a Class 1 came to somewhere between an inch and an inch and a half thick.
Under the pressure of a torrent, this ship's central deck plates quite simply fractured. Carlsen
himself reported the noise as "a terrific, loud
snap like a pistol shot."

She righted herself after a fast, initial listing,
and sailors looking out of the accommodation-
block portholes could see the split. Robert
Lumpkins, a cook from Boston, told the inquiry board that it was "wide enough to stick a
silver dollar in edgewise." One of the passengers, Rolf Kastenholz, seasick like almost all
the others, also "heard a terrible crack"—and
Lumpkins told him to put on a life vest.

At that time, the seas were running forty feet
high from trough to crest. Each wave spooled
out as long as three hundred yards. If giant
hands had kept pressing down on the bow and
the stern, **Flying Enterprise** would have been
bent upward in the middle and would have en-

tirely split in two amidships, along this new, horrible fault line, and every person on board would have been catapulted into the air. But even though Carlsen knew that his freighter had suffered critical damage, he also knew that he had been lucky, because the cracks attenuated into hair-thin lines as they stretched down each side of the ship, toward the water.

In December 1941, in anticipation of American involvement in the Second World War, the president of the United States, Franklin Delano Roosevelt, famously launched a series of freighters as the supply vessels of the U.S. Navy. Since the first ship off the blocks had been christened **Patrick Henry,** after the Revolutionary War patriot who said, "Give me liberty or give me death," they became known colloquially as "Liberty ships," made, broadly speaking, to an original English model. They had riveted keels—but these proved liable to cracking under storm pressure. The C1 class, of the same workaday, workhorse design, had predated and then overlapped the Liberty ship, and the C1-B had been built with a welded keel, countering, it was believed, this tendency to split. And yet the Coast Guard experts concluded, from all the anecdotal evidence, that S.S. **Flying Enterprise** "on 27 December,

1951, in approximate position 50°41'N 15°26'W, suffered a complete fracture of the weather deck."

8.

INCLUDING OFFICERS, **FLYING ENTER-prise** carried forty crew. Some dozen of them had to do with engine work, including oilers and wipers—men who do exactly what it sounds as if they do: they oil the machinery and they wipe it clean. A steward and two messmen, who served and cleaned, supported three cooks.

Typically, merchant marine ranks descend from captain to first (or chief) mate, second mate, third mate, to fourth mate, able (or able-bodied) seaman, and ordinary seaman (also called "mariner one" in some seas). On this voyage under Carlsen, six able seamen sailed and three ordinary. As well as chief, second, third, and fourth mates, he had his boatswain, Janssens, who had been on **Flying Enterprise** for two years. (The boatswain ranks below the second mate.)

Carlsen learned the drama of the fracture at

the mate and boatswain levels. These were the seamen with sufficient training and experience to grasp that a cracked ship could crack wider and worse. Water had already flooded in through the fissures, and Janssens went forward to the bridge.

"I told the old man it was cracked. 'Where?' he says. I said, 'On port and starboard, just outside my porthole.' I didn't know yet that she was cracked on the after-end of number three hatch on the port side. I found that out afterwards." The boatswain then asked Bartak, the chief mate, to muster all hands on deck. "I said, 'You must get everyone out. This is an emergency case. My life is just as important as everybody else's.' So he says, 'What are you going to do, Boatswain?'"

Janssens knew what he was going to do: he was simply going to follow the captain's orders. Carlsen, the intuitive and practical man, told him—and saw nothing extraordinary in the suggestion—to try to lash the ship together again. The crewmen went out on deck, into winds above ninety miles an hour, into driving rain and spray, with waves up to forty feet high smashing over them. Using lengths of stiff cable and wooden blocks to tauten them, Janssens and his crewmen winched yards of wire around the bitts, the metal stanchions or bollards welded to every ship's deck for making fast anchor chains or deck cargo.

The boatswain reckoned that the crack at its worst point measured an inch and a half wide. If they succeeded in tightening it by at least half an inch, they would achieve a great deal. It might control the volume of water pouring in and keep it low enough to avoid drenching the mailbags in No. 3 Hold, directly below the crack. And it might save the coffee used as dunnage. And preserve the grass seed. And the bales of rags and the animal hair. And they didn't even know about the Old Master paintings and the Stradivarius violins in the steel container vans. Or the bearer bonds. Or the stock certificates. Or the cash. Most crucial of all, if they could reduce the volume of water that got in below, they would not only protect the cargo, they would prevent the split from widening further. So they winched, they hauled, they tightened wires from every available binnacle to every available spur, and gradually they could see the crack, at its widest stretches, squeezing closed.

Janssens now relayed the next stage of Carlsen's orders to his able and ordinary seamen: "Get a two-by-four and start to make a ladder, a scupper on both sides of the crack and secure them so that they can't be washed out."

Good boatswains work like magpies. They gather seemingly random objects and store them; later on, they press them into service, for stowage, dunnage—all sorts of purposes. Janssens had kept on board some balks of two-by-four timber from the day some months before when he had had to construct a catwalk for loading U.S. Army cargo in Norfolk, Virginia.

"I have been going to sea many years," he told the inquiry board, "and whenever I am able to get a piece of wood, I'll save it. It always comes in handy in emergencies."

When he was satisfied that the wires might indeed hold the cracks closed tighter, he had some of his crewmen use these two-by-fours to construct a frame, a breakwater, on either side of the most vital parts of the cracks. During this exercise, Janssens ordered other sailors to start mixing cement. He then had them pour the cement into this long, narrow wooden frame that ran across the deck over the fissures. They did this while being washed over constantly by waves falling across the decks, with whipping spray biting into their faces. In short, in the middle of a storm, Carlsen had asked his boatswain to repair a cracked steel freighter with concrete—and they had literally plastered over the cracks.

By now, the truth about the "gunfire" was spreading throughout the ship. Richard Cosaro, the third assistant engineer, described **Flying Enterprise** as his first ship. Age twenty-two, he had received his license only that very month—and he was now awakened by the steward, Ross Thomas. "He said, 'Dick, the ship is got a crack.' I told him he's crazy, I didn't believe it. He was kidding." Cosaro, who came from Chicago (and still lives there), said that by the time he got up to see the crack—he was going on duty—the repairs had been effected. "They had placed a canvas sort of a screen across the deck where the crack occurred in the deck," he recalled, "so the water wouldn't go into the crack [at] Number Three Hold. A canvas nailed to two pieces of board acted as waterproof covering."

Cosaro then traced the extent of the ship's damage.

"I hung over the side for a while, the crack extended down the garboard strake and it looked like it ended at the garboard strake" (the lowest part of the ship's side, the strip of planking or metal plates just above the keel). Whether it was repaired or not, he felt less than secure. "I couldn't be sure of her," he said. "I could hear the crack working once in a while."

In other words, even after being fixed, with

cement poured into the crack, with long, narrow wooden walls shepherding it, and with a canvas shield erected over it, the ship creaked along her new fault line—as if the same ogre that had split her had come back and was trying to force her open. So, to secure the job further, to stop the cement from fraying or melting in the flying waters, and to keep the deck water from leaking down to the holds, Carlsen then instructed the crew, as a final measure, to pile sacks of the volatile naphthalene from the deck cargo on top of the wooden breakwater, as extra protection over the fissures.

And it all worked. It all hung together. Luckily, the ship had righted herself immediately after she'd cracked. The pumps, after six or seven heaves, made the sucking noises that say they've run dry. As Janssens himself put it, "The crack and the leak caused by the crack, we had actually under control and she was not taking on any more disturbing amount of water than the bilges could take care of." In fact, one of his men went into Hold 3, found very little water, not more than seepage, and could not see daylight through the crack.

Carlsen still felt confident in his ship, even in that weather, even with her decks patched with still-wet cement. He also felt confident in his own seamanship and saw no need to declare an emergency or ask for help, and he wrote a signal that betrayed no panic, no anxiety—nothing but professional concern. Sent out with difficulty over that turbulent ocean, and delayed until David Greene, the radio officer, found a station that could receive it and then forward it, the message went at half past two—a simple notification to Hans Isbrandtsen in New York that his ship had cracked. No further details were included, and at four o'clock (eleven in the morning New York time) **Flying Enterprise** received an acknowledgment that merely said, "Your No. 8 noted." (The Isbrandtsen Line gave numbers to all messages from a traveling ship.) Later, a fuller reply said, "Please radio your dispositions or intentions."

AT SEA IN a gale you can do only two things advisedly: stand still or go forward carefully, perhaps making for port. Carlsen had already tried heaving to and had been punished by the sea for doing so. And he knew that if he reached the lee of a landmass without getting deep in by the harbor wall to a good mooring, his anchor might not hold under the pressure of the storm. As the lighthouse men know, the land is the danger.

This left him only the option, for the moment, of steaming on carefully; his position left him too far out for a realistic return toward a landfall. Sinisterly, in that bearing, south of Ireland's Cape Clear, the ocean runs roughest and deepest; here lies one of the northeastern Atlantic's fullest graveyards. Furthermore, Carlsen's course, common in transatlantic freight shipping, would soon take him across serious geological badlands. In the early eighteenth century, a wave of tsunami proportions arose from these waters and had the power and momentum to reach the southern Irish shore three hundred miles away.

A ship in a storm has the advantages with which she was constructed: her built-in marine dynamics, her checks and balances, her expected buoyancy. In a great storm, these assets begin to flake away, stripped off one by one. Carlsen, his ship severed, cut close to the bone, began to count his blessings. He remained afloat; indeed, the U.S. Coast Guard eventually observed that the crack "did not cause Flying Enterprise to founder." Any flooding below had been expelled with a few strokes of the pumps. He had survived a horrendous beating and stayed seaworthy.

Now he decided not only to continue the voyage but to set a salvation course. Hedging his bets against further misfortune, he turned south to get into busier shipping lanes, hoping, in case the ship did not survive, to be found by any traffic making for Europe through the English Channel. If worst came to worst, he might at least get his passengers and crew onto a passing boat.

In easier straits, with, if necessary, another vessel as shepherd, he might make it to the Azores, where he could put in for repairs. Brest, in France, southeast of him, also had possibilities, as had Bantry, to the north, in Ireland. Bantry, however, has a bad-weather history: an eighteenth-century Irish insurgency failed when gales blew away the French ships bearing troops to support the rebels.

Carlsen's own gale continued its appalling barrage. **Flying Enterprise** heaved and swung. Waves hard as marble slammed her hull. The captain came down from the bridge to meet the passengers, who had already heard that the ship had cracked. He made no effort to conceal the damage suffered by the ship, even though he believed that he could get to safe harbor. He would go on, he would find the lanes—or a port for repairs—and if the weather improved splendidly, he might even make his home port of New York.

Appearing at the board of inquiry, John Edward Drake, the first assistant engineer, described the crack as "like taking a heavy mall (maul) and beating a piece of sheet metal, just a sharp crack, something like that. Like it was hitting something solid instead of bouncing off." But Drake corroborated Carlsen's instincts. He believed that **Flying Enterprise** had every chance of making it to safety: "After the crack occurred [for] two days she stayed on even keel."

Not everyone else on board felt as easy. One of the able seamen, Clark Hall, from Kentucky, had been steering until an hour before the "gunshots." He put the time of the crack at "eleven before seven," and that afternoon he found himself approached by a number of shipmates. Hall had been one of "the spokesmen for the crew and a lot of times whenever they had any beefs, always went up to the captain, tried to settle them," he said. Now some of the sailors wanted him to do so again.

"Several of them begin to get a little frightened," he reported, "was coming to me asking what they was going to do and everything. So I went up to the radio operator's room and asked if they had sent out any sort of distress or standby message for other ships. That the crew, some of them wanted like, to see her head back the other way. Sparks, the only thing he sent out, was a message to New York, Isbrandtsen Company, that the ship was cracked, await for further orders."

In the radio shack, David Greene took Hall through the charts and showed him how far they now lay from the nearest landfall. "And then," said Hall, "I went back down and talked to the part of the crew in the messhall."

The criticisms had started. Many of the sailors now spoke openly. Why wasn't the skipper heading for a port—any port in a storm? Would he not turn back? Had he sent an SOS? Hall caught their fear. He had a wife in Germany; he knew she'd be worried by the weather reports and he wanted to reassure her.

"So I went back up to Sparks," he testified, "asked if he had received any message, he said 'No.' I told him I like to send one myself, personal message. He said he was sorry, he had to keep the wire off the line, keep it open, the message might be received from New York."

At this refusal, Hall continued on his mission to see Carlsen, even though he learned from the engineers that "the ship is making headway." Instead, he met another delegate, from the steward's department: "He just come out of the room, he say the captain was pretty much worried, it was no use to talk to him because he had too much on his mind. So I didn't bother him."

9.

FRIDAY, DECEMBER 28, 1951, DAWNED gray. the wind had dropped a little in the night. After showers of rain and hail, some nervous sunshine almost broke through. As the pale sun gained strength, the winds climbed again and veered from southwest to northwest— Force 9 to Force 10 to Force 11 to Force 12. By mid-morning, a vicious cold front was skulking across the sea like a man with a grudge.

Twenty-eight hours had passed since the deck had split open. The waves still ran high, twenty, twenty-five, thirty feet. No calm promised to come in; nothing looked as though it might subside, not the wind, not the water, not the spray, but Carlsen, on the bridge all the time and watching everything, found that his ship was laying very easily. "Not too stiff and not too tender," he said; she was "comfortable."

Carlsen understood that he must go on, yet he knew the direction he most needed would have the effect of taking him headfirst into this weather—not a good idea with cracked metals.

So, while staying within his general direction, he set a course that kept the wind and the sea just off center of the starboard bow.

In the huge **smack!** that opened the fissures, some **Flying Enterprise** passengers suffered minor bruises. They had been bounced out of their bunks, crashed into metal walls, landed on metal floors. Their hairbrushes, the books they were reading, their personal belongings cascaded on top of them. They were all frightened; they could see the size of the waves that were still hitting the ship.

Now the crew began to calm them: yes, the deck repairs seemed to be holding; and yes, the ship was making progress. Everyone cheered up just a little. Fearful, and in some cases miserable with seasickness, most of them elected to stay in bed as the waves went on lashing at the portholes.

The morning moved forward to eleven o'clock.

Every mariner in the world, every liner captain and lobsterman, every yachtsman, yawler, and trawler, every dinghy, dhow, and deep-sea fisherman has seen big seas. All sailors, male and female, serious and sport, will thus have known the experience of trying to escape those great, half-hanging waves that, in a "normal" storm, rear and fall—fall over themselves and all over every ship in their way. And all sailors have also known the roaring winds; they come, in every sense, with the territory. But few have encountered—and fewer have lived to describe—a different sort of wave. This wave will have the backing and grandeur of the vast ocean, out of whose depths it sucks its power, and it will have the direct support of the waves nearest to it, from whom it draws its energy. This wave will race toward you so fast that you can't get out of its way. It will loom far above you, drive straight through you, travel over you and continue beyond you, until it decides to subside into anonymity or break upon some far-off shore that you can't even see and, now, could probably never reach.

If it hits you instead of lifting you, that wall of water might as well be a wall of concrete falling across your decks: ask any sailor who has had a limb broken by the weight of water in bad weather. If its timing is such that you drop into the black valley of its preceding trough, you will disappear without a trace into eternity.

Today, this marine terror possesses an acronym and an official name: ESW, extreme storm wave; or, in the cruder language that better suits it, a "rogue" wave or a "freak." **Flying Enterprise**'s crack had surely been caused by an extreme storm wave—a freak, a rogue.

Believe it or not, Carlsen enjoyed relatively good fortune on the morning of the crack. Lloyd's of London estimates that more than forty vessels a year are lost to the savagery of the oceans—whether tankers or fishing smacks, they vanish mysteriously and without trace. For decades, no one would dare suggest what caused these inexplicable disasters. Today, we know, in many cases, what happens and what some mariners have always known. This ESW, this giant wave, an ocean phenomenon that was once no more than an undocumented—and doubtful—part of sailing lore, has become an established fact of marine science.

My grandfather's tall tales of the sea and ships belonged to a great tradition. Sailors have always been famed for their embellished yarns—therefore, who could believe an old salt describing a spectacular wall of water? Did he also see a mermaid? Until the early 1940s, most of the very few seafarers who had encountered and survived these freak surges kept their mouths shut. They knew that no one would believe them. However, off the coast of New-foundland, more than a thousand miles northwest of Carlsen's encounter and less than a decade earlier, Cunard's **Queen Mary** made credible the freak or rogue wave.

For the World War II effort, **Queen Mary** had been converted to a troopship, her speed being invaluable—five days to cross the Atlantic. In December 1942, she was headed east for Europe with over a thousand crew and twelve thousand American service personnel who would soon fight Hitler. (President Roosevelt had sometime beforehand decided to join the European battle, but he hadn't yet told the world—and would not for almost another year.)

Queen Mary was 975 feet long, 118 feet wide, and, at her tallest point, her forward smokestack, 70 feet high. In other words, this liner, all around, bulked out at almost three times the size of **Flying Enterprise.** A gale as wild as Carlsen's came up, and out of that gale strode a rogue wave. Over a hundred feet tall, it hit the eighty-thousand-ton ship broadside and all but finished her. The liner heeled right over, to about seven degrees short of horizontal. Lifeboats, personnel, fittings of all kinds flew overboard and four people died, skittering down the near-perpendicular decks into the sea; hundreds of soldiers suffered varying degrees of injury and shock.

If she hadn't been so big, hadn't weighed so heavy, or had been less expertly constructed, **Queen Mary** would have gone down with the probable loss of over thirteen thousand people, because the wall of water hit too hard and fast for any rescue possibilities. Fortunately, she didn't need them; slowly, carefully, "the Queen" came back up, righted herself, and recovered her poise.

For reasons of wartime propaganda and security, Cunard suppressed any word of the incident. It eventually leaked—how could it not with all those people on board? After the story was verified—and thus a tacit validation granted—a thousand tales of these rogue waves burst forth. Everybody reported along the same terrifying lines: the wide, high, sudden rampart of water walking or running straight at them. If luckier, they saw it in the distance heading in a different direction; seventy feet high and more, they said, often appearing out of nowhere, even on a calm day. A hundred feet high is not impossible for these ocean monsters.

After the **Queen Mary** incident, coastal authorities and meteorological services came out of denial. They began to assemble loose knowledge of this phenomenon and felt free to gather evidence from all over the world. Soon, the other interested parties, the ship owners, the insurance underwriters, had possible explanations for the mysterious disappearances of many ships—such as, two decades later, the German supertanker **München.**

Almost three football fields long, the pride, at the time, of Germany's maritime commerce, she disappeared—in seemingly normal weather—on December 7, 1978, while on a voyage from Rotterdam to Savannah. Just before she vanished, **München** sent out an abrupt, confused, and very brief distress signal—and then not another word. Weeks later, a mangled lifeboat was found on the waves but no sign of anything else. Part of her death lore says that a Russian submarine picked up on its sonar **München**'s dying fall to the ocean bed. A stronger assumption then began—and persists: that **München** succumbed to a rogue wave, either overwhelmed by its walls of water or sucked into the vortex of the trough.

ESWs derive from different forces: the shifting of tectonic plates, severe weather coincidences, or self-feeding extremes—and most accounts of them are associated with storms (though there have also been many sightings of such waves appearing vicious and unannounced on a flat, calm sea). Given the optimum combination of wind, wave, and weather, an ESW simply climbs up out of the waters, annihilates everything in its path, roars on, and falls away—as it did when it cracked **Flying Enterprise.**

Even though Carlsen heard what he called the "pistol shots," he never saw the culprit. When you sail an ocean, you change your clock by an hour every day. At ten minutes to seven in the northeastern Atlantic, his clock had been put back only one hour in the five-hour time difference between western Europe and eastern America. In Carlsen's time zone, the sun hadn't yet risen; it was too dark to see the wave that cracked his decks.

But on the next day, Friday, December 28, he saw every wash of the second rogue wave that hit him.

AT TEN MINUTES past eleven, John Crowder, the second assistant engineer (who, remember, had been thrown off his feet in the engine room on the morning of the crack), was sitting at his desk typing. In rough seas, typing is never a simple job. "I had the typewriter turned so that the carriage wouldn't slide down," he said. "If the vessel rolled and I didn't have it turned around it would stop moving or slide back and I would type over the same letters."

Crowder left his typewriter and looked out of the afterhatch, the entrance to the aft passageway. "The howling of the wind was very great. It made a lot of noise. And the waves were very high. It was the roughest weather I have ever seen." He knew what he was talking about. "I have been in one typhoon, September 1945, in the Navy, in Okinawa. But this lasted much longer. It was much worse than that."

At that precise moment, Carlsen was seeing his ship carefully through the heavy and freezing seas with all her patched wounds. Sometimes he hove to, sometimes he asked the engine room for eight knots; he constantly changed course.

In these maneuvers, he still aimed at trying to keep **Flying Enterprise**'s bow at an angle that might deflect the sea's sharpest brunt. This could prevent the freighter from flooding too heavily through the lower cracks in the plating, the thinner fissures that they hadn't been able to reach with cement. As far as he and his crew could judge, no water had ever come through them, not even on the crack's impact. Twenty-four hours after the repairs, she still wasn't suffering any more water, but he could now take fewer chances than he might otherwise have done. If he could keep her steady until the storm abated—as it must eventually—he stood a good chance of weathering the ship's disability.

Suddenly, that chance disappeared. Carlsen, on the bridge, looking to his right, saw an awful sight. Over sixty feet high, traveling at enormous speed in the fitful sunshine, a green wall of giant water came from the north, much too fast for any ship to get out of its way.

First the swell of the sea set up the freighter on the palm of the ocean's hand. Then the wide, flat, high slab of water, big as the side of a marble quarry and weighing just as many tons, hit **Flying Enterprise** on her fore starboard.

This liquid monolith stove in the wheelhouse windows, flooded the interiors, and sprayed every exposed part of the ship with sheets of icy water. It shredded the starboard lifeboat. It tore compasses and iron furniture from their bolted deck fixtures and sent every loose object on board flying in one direction or another.

Glass exploded into shards as the water hammered it against the metal walls. Sounds of rending and tearing ripped through the ship. In the cabins, bunks were ripped from their bulkhead moorings, metal lockers and night tables were prized off the walls, and people were pitched around like dolls.

The incident lasted less than half a minute. At the end of it **Flying Enterprise** was hurled down like a child on her left side. She lay there, listing to port, the kicked and pounded victim of an unequal fight with a bully—John Crowder gave evidence that **Flying Enterprise** took a list of twenty-five degrees and "never righted itself from this angle. And the lights began to grow dim," he said. Then the ship heaved down again, and deeper.

Official observations for that day and that time confirm the severe weather. A British ship some hours away, M.V. **Sherborne,** logged "screen and thermometers broken by sea hitting bridge. Present and past weather reports included squalls. Waves 280° period 13 seconds height 30 feet. Remarks: 'Hurricane force winds, visibility nil. Waves at least 40 feet at times.' " Translated: **Sherborne** was getting hammered every thirteen seconds by waves thirty, forty feet high and higher. Meanwhile, S.S. **War Hawk** was "taking seas and heavy spray in high, rough seas. Using various courses and speeds in trying to ease vessel."

. . .

A SHIP, ESPECIALLY a working serf such as a freighter, is made of various metals—steel, iron, myriad alloys—because she must prove relentlessly functional. Doorways and hatches do not open and close sympathetically, with a gentle click or hiss—they hammer and clang, with metal wheels and levers to lock them shut. Ladders and companionways also ring to the boot; all fittings and fixtures have been fashioned for the heavy duty of survival.

The space used by the sailors resembles a house no more than a tin can resembles a glove—a cargo ship must be hard and unyielding. Even if she contains the more benign onboard material of timber, the shipwrights will have used hardwood: teak, afromosia, oak, mahogany, lacquered to bullet hardness.

On deck, the accoutrements, kept to a minimum, haven't an ounce of give. The iron bitts (when an anchor is played out from them, its chain has reached "the bitter end"); the steel hatches, beneath which the holds yawn like mine shafts; the tough machinery for hauling, winching, and reeling—this is a rigid world designed to defend itself rigidly while fulfilling its rigid purpose.

But when a hurricane throws a ship around the sea, what makes it strong also makes it dangerous. The ship's very being becomes, in part, an enemy. Her iron substance becomes the sailor's foe as well as his friend. The walls and floors bruise, and bones break against them. Blood flows from the cuts and abrasions they deliver. The cabin or corridor, secure and iron hard, changes into a doubtful ally who fights on both sides.

And it gets worse. At sea in a Force 12, the hurricane will turn a ship and her fittings into an armory—even to the point of ripping a chain from its moorings and swinging it like a hoodlum in a gang fight.

When a sailing vessel is attacked by the weather, her master is her guardian—that requirement lies at the core of his job. He must try to save his ship. Only one requirement supersedes that maxim: he must first of all save any human life aboard. What he fears, however, is that his ship will somehow let him down, that when the test comes she will be found wanting. (He dare not even think about his letting her down.) No seaman ever imagines sinking—but those who have known life in such a gale never forget the havoc stemming from those iron protections upon which they had depended.

Meanwhile, the captain's getting drenched to the skin by the freezing water that's washing like a tide all over the decks. He can't see through the blinding spray to defend his ship, or to protect himself. He can't breathe without gasping. He can't stand upright. He can't watch where he's going. All he can do is grab for any fixed handhold aboard and then hope that the iron unyieldingness of the ship will stave off the water and the wind until he can get things back to some semblance of how they should be.

His main hope is that, with him helping her with such seamanship as the elements permit him to use, his ship will somehow know how to ride the storm. By now, the master is checking everything. He's checking for fire, in case an oil line has fractured; sailors fear fire as much as cats do, or airline pilots or oilmen. He's checking for deep damage, such as holes beneath the waterline. He's checking for power—does he have a means of propulsion? He's checking for electricity—does his ship still have her lights?

And as well as looking, he's listening. He will hear the cataracts falling on her superstructure. He will then hear the sharper noise of fittings crashing around and about the decks. He will hear the wind screeching through whatever mast, rigging, or antennae the ship still possesses.

If those angry and distressed noises do not soon or slowly abate, he will begin listening in dread for two much more fearsome sounds.

One will range upward from gunshot to cannon fire to the crack of doom: the ship's metals cracking. The other will groan and boom frightfully: the sound of his cargo shifting. If he hears one of those sounds, it's bad. If hears both, he knows he's in peril.

And finally a master mariner understands his lot: women and children first; the captain will be the last man to leave his ship; and he may have to go down with his ship.

Carlsen had already heard the metals cracking. Did he now hear the huge groan of his cargo shifting as his ship listed to starboard at an angle of between twenty-five and thirty degrees? Others did; and not only was the black freighter not righting herself from that angle— she was slipping farther down. Every movable article on board, every person and unfastened thing had tipped violently down to the left, and then down again—and again.

John Crowder did what was expected of an engineer: he headed for the engine room. The chief cook walked out; as his crockery and pans crashed about his ears he said, "I can't cook in this galley." Able Seaman Ralph Innocenti had been sleeping after his early watch when Able Seaman Clark Hall opened his door to say, "You don't want to be dead, better get dressed . . ."

10.

Matias Lopes Moraes, from Brooklyn and in his twenties, stood the eight-to-twelve watch on that Friday morning. He had charge of the wheel when the second rogue wave struck. The sudden sharp list sent him spinning; green waves shattered the wheelhouse windows and sent him flying. He crashed into a metal fitting and sprawled on the floor, damaging his arm; flints of glass cut his hand.

From outside, on the wing of the bridge, Able Seaman George Bulhak, though blinded by the wind-blown spray, dashed into the wheelhouse and grabbed the wheel, giving Moraes, with his damaged arm, time to get up from the floor and its slopping waters.

Moraes took the wheel again as the sea continued to surge through the glassless portholes. "Everything now stopped," he said in evidence. "The electric stopping. I told the captain everything stopped."

Carlsen, also in the wheelhouse at that moment, sent Bulhak off to get a life jacket and fetched one from his own quarters for Moraes.

Few men on board this vessel had the experience, presence of mind, or resourcefulness to deal with these violent circumstances. Carlsen had, and he led accordingly. He needed to achieve two things at once: correct the severe listing to port and change his course again to avoid the brunt of the seas in the wake of the wave.

First, he asked the engine room for more speed. Next, he told Matias Moraes, "Hard to starboard," hoping that a sudden change of direction to the right might straighten her. Matias did his best; he had, after all, just been flung the length of the wheelhouse. He recalled, "I turn the wheel. I am slipping on deck . . . I have a lot of blood."

The ship didn't respond. Carlsen gave a different order, this time trying to swing her to port, hard left. No response. He called the engine room. They told him that the steering gear seemed to be working. Carlsen, puzzled, tried his next tactic—he asked the engine room for "full speed ahead."

After a short delay, back came the tinny reply up the voice pipe: "The plant has kicked out."

Carlsen set them to work on trying to get the

engines going again. Ordering Matias to stay at the wheel, he left the shattered wheelhouse to embark upon actions that, by any standards, could only be considered extraordinary and are still counted as such. He understood how grievously he had been hit. He could hear the repeated efforts as great machinery kicked in and died, kicked in again and died again, meaning he was now losing power. **Flying Enterprise** had already refused the wheel, so even if she had full and lasting forward drive, where could she go? Carlsen could now only steer her to nowhere—even if he had engines.

He went out into the storm and forward on the bridge deck. Up at the highest point of the ship, he flung an arm around the radar mast and hung on. From there, through the rain and spray, he surveyed the situation.

The seas continued to hammer. Water formed pools on floors, it swirled in tides along the decks and down the stairways, it ran freely through shattered portholes. His freighter was barely coming back up from her sudden listing and was not staying up—worse, she was rolling a little deeper with each heave.

Michael Staikoff, the fourth mate, who had earlier been blowing the foghorn constantly on account of the spray's thickness, recalled saying to another crew member, "The ship was defying the law of gravity by rolling so far and coming back. It was rolling to seventy-three degrees."

At the radar mast, Carlsen took one more look and judged that if the engines did not revive, he must abandon ship.

11.

FROM THE SHIPBOARD TERM **ENGINE room,** dismiss the word **room.** On **Flying Enterprise** and all freighters of her size, what they called the engine "room" was longer and wider than most people's houses and almost twice as high. This chunky cathedral of mechanisms resembled the underground workings deep in the mountains where, in all the best boyhood books and movies, the mad scientist lived.

Endless pipes, some thick as a thigh, some thin as a pen, snaked around the interior, making the walls look like a huge, fat subway map. They curved at soft right angles across the ceilings, they ran up and down the riveted metal girders that served as flat pillars, they disappeared into dark corners and then reappeared.

No ship's engine room wastes space; each

wall has something using it. On **Flying Enterprise** and all of her class, clanging ladders veered here and there, ladders so narrow that each stair tread seemed no bigger than a child's shoe. These ladders climbed the height of three office floors, linked by narrow companionways along which someone slim as a snake might just about manage to sidle. On random walls, above workbenches, on oil-smudged pegboard, sat rows of tools in neat lines.

In the middle of this church of power and force sat a giant cog, seemingly big enough to turn the Wheel of Life. Its massive cage had bars made of metal girders four inches thick and a yard apart. The oilers and wipers, reaching in with their rags and wadding stuff, kept the vitals of this cog lubricated and clean—the brass pistons, the shiny black plates, the glass valves and gauges, with their complicated and vital information.

Generators, the ship's power source, turned open faces to their handlers—to them, the round dials with big faces and quivering needles read as easily as a clock. **Flying Enterprise** had three boilers; and a man standing on the shoulders of another man who balanced on a third would just about reach the top of one. Everywhere hung the unique and energetic smell of oil. The oil fired the generators, which drove the boilers, which boiled the water, whose steam pressure turned the giant cog. From the cog's hips ran a long, fat, tubular case about three feet high, and beside it ran an enclosed passageway, the shaft alley—because within the plump tube ran the shaft, which turned the screw, which drove the ship.

Not one system or surface in this coiling, oiling cave had anything sympathetic in its making. In demanding times, when unusual calls were made from the bridge, the temperature in the engine room could hit 125 degrees. Those who worked an engine room's around-the-clock shifts had long been called, by tradition, the "Black Gang," because in the early days of steam, these men had coal dust on their faces; nowadays, they glistened with the lighter tan of oil. **Flying Enterprise**'s Black Gang was led by a remarkable chief engineer, George Brown.

George Brown, from Baltimore, Maryland, was thirty-five years old. If action be the judge of character, he had matured beyond his years. The Coast Guard inquiry officers acknowledged this, in the great length at which they required him to give evidence and in the obvious respect that they accorded his answers. His conduct of his part in the entire crisis speaks to his simple courage and integrity as a human being—and also tracks the course of the **Flying Enterprise** incident.

After the first rogue wave, Brown ascertained that the machinery had risen easily to the challenge of the fractured decks and had pumped the holds dry. He had also established that Carlsen need have no worries regarding ongoing water problems at that time; the repairs had worked. When the second freak wave struck, Brown registered that the ship "took one roll, one pretty bad roll and didn't come back again like it should have." Before that she had not, he believed, been rolling much, despite the crack. In response to Carlsen's "hard to starboard" request from the bridge, Brown went to the steering gear room.

"I called the Mate from there and told him to go ahead and swing her a little one way or the other," he reported. "The arms were working and I called him back and told him she was answering all right." She wasn't—she only seemed to be, for reasons that neither Brown nor Carlsen yet knew and would only find out much, much later. The fact was that when Brown tested it, the steering gear responded only to its own electric controls, rather like a gauge that seems to tell you how much oil is in the central heating tank—but is actually only reading how much is in the gauge.

Brown clambered from the steering-gear room back down one of those narrow ladders to the engine room, a place about to turn into hell. By then he knew what had happened to the ship under his feet: "She took a decided list about three times—not just one big list—and stayed there."

Consider the word **list.** Although seamen understandably hate and fear it—because it means to tilt unwontedly, and in a ship always suggests danger or failure—it reaches back in its origins to a word that sailors are supposed to personify: the word **lust.** With an archaic **y** spelling—**lyst**—it meant **desire** and thus (delightfully) **inclination;** thence it reached the word **incline.** To be listless meant to be, at best, passive, at worst without energy. But at sea, "listing" means something much worse.

WHEN JOHN CROWDER got to his post in the engine room, water covered the floor; everything now tilted at an angle, more than halfway out of true. The "slope" of the ship, he said, was the worst he had ever seen. "It was impossible to move any place without having rails or machinery to hold on and pull yourself along. Progress was very slow and footing treacherous."

Richard Cosaro, the third assistant engineer, had come off duty earlier and was still "in the sack" at eleven o'clock.

"The list had me woke up," he recalled. "I mean, I am out of sleep through the list. I was standing on my head." He got his feet down and also headed for the engine room. "In the passageway, which I was going towards the Officers' Pantry, I was going to the steward, [and] he said, 'It looks pretty bad.' I said, 'I don't believe you, it's a lot of baloney.' So by the time I was going down the ladder, the lights got dim."

The chairman of the Coast Guard inquiry board, Captain Lewis H. Shackelford, asked Cosaro, "What was the condition of the engine room when you got there?"

"Total blackout, lube-oil coming out of the generator due to the list. Lube-oil on the engine-room decks and port side due to the list and the turbine was coasting to stop, no steam on it."

Frisco Hoivoya Johnson, a Californian who held the license of third assistant engineer, was on duty in the engine room during the second wave's attack. When "the ship was rolling

pretty bad," he found the chief engineer standing beside him as the bridge asked for power.

"So I looked at him," he told the inquiry
board. "I says, 'Shall I give it to them?' He said,
'Give it to them if they want it. Open up the
throttle wide open,' and after I had it wide
open, the ship just listed way over on the port
side and she never did come back."

When she listed, Frisco Johnson saw water
from one of the boilers spill into the generator
and the lights start to go out. The emergency
generator took over, and the lights came back
on. But he knew the main power had gone—
and perhaps for good. This happened, he said,
around ten minutes past eleven. In other
words, the ship lost power that morning at the
moment she listed. Which means that she lost
power just after the great wave struck.

Trying to keep his balance as the ship heaved
and swung, George Brown saw the lights on
the generators dying one by one and he knew
in his bones the extent of the trouble in store.
In fact, he saw many different, major problems
breaking out simultaneously.

In the engine room, everything depended
upon everything else—the boilers, the generators, and, crucially, the pumps: pumps to feed
oil, pumps to feed water, pumps to maintain

lubrication, pumps to clear the bilges. All had been fitted to work more or less vertically and in dry conditions.

Typically the ship was accustomed simply to driving onward through her voyage, day in, night out, steady as she goes, her motor power nursed by her Black Gang. Generally, a chief engineer makes himself as much a watchman as anything else—there to fix problems should they arise. Almost paradoxically, the better he does his job, the less he will have to do. Brown's first steps in the raking, sloping, oil-leaking engine room had symbolic as well as practical application: he took back manual control of as much as he could get his hands on—boilers, generators, pumps.

Some machinery responded, some responded not at all, some responded and expired. "The emergency generator kicked in and took over the lighting," he testified—which meant that the passengers and crew need not have their alarm turned to panic by a sudden loss of power and light. "In the meantime my other engineers had begun to come down below by that time when they saw the lights [flickering off and on,] and one of them headed for the steam lube oil pump."

There lay the critical problem. The tanks operated on gravity feeds, and because of the angle at which the ship lurched, no lubricating oil could get to the generators. From now on, **Flying Enterprise** had little chance of recovery, a fact that was not lost on George Brown. Yet it never stopped him from trying. Feed pumps, breakers, emergency generators, vacuums, main engines, condensers, fans—one by one, he focused on every component that makes a ship run or protects her under pressure. But as she began to keel over even farther, he found massive difficulties everywhere—and on the increase.

The fans for regulating the boiler temperatures flapped out, creating risk of fire. He "secured" the main engines, meaning he shut off the throttles. "Plus," he said, "oil was coming out of the emergency generator, plus water had run out of the radiator, plus acid was running out of some of the batteries." And the electrician, Adolf Fuerst, told him that now there was smoke pouring out of the back of the main wiring board. Brown next found that the emergency generator "was not coming up to speed. She was running fast enough to carry the emergency lighting." And not much else.

As the engine room of **Flying Enterprise** darkened into shadow, steam was escaping ominously, the temperature was rising, and oil was pouring from the machinery down the steps of the different levels. All hands needed to hold on to anything that would keep them on their feet while viscous water slapped and slopped around their ankles.

12.

AFTER HIS BLEAK SURVEY OF HIS chances up above on the weather deck, Carlsen clambered back down the sloping, rolling levels of his afflicted ship. He lurched his way to the radio shack and dictated a signal to David Greene, the **Flying Enterprise** radio officer: "Encountering severe hurricane, position 49-20 north; 17-20 west, situation grave, 30-degree port list"—the subsequent heaves had not yet kicked in—"and just drifting. Ships in vicinity please indicate. Signed Master." Greene sent this with the "XXX" international prefix indicating "urgent."

It was twenty-five past noon Greenwich mean time, twenty-five minutes past eleven on the ship, a quarter of an hour after the wave hit. The stinging edges of a rain shower passed over and Greene went to work. He knew that whatever the urgency, it would take some time before the necessary relay stations picked up his message and passed it on.

The day and the events now took on a long, slow darkening. As the radio officer began to call for help, Carlsen looked over the ship again and finalized his grave strategy. He had to assume the toughest possible scenario—of everyone jumping into the sea—because he had no certainty as to whether he could use his own port lifeboat. It had not been taken out of commission, as had the starboard boat, but he suspected that once he began to commission it, the metal davits that lowered it would hammer down on the heads of anyone trying to get into the boat. If he took a chance and hung it out unmanned, the sea would surely drive it back against the side of the ship.

Those who observed Carlsen said that he exhibited no anxiety, no haste, no fever, no excitability, no distress; he spoke clear, simple words and maintained an unworried expression. Already he had made the decision not to ring an alarm bell; now, he ordered Michael Staikoff to find the chief mate and the chief steward and relay orders to them—that each passenger should fetch from their ruined cabins such warm clothing as they could still use, and then be issued life jackets. Next, the passengers must congregate in the starboard corridor of the accommodation block, the highest indoor part of the ship at that time.

When Staikoff found Frank Bartak, the chief mate, in the passageway outside the wheel-house, he also found a passenger badgering Bartak. Nikolai Bunjakowski, an awkward man about whom nobody knew much, had two conflicting listings in the passenger manifest: "German" and "Stateless." Insofar as anyone could see, he had either been friendly with or had befriended Mrs. Nina Dannheiser from Hamburg, the oldest of the women passengers, and he had also taken a shine to Mrs. Dannheiser's small white dog.

Now Bunjakowski sought reassurance from the chief mate, and Bartak tried to soothe him. Staikoff, seeing Bunjakowski's agitation, did not want the passenger to hear Carlsen's orders, with their evident urgency, so he eased Bartak away. Bartak then began to act on the orders relayed from Carlsen.

At least one member of the crew had anticipated the captain. Ross Thomas, the chief steward, had already prepared the life vests—"so I could have them ready within a split second in all the rooms," he said. In anticipation, too, of the captain's need for calm, the steward hadn't yet shown the life vests to the passengers.

In due course, however, crew members began to help the passengers put on the flotation vests. At the same time, with as much tact and calm as they could muster, they passed on an even more dismaying order: "Vacate all cabins." If the sea decided to take the ship down soon, a swift escape from the cabins could prove impossible.

In some ways, though, the order came as a relief. Shipboard life had already been significantly unpleasant for days; when the second wave hit, most of the people had been huddled in bed, in nightwear and overcoats, seasick, miserable, and scared. Now the sea came into their rooms and soaked everything they owned.

Leanne Müller described the circumstances: "The ship was rolling very heavily and she took one roll and stayed over on her side. Then a man, he had us put on life jackets. Then we had to go to the floor of the ship, to go out the door." Her crawl along the floor of her cabin took her into the long corridor. "We were all in our night clothes. And a man fetched us some blankets to put over us. And my father was able to go into the room and fetch a coat and a pair of pants for me. And then we were sitting there; we got a little to drink."

Carlsen had now obtained from his passengers what he needed in order to try to save them: assembly in one place, with easy access to a deck to get them off fast. All ten passengers crowded obediently on the floor of that corridor, as close as they could get to the doors.

Such an experience: cold, frightened, severely uncomfortable. No matter how they wished to sit, they would tilt sharply down on the steep list of the decks. Leanne Müller, at that moment, "felt tremendous respect for my parents and brother. They were not panicked. And the waves were so high. It was so horribly wet. And dark."

Presently, Carlsen himself arrived and told everyone to be calm. Help had been summoned, he said, and they must conserve energy in case they had to swim. This assembly took place on Friday afternoon and the passengers, who had boarded so hopefully in Hamburg, sat there all evening and all night, huddled together in groups.

They endured the noise of the waves lashing the decks. They endured nauseating uncertainty each time the ship wallowed or rolled. They endured the terror of the lights going out on **Flying Enterprise.** They endured minute after minute of total, icy, wet darkness—and their ordeal would last for twenty-six hours to come.

Carlsen's crew did their best. The chief steward, Ross Thomas, said, "We had blankets and things there and wrapped them as warm as we possibly could."

TWENTY MINUTES AFTER David Greene sent the distress signal, his first acknowledgment came through—from a U.S. Navy vessel, **General A. W. Greely.** She said she was making no more than four knots because of the appalling weather and therefore could be, she feared, as much as twenty-four hours from **Flying Enterprise. Greely** was a big, thirteen-thousand-ton troopship, five hundred feet long, seventy feet wide, named after an American Civil War veteran.

Next, a freighter out of Savannah, S.S. **Southland,** received **Flying Enterprise**'s distress call at three minutes before one o'clock. Fifty minutes later, the British ship **Sherborne** called **Flying Enterprise** to say that she was coming and would Carlsen's ship please respond. Greene sent the original distress message out again, this time changing it from "XXX" to "SOS," which left no doubt in anyone's mind, anywhere, as to **Flying Enterprise**'s plight.

Just after two o'clock, three more ships came through within minutes of one another; the

Norwegian S.S. **Westfal Larsen** said she'd reach **Flying Enterprise** by seven in the morning and offered oil to calm the waters, to stop waves from breaking in the freighter's vicinity. Two more Norwegian vessels answered, S.S. **Norse Mountain** and S.S. **Noordam,** a passenger ship, who said she was proceeding in the general direction and also offered help.

Fifteen minutes after this, M.V. **Sherborne** came through again and asked, "Is your engine broke down?" David Greene replied, "Yes, our plant kicked out." At twenty minutes past three, a further British ship, not identified in the signals but almost certainly S.S. **War Hawk,** asked, "Do you want us?" At twenty-five past three Greene replied, "We are making water and have a 45-degree list." At half past three, he radioed, "Change our urgent to 'distress—engine dead'."

Look down with God's eye; look down on that roiling, boiling, gray-green, white-foamed segment of the North Atlantic that afternoon, and you will see at least half a dozen ships plowing from all directions, heaving up and down through the seas, converging from many angles, hoping to throw a cordon of ready assistance around a sister ship lying on her side.

The approaching vessels all knew what Carlsen must have been through. **Greely** recorded winds at ninety miles an hour, and **War Hawk**'s log gives a kind of representative running commentary; that morning, she too had been "taking seas and heavy spray in high, rough seas. Using various courses and speeds in trying to ease vessel." The log continues: "1245 Radio operator reported urgent signals for assistance from S/S **Flying Enterprise** and requesting us to rush to his position in about Lat. 49-20N Long. 17-20W." **War Hawk** changed course and at half past two noted, "Signals changed to SOS." Finally, just after midnight, **War Hawk**'s bridge "sighted lights and flares about 2 points on port bow. Proceeded to area under reduced speed and shuttled back and forth awaiting daylight."

Carlsen had already told the arriving ships not to come near **Flying Enterprise** in the dark. He had no intention of mounting a rescue operation at night when he had no lights and with the Atlantic Ocean still climbing all over his unfortunate ship. So he warned **Southland, Sherborne,** and **War Hawk** not to send boats until he told them to—not to attempt any rescue until they could see more clearly in such light as day might bring. And he added riders of advice about the dangers: when they did dispatch their lifeboats, they must take care not to get dragged in under the listing side of his ship.

He also placed watches permanently on the highest point of his own ship, lookouts who, in the words of Otto Michaels, the second mate, "waited for ships approaching and kept on giving lights so that they wouldn't hit us."

DOWN IN THE engine room, the frantic pace of the day and the frenetic mood continued, led by George Brown to the point of his own total exhaustion. He was using every means he had ever learned or heard of to get his ship's engines started. Finding that his emergency measures were not giving him enough, he "kicked in the access doors to both furnaces on the boilers, fired both boilers."

For a time this maintained steam; at ten minutes past seven he fired the main engine. Daring to hope a little, he went and told Carlsen—who then directed, "Whatever power you have down there, use it for the pumps, nothing but the pumps." Carlsen knew not to hope too much, and after twenty minutes the revived engine died, unable to work on one boiler.

Then, as Brown himself acknowledged, three more major things went wrong. First, "There was no means whatsoever to tell how much water was in the boilers on account of the list. The gauge glasses were useless." Second, the starboard boiler threatened to go on fire imminently, and he had to shut it off. Third, and most serious of all, a new source of water poured into the engine room and flooded areas of the floor already lapped with seawater. Brown looked at it, puzzled, and bent down and cautiously tasted it.

"I'm under the opinion that it definitely was fresh water," he said. "And you should have heard it—things were crashing—tools, barrels, everything under the sun. It's my opinion that it came from some place down there, a pipe maybe, on the fresh-water system."

Not salt water, fresh water—which meant that one of the ship's own supply lines had fractured and was leaking into the engine room. Were it a fire line, what would happen if they needed water to fight a fire in the engine room? And all around him, Brown's men, his Black Gang, were skidding, falling, crawling along the floor, trying not to touch metal surfaces that had now become roastingly hot. Steam leaked everywhere, stinging their faces, and they were addressing all this at an impossible angle, with water and oil in their boots, drenching their legs to knee height.

The biggest man in the Black Gang, Cyril Francis, stood six feet six and weighed 230 pounds. He gave the most telling description: "I had to lay on my stomach and put my fingernails in the crease of the floor plates and slide myself along on top of the floor plates and pull myself over to the generator. It took me about five minutes. That is how steep it was down there."

Said George Brown, "Anybody can gather that we were working down there under terrific conditions. There was oil on the floor plates; the ship was listing forty-five to sixty degrees. Where you may [ordinarily] go from one side of the engine room to the other in ten to fifteen seconds, it [now] takes you a good five minutes to work your way from one side to the other and the heat was terrific."

The rogue wave had done its work at just after eleven o'clock in the morning. **Flying Enterprise**'s Black Gang had four assistant engineers (John Drake, John Crowder, Richard Cosaro, and Frisco Johnson), a plumber-machinist (Cyril Francis), three oilers (Jose Marti, Georgy Miterko, and Herman Banks), two wipers (Louis Rodock and Miguel

Cordero), and a fireman (Gene Lacy). The electrician, Adolf Fuerst, had been twenty years at sea.

Directly after the hit, all of these men (those who hadn't already been on duty) went straight to the engine room—which means that most of the Black Gang worked all through the late morning, all through the afternoon, and would now go on, one way or another, all through the night.

OUT ON THE SEA, S.S. **Southland** made good time, even in those waves. At five o'clock, just after nightfall, her radar picked up **Flying Enterprise**; at half past five, she knew that the sprawled freighter lay five miles ahead; ten minutes later, Nikolai Nielsen, her radio officer, told David Greene, "We see you." Moving steadily in, Nielsen asked Greene at six o'clock, "What lights are you showing and are you under way?"

"Showing mast and running lights. Not under way."

Four minutes later, Nielsen asked, "How long can you hold out?" Two minutes after that, the British ship **Sherborne** radioed Carlsen to say, "We are four miles astern of the **Southland**."

Greene replied bluntly, "Have ten passengers." Seconds after that message, all the lights on **Flying Enterprise** went out and her signals went dead; Carlsen had lost all electric power at seven minutes past six, just as the dark of night intensified. Ten minutes later Greene broke this worrying silence to say, "Trying to hold out until daylight."

By now, **Southland** had arrived at **Flying Enterprise**'s side. Greene had earlier stipulated that he must try to conserve his batteries; if **Southland** needed to talk to him, they should flash a signaling light and he would acknowledge by radio. Nielsen agreed and then devoted himself to scanning for any other ships coming to the rescue. He broadcast a signal giving **Flying Enterprise**'s bearings in case the new arrivals didn't all have radar.

"And then the night came and we saw the lights of this ship," said Leanne Müller. "Imagine how happy we are to know that somebody was around to take us off."

Indeed—but now a new danger had presented itself: **Flying Enterprise** could not be seen in the water. At just after nine o'clock, **War Hawk** said that she was approaching and intended to direct her big searchlight into the air so that other ships could give her a bearing on **Flying Enterprise**—but she admitted to having difficulty with the waves and weather. To which **Sherborne** replied, "Request you keep well clear, we standing by and steering poorly."

At six minutes before ten, the passenger ship **Noordam** asked, "Can we give you any further assistance?" Three minutes later Carlsen said, "Can you stand by until daylight?"

Noordam replied, "With two ships in close vicinity, do you think we are necessary?"

David Greene answered, "Master thinks it necessary."

But at one twenty-eight in the morning, **Noordam** sailed away, reassured no doubt by the size of the gathering support team and concerned for her own passengers in such weather.

None of these ships had specific training for, or experience in, sea rescues. In a port, tied to a mooring, they would not have looked much different from the rusting traders that my grandfather showed me on the quays of Limerick. They plied the sea, fetching and carrying, one port to another, hemisphere to hemisphere, and they never saw themselves as anything other than ordinary, respectable vessels of trade. And yet, that Friday night, all these seamen knew that when the next day dawned—or that night, if the freighter went down—they would have to take part in a rescue of passengers and crew in weather that was making it nearly impossible to control even their own destinies. In fact, at just after eleven o'clock, Nielsen, on the hale and hearty **Southland,** had to switch on his own emergency transmitter because his main generator had failed.

ON THURSDAY, THE day of the crack, the radio antennae had disappeared, swept into the sea, so at the height of that phase of the storm, David Greene rigged up an emergency replacement. After the second wave struck, he began to test this emergency equipment in relation to all batteries and had just proved it in working order when Carlsen arrived to send the climactic SOS. Subsequently, Greene worked unceasingly, in near-impossible conditions, to provide Carlsen with a broad view of the rescue hopes coming toward them.

When Hans Isbrandtsen received Carlsen's "encountering severe hurricane" SOS message, he signaled back, "We have been anxiously watching your precarious position STOP Presume you unable to communicate with us STOP Weather reports indicate sharp improvements next few hours STOP We trust you will be able to make nearest safe port Isbrandtsen."

Captain Carlsen had Greene reply, "Hoping

to stay afloat until daybreak STOP Will transfer passengers and crew then Carlsen." That message went out at five minutes past ten on Friday night.

Later that night Isbrandtsen radioed, "Suggest endeavor have rescue ships stand by if you must abandon as derelict STOP Dutch tug Oceann [he misspelled **Oceaan**] on way to you 700 miles distant noon today understand weather moderating we endeavoring determine arrival tug Oceann STOP We extremely worried your situation keep us advised especially safety crew and passengers Isbrandtsen."

Carlsen spent most of the night in the radio shack with David Greene. He needed to assess such other ships as might come through, vessels with potentially better, easier facilities for the task that lay ahead of him.

At seven minutes to six the next morning, Greene sent this message to Hans Isbrandtsen: "Confirming STOP Vessel floating but 60 degrees list port and plant dead also taking water number three cargo shifted no casualties passengers or crew who have been hanging on to deck all night we will do our best however it is even problem to move few feet as she rolls over to 80 degrees unable communicate with you direct now saving emergency transmitter for SOS Carlsen."

13.

THE BLACK GANG DID EVERYTHING they could. none of them had ever before faced such odds. In parts of the engine room the paint began to blister with the heat; flames roared out of the furnace doors. They fed in lube oil by hand because the gravity feeds had been wrecked in the ship's tilt.

But there came a point when George Brown finally gave up and lay on the floor. Nobody could have worked harder to revive these huge pieces of machinery, and his men had watched him in ferocious action, trying to keep his feet, addressing the plant directly, as if he could somehow drive the ship on his own great energy. Richard Cosaro had never seen his boss so exhausted and now lay down beside him.

"I was so tired I couldn't move," Cosaro testified. "I was laying there, and the water kept coming over the chief and I. The Junior Third [Frisco Johnson] was next to us."

Oil had leaked everywhere. Water—some of it hot from the boilers—sloshed down stairways. The floor had grown unmanageably slippery and the heat unendurable as a result of re-peated efforts to get the turbines started and running.

The other men took breaks—they had to. Cosaro himself went up for air every hour or so, then back down to the floor plates of the engine room, until two o'clock in the morning. Someone fetched fruit juice, and they all compared notes, tried to control this piece of machinery, shut down that generator; they abandoned yet another pump. In the upshot, when everything failed, at half past two in the morning Brown, Cosaro, and Second Assistant Engineer Crowder quit their efforts. They spent the rest of the night in a passageway in the crew's quarters. Cosaro said, "We thought if the ship capsized it would be as good a place as any to get off."

According to John Drake, the first assistant engineer, the ship finally lost all remaining power from all emergency sources at "about one o'clock in the morning"—the lights had gone seven hours earlier. He had been man-ning a futile pump, trying to clear the water from Hold 3. Drake spent nine and a half hours in the engine room, which he described as "very hot" and with "no ventilation at all."

Like the others he took breaks, and like the others he saw, late at night, in all the smoke and gloom and steam and water and oil, the writing on the wall. It was time for the Black Gang to begin saving itself.

Here is the exchange between the recorder of the Coast Guard inquiry, Lieutenant Commander Clinton J. Maguire, and the chief engineer of **Flying Enterprise.**

> Q. Mr. Brown, on the 29th did you
> receive any instructions with regard to
> leaving the ship?
> A. This was the day we left the ship
> actually?
> Q. Yes.
> A. Well, I remained at the top of the
> engine room that night. The next
> morning I worked my way up to the
> next deck where the passengers were
> assembled and also the crew was
> assembled. The first thing I heard was
> to get the passengers ready for
> going over.

Dawn had broken. Some god somewhere had taken the weather and the seas a little in hand—but only a little. The time was nine o'clock; George Brown began to take care of his men.

John Crowder had stayed in the engine

room, he said, "until eight o'clock that night. I did go up a few minutes several times for a breather." Louis Rodock, a wiper, got out just before ten that night; Jose Aurelio Sanchez Marti reported for duty as usual. "But," he said, "no can do. No light." When he got down to the engine room, he couldn't even see adequately to get to his post: "I feel to walk but had to make sleeping." He concluded that he had "nothing to do down there with no light."

Frisco Johnson stayed in the engine room longest of all. At a moment he described as "some time during the latter part of the evening," he went up on deck "to get some air." He headed for his cabin, lay down, tried to sleep, couldn't. "I finally got up and I went down below again." Lying on the hot floor plates, lapped by oily water, Johnson, a Native American nicknamed "Indian," slept in the engine room until seven o'clock in the morning.

"I heard the chief hollering from the topside," Johnson recalled. Brown by now knew clearly the risks and had begun to yell in general, "Is anyone down there?" "I hollered back. I said, 'I am.' 'Is that you, Indian?' I said, 'Yes, sir, that's me.' He said, 'Come on up.' So then I came up topside.'"

When Frisco Johnson joined a bunch of the other crewmen in the port passageway, the last of the Black Gang had emerged. It would have been so easy for one of them to have fallen asleep down there in the dark, been overlooked, been injured or otherwise trapped by the very momentum they had so willingly maintained, above and beyond the call of duty.

All through the night, other seamen had been in different parts of the ship, sheltering as and when they could, waiting for the dawn. Matias Moraes, cradling his injured arm, sat in a crew accommodation-block passageway. "There was no food," he said. "I no eat all night. It was me and the boatswain, one more AB, a tall guy on the twelve to four watch, the second mate, and the third mate and the chief mate on the boat deck over night. The next day in the morning there's another ship—I forget its name—all the time in the night time they put a light on like somebody on the ship make a silhouette."

14.

THE PREDAWN WEATHER AROUND **Flying Enterprise** brought westerly to north-westerly winds at Force 7 on the Beaufort scale.

As the morning broke, the wind eased back to Force 4, and the sun tried to sneak through. The wave patterns, though, continued to exemplify that euphemistic description: "confused." None rose lower than a recorded thirteen feet high; they would soon again climb much higher.

As the morning strengthened, a number of crewmen, including the chief steward, Ross Thomas, cautiously led the ten passengers out on deck and helped them find binnacles, spurs, or projections of any kind to which they could cling. The bedraggled passengers had, said Ross, "remained in that alleyway from about 1600 in the afternoon until about eight o'clock the following morning when I started to get them out of there."

To get to the point whence Carlsen had elected they should jump, they needed to climb from the main deck up to the higher—highest—weather deck and then descend to the boat deck. The crew produced ropes, which they rigged as lifelines to help the passengers up the steep and rocking, swaying ladder. They then laid a ladder down to Carlsen on the boat deck and loosely roped each passenger to this ladder.

Each person to jump would be sent for when needed, and then helped down to the jumping point—the stretch of the boat deck rail to which Carlsen judged that the arriving lifeboats could get nearest. All of this was taking place in winds gusting up to Force 6, with waves slashing at people's legs.

Most of the passengers responded well, meaning that they remained helpful and quiet. Nina Dannheiser, at fifty-six the oldest woman there, began to scream, and the cook, Robert Lumpkins, went to her. "I had to keep her comfortable," he said. "I got her quieted down by deliberately lying to her—I had to."

On the boat deck, as Carlsen stood looking out for lifeboats and preparing to direct the rescue operation, four of his crew approached him and said, "Captain, if you want us to, we're willing to stay with you." Carlsen respectfully but formally declined their offer. The four were two Black Gang members, Richard Cosaro and Frisco Johnson, with Able Seaman Edward Higgenbotham and Ordinary Seaman Frank La Buda.

On the sea, visibility grew poor again; soon it would be described as "nil." By now, a flotilla had settled nearby to help this ship, which they couldn't see through the spray but could almost feel: **Southland, War Hawk, Sherborne, Westfal Larsen** (which, at twenty-five minutes past nine, began to pour oil into the rescue area), the German freighter **Arion,** and **General A. W. Greely. Greely** had taken twenty hours since the distress signal to arrive and had, to Carlsen's delight, a Danish commander, Nils Olsen. His first glimpse of this ship that he had come to help moved him to write an arresting entry in **Greely**'s log.

> The **Enterprise** was laying on her port side listed from sixty to seventy degrees and wallowing about helplessly in the trough. Her port side weather decks and cabin decks were awash and with a heavy roll to port it appeared as if her cross trees would almost touch the water. At the time it seemed impossible for her to stay afloat much longer and in the event of another gale I believed that what watertight integrity she retained would collapse sinking her immediately.

By that vision, of a ship so reduced, did he and all the other masters in the vicinity assess the demands of their task. Some had already been gearing up for this effort and, as **Greely** prepared her own rescue team, Carlsen saw his first potential rescuer, the **Southland** lifeboat, materialize through the gloom. Now, all on **Flying Enterprise** could see the rescue about to begin.

CARLSEN'S CANDIDATE TO lead off the abandon-ship order, Frau Müller, reached his side; he talked to her nonstop, reassuring her. As the boat came in, she was seen to respond to his gestures and climb onto the ship's rail. When Carlsen tapped her on the shoulder, Frau Müller, with heartbreaking courage, jumped into the Atlantic—and sank. She surfaced immediately; her face and her hair and her clothing had been coated with the thick oil from **Westfal Larsen.**

The oil may have helped somewhat—but how does one measure "somewhat" in waves that rose higher than a house? Elsa Müller wiped the oil from her eyes—and lost the rope. She found it again and yanked on it, as though she might haul the lifeboat toward her. On the drenched and swooping deck above, her husband and children looked down at the small figure fighting this massive sea. The **Southland** men drew her in, and all hands helped her aboard. Immediately, the boat retreated as though positioning itself to return for another passenger. But instead of coming in again, the lifeboat moved farther out—and disappeared into the spray.

What Carlsen couldn't have known was that the crewman in charge of the **Southland** boat had headed back to his own ship, where he was about to tell his captain that he greatly feared being swept in under the overhanging hull of the heaving **Flying Enterprise.** He feared it with good reason.

Henry Brazil, the second mate of **Southland,** who ran his ship's rescue effort, recalled the danger: "On the first attempt I came about twenty feet away and threw a heaving line, but the decks of the **Enterprise** was awash, and every time as I come up, the sea would go below the bulwarks, and I was afraid I would get caught in the wash, and then I couldn't get away any more. So from then on I decided to lay off. When I rescued the first passenger, it was by throwing the heaving line."

As Brazil batted through the waves back to **Southland,** his one survivor, Elsa Müller, repeated over and over to the lifeboat crew one of the few words of English she knew: "Children."

The skipper of **Southland,** William Lawton, agreed with Brazil on the risks of getting trapped by the wash under **Flying Enterprise**'s port hull. Yet Brazil went back again, if more cautiously than before.

During his absence, Carlsen and George Brown puzzled over the disappearance of the lifeboat, and Brown said, "Why don't we launch our boat?" On Carlsen's orders, John Drake, his first assistant engineer, and John Crowder, his second, climbed into the port boat. Brown watched: "Then the weather was getting rougher. It was definitely getting rougher." He went to help.

As Brown began to loosen the metal-and-canvas gripes by which the boat was fastened to her davits, the watching crew members—and Carlsen—suddenly yelled at him to stop. Not surprisingly, Carlsen's pessimism had proven strongly founded; any attempt to launch the port lifeboat could bring serious injury.

Drake and Crowder killed the lifeboat engine; Brown went back to Carlsen at the rail. They stood there for minute after long minute, wondering what was happening to the other, promised boats. But they might have gone ahead, taken the risks and launched their own lifeboats, had they known what was happening out on the sea, where a god of chaos had moved in on the other would-be rescuers.

With winds rising to Force 6 and falling back to Force 4, M.V. **Sherborne** launched her boat, which made a journey toward **Flying Enterprise.** Her crew saw that no passengers could be rescued easily or securely in those seas and turned back toward the mother ship— whereupon she capsized, pitching her four men into the water. **Sherborne** herself managed to pick them up.

Next, **War Hawk** launched her boat, and its crew never even got near **Flying Enterprise**— the lifeboat capsized almost as soon as it pulled away from **War Hawk**'s side. Those lifeboat crewmen also managed to get back to their mother ship.

On **Flying Enterprise,** only one person knew of these—quite literal—upheavals. In the radio shack, David Greene monitored transmissions from the other ships to each other and to him. His main difficulty lay in trying to conserve his batteries and yet get on the air often enough to eavesdrop on the exchanges between the rescue ships, in case they had difficulties that might jeopardize the rescue. That was how he heard that boats were capsizing out there in the spray. He relayed each development to Carlsen.

At one stage, judging from the "traffic" he was overhearing, Greene feared that no more boats were going to come; then, luckily, he said, "Somebody hollered in the doorway and said, 'Here come the boats.' It was a surprise to me." Also, he had begun to learn, usefully, that the rescuing ships had a different perspective on how **Flying Enterprise** rolled, how she lay in the water. Greene took in the observations that they offered—how and from where people might most safely jump off the ship to be picked up—and got that advice out to Carlsen on the boat deck as fast as he could.

The **Southland** lifeboat came back, having deposited Elsa Müller—but it stood off for about an hour. A kind of grim comedy of hand waving began, in which the men in the **Southland** lifeboat waved to **Flying Enterprise,** indicating that passengers should begin jumping into the water, while Carlsen gestured emphatically at the lifeboat to beckon it in. Carlsen, irked, said to Brown, "We got to get these passengers off, why don't he come in closer?"

Brazil remained cautious—understandably, in waves now so high. "I would say that I could walk off the lifeboat to the deck sometimes and at other times I'd say I was more than 15 feet below," he recalled. He couldn't see **Flying Enterprise** half the time because he went so far down in the trough.

By now, nineteen-year-old Leanne Müller had descended the ladder and, hand over hand along the rail, came to where Carlsen stood on the boat deck with George Brown. The rescue had run into a deadlock—with a boat that felt it could not come in closer and passengers who did not want to jump in and swim so far. Brown made a decision.

"I told the Captain that if he wanted, why, I would take a chance with one passenger, and jump. He was scared to let us go at first." Not scared—perhaps justifiably concerned; the sea continued to wash up to where they stood, visibility waxed and waned, and the weather seemed to be worsening again. As Brown reported, "I know what he was scared of. He was scared that we would get washed back into the ship's plates."

Brown testified that Carlsen finally told him, " 'Well, all right, Chief; wait until this boat comes in.' So I got this one girl and I tied her [life]jacket on tighter than what it was—it wasn't too good—and we stood at the rail ready to go. So then the last thing the Old Man said to me was, 'O.K. Chief, God bless you. Go ahead.' So I went over with her."

Today, the "one girl" in Brown's evidence, Mrs. Leanne Müller Smith, lives in Sandy, Utah. A devout woman with a doctorate in education who spent sixteen years as a high school principal, she speaks perfect English with an undertone of her German birth accent.

Her memory seems generally dustless. She recalls the texture of the weather, the temperature of the sea, the stench of the oil.

"When you jumped in the water," I asked her, "do you today have a memory of how you reacted?"

She paused, then said, "I struck the water and I laughed. I remember laughing. Yes, I laughed."

I thought but didn't ask, "Not too much to laugh about in forty-foot-high freezing waves?"

She continued: "It felt like being freed. You see, I was so glad to leave the ship. The ship was by then a greater danger to us. It had become a dangerous place. Now God had given me the chance to get out of that danger, and I would respond to His will. It was amazing, knowing what I know today," she said. "The sea was freezing. I might have died of hypothermia. And I remember how devastating it was to worry so much about my little brother. And about my father."

Curt Müller remained among the passengers on the weather deck, watching the attempted rescue of his wife and daughter and awaiting his turn. His son, Lothar, had yet to jump, a fact uppermost in Leanne's head—and heart.

"That was when I cried, at the thought of my little brother. I cried much harder about him. My nonpanic came from my Heavenly Father. That is why I laughed when I struck the water. The oil totally covered my coat—I must have swallowed some of it; I do not recall. But the reason I laughed was, I thought, 'I am more in control now.' And then I cried for my little brother. The cold—oh, the sea was so cold. I was gasping."

Her voice has scarcely changed since she spoke to the world's media when she eventually landed at Rotterdam. George Brown had taken her hand, shown her how to be courageous, jumped over the side of the ship with her, and quite possibly saved her life.

"We were not roped together, we did hold hands, we did make an attempt at swimming. The men in the lifeboat, we saw them off and on. But there was calm, no panic."

WHEN CARLSEN WATCHED George Brown and Leanne Müller jump, he made an important modification to his rescue plan. He recognized that two people in such a sea would be easier for a lifeboat to find than a lone head bobbing in the high waves. Now a crewman would jump with each passenger, two by two; this tactic would also reduce the great fear among the passengers.

John Crowder also saw Brown's jump with Leanne Müller. "After the lifeboat picked them up," he reported, "they gave the signal from the boat for the next two to go. We went one passenger to one crew member, right over." Next went Robert Lumpkins, the cook, with young Lothar Müller. And after that John Drake jumped with forty-five-year-old Maria Duttenhofer.

So that the lifeboats would see them, everyone who went into the sea that day was instructed to raise a hand and gesture with each rise of the swell. Forty-two-year-old Harold Gleaves, the crew pantryman from Boston, went over with Leonore Von Klenau, the photographer, who was also, Gleaves recalled, comforted by Carlsen. "He spoke in German to these people. And he gave this lady I was with a pair of woollen socks to put on."

Any comfort would have been welcome at that point. During the preceding nights, Leonore Von Klenau had had to hold on tight several times to avoid falling out of her bunk. Now she had Harold Gleaves as her savior.

Gleaves said, "The Chief Engineer was the first one to say, 'We jump, I'll take one passenger with me.' Mr. Robert Lumpkins, the Third Cook, said, 'I'll go next with this passenger.' This was the young boy, eleven-year-old boy.

Then last but not least, me. I say, 'I'll take charge of this young lady, Miss von Klenau.' "

Miss Von Klenau, Gleaves reported, was not panicky. She, when her turn came to bear witness, said that even though she couldn't swim, she could "make the movement. You couldn't swim much because the waves are very high." She lost Gleaves in the beginning. "But," she added, "I got hold of him again. He can't swim either."

All in all, **Southland**'s lifeboat rescued eleven people.

Of all the survivors, Frau Dannheiser suffered most. The crewman who jumped with her, the plumber-machinist Cyril Francis, from the Bronx, selected himself as her helpmeet on account of his physical size. "She weighed about 230 pounds. Each crewmember was supposed to jump with a passenger, and when her turn came everybody refused to jump with her. So I climbed along the handrail by hand and I shouted to the captain, 'I'll jump with her' and he says, 'That's fine.' And she didn't want to jump. She was very nervous. And she had a little trouble getting started. She got one leg on the rail and I leaned over, and my weight pulled her over the side."

With massive exertion—"She had me very tightly. I thought that I was going to drown myself"—Cyril Francis, his fingers locked into a bracelet that Frau Dannheiser was wearing, hauled her through the water to the **Southland**'s lifeboat, where some survivors and the crewmen tried to pull her aboard.

By now Frau Dannheiser had all but fallen unconscious from the combination of shock and hypothermia. She could give the men no help whatsoever in getting her into the lifeboat; she lay in the water, her deadweight supported by Cyril Francis. He tried to lift her, but he had to address his own exhaustion. The men in the boat, in the process of trying to get a grip on her oil-soaked person, pulled off her clothing, thereby exposing her to further danger from the temperature.

One of the boatmen got a line around her waist, but it slipped and hooked around her leg. After twenty minutes of this struggle they had to stop and rest, so they laid Frau Dannheiser in the sea alongside the lifeboat until they recovered some strength. Finally, with one man leaning out of the lifeboat and cradling her head to keep it up out of the water, and another holding the bracelet, the crew motored back to the side of **Southland.** From there, they hoisted the exhausted woman up on a litter, barely conscious, half frozen, naked, and slimed with oil.

William Lawton, the **Southland** skipper, watched through binoculars. "It was a hell of a job getting her on board," he said. Even at that distance Captain Lawton could see that she "was unconscious, and helpless."

While Henry Brazil was taking **Southland**'s boat back to her ship, with Nina Dannheiser being literally towed alongside in waves now nearing thirty feet high, Commander Olsen on the **Greely** was being informed of his ship's contribution to the rescue. It proved initially problematic, and then astonishing.

The first officer, George Jullien, took seven crewmen with him, launched a lifeboat, and headed toward **Flying Enterprise.** When the gray navy transport appeared through the waves, John Crowder told Carlsen that he possibly knew somebody aboard this boat and asked whether he might be allowed to jump for it. Carlsen agreed—he had, by now, seen his women and children safely off. He directed Crowder to twin with a passenger: the young German man, Rolf Kastenholz. Crowder jumped behind Kastenholz and swam with him to the **Greely** lifeboat. Kastenholz, Crowder recalled, "didn't seem hysterical or anything. In fact, he was telling me in German that he was seasick and he hadn't eaten for five days."

Then two crewmen jumped—Louis Rodock, a wiper, and Luis Pagan, a Cuban messman. Rodock also had a bad time. To get to the jumping point he went down a rope from the weather deck to the boat deck, but he hit his head on "one of the pillars that support the lifeboat." This left him, he said, "a little dizzy but not much." Rodock then jumped straight into the sea—he called it a "hasty jump."

As he floundered in the water, the **Greely** lifeboat actually ran him over; he went under the boat, which struck him on the head. He managed to get the attention of the lifeboat crew, but it was his own colleague, John Crowder, who hauled him out.

With Rodock, Pagan, Kastenholz, and Crowder safely aboard, the **Greely** lifeboat crew immediately found themselves in difficulties: their engine cut out. No amount of effort would restart it, so George Jullien gave the order to begin rowing.

They found that they couldn't make it back to **Greely** under oars; the swells proved too enormous and rough. **Southland** seemed nearer, and they opted to row to her.

Brazil, in the **Southland** lifeboat, had already reached his own ship. He wanted the **Flying Enterprise** passengers off and safe, and he wanted his lifeboat crew relieved. He had left **Southland** before ten that morning, and he hadn't gotten George Brown and Leanne Müller into his lifeboat until one o'clock. Now he supervised as the survivors climbed up the precarious ladders that **Southland** had lowered over the side.

In the course of this operation, one of Brazil's own crew almost died. Able Seaman Herman Nungezer, who had contributed effectively to the rescue of the passengers by pouring extra oil on the sea beside the lifeboat, set out to climb the pilot ladder up to **Southland**'s decks. In Brazil's words, "A big sea was coming along and took the lifeboat away over his head and he was between the ship and this boat." Nungezer survived and got aboard his own ship. In the last movement of that perilous dance, they raised Frau Dannheiser aboard.

Now the **Greely** lifeboat arrived alongside **Southland**—and alongside **Southland**'s lifeboat. The waves bounced the **Greely** boat off **Southland**'s hull and holed the **Greely** lifeboat, which then collided with **Southland**'s lifeboat and ripped off its rudder.

Which meant that the only two active lifeboats in the rescue operation so far had been taken out, bringing the total of lifeboats damaged to four. A few minutes later, that number rose to five: **Westfal Larsen** launched its lifeboat, which promptly capsized. Five lifeboats launched, five lifeboats gone: from these smaller but no less dangerous catastrophes we may judge the chaos of the seas on that Saturday afternoon.

First Officer Jullien got his four **Flying Enterprise** survivors and his seven-man crew off the lifeboat and onto **Southland.** Survivors now themselves, they climbed the pilot ladder just behind the **Flying Enterprise** survivors, and then Jullien had his boat winched up onto the **Southland** deck, where repairs began. **Southland**'s Captain Lawton spoke to **Greely**'s Commander Olsen and told him of the accident. Olsen had already heard from David Greene on **Flying Enterprise** that the **Greely** lifeboat engine had died.

Through Greene, Carlsen asked Olsen to send another boat from **Greely.** Olsen waited until he had ascertained that his own lifeboat crew and the survivors they had taken from the water had been safely brought aboard **Southland.** He then sent a message to all ships nearby, asking them to give him room to maneuver close to **Flying Enterprise,** because he was about to launch a second boat.

Someone needed to do something. **Southland** had had enough; **Westfal Larsen** was still trying to pluck her lifeboat crew from the sea (she lost the boat but not the men). The German freighter **Arion** stood by. **Sherborne** and **War Hawk** had left the area, licking their wounds and with no rescues achieved. Thirty-five people still had to be saved. And Carlsen.

15.

ENTER NOW A TWENTY-FIVE-YEAR-old U.S. Navy officer whose skills of seamanship and almost casual heroism seem to have gone unnoticed by the world—and yet, besides Carlsen, he proved the most significant participant in this rescue. His name was Robert Husband, and my last possible trace of him—and I don't even know that it was the same man—led me fruitlessly to Sulphur Springs, Texas. There, the trail that had wound for years though service records, navy pension archives, contacts with veterans, and old comrade organizations, reaching from World War II to Vietnam and after, finally died on the spike of a telephone that had been disconnected.

At a quarter to one on that freezing Saturday afternoon of vicious waves and howling winds,

Robert Husband launched a lifeboat from **General A. W. Greely.** Taking no chances, he manned it with a crew of nine; **Flying Enterprise** lay almost three-quarters of a mile away. He later made a full report to his commander.

"I crossed the bow of the **Enterprise** and proceeded along her port side checking her drift and set. As our boat came abreast of her midships house, four figures jumped into the water. I saw that they were being tossed forcefully by the action of the sea." While Husband and his crew watched, he saw that "these four survivors which were in the water were being thrown back on board by the seas, some of them one or two times."

The "four survivors" were the oiler Jose Marti, who confirmed Husband's account; he related how he jumped from amidships and "the wave sent me back all the time to the ship." Jumping along with Marti went a steward, Samuel Miller, from Michigan; Ordinary Seaman Yan Sang, a deck-maintenance hand; and the agitated, terrified Nikolai Bunjakowski, who stood on the deck, life-vested and shaking with fear. With one hand, he held a hat clamped tight on his head, and with the other he held on to Nina Dannheiser's little white dog. He showed no inclination to jump.

The boatswain, Arthur Janssens, went up to

Mr. Bunjakowski and pointed to a ladder that he had just rigged to get the jumpers nearer the water and more likely to clear the ship. "I told him, 'Don't be afraid. You're only going to be a few minutes in the water. You will be picked up,' " said Janssens. "Brr. Brr," he added, indicating how Mr. Bunjakowski trembled.

Earlier, Carlsen had put a life jacket on the dog, a child's life jacket that had been worn by his daughter Karen during boat drill on a voyage with her father. According to Janssens' evidence, before Bunjakowski jumped, "They [the crew] dumped his dog overboard and then he jumped." As he hit the water, his hat came off, and from beneath it fluttered a billow of currency notes. He tried to reach them. At the same time, the deck-maintenance man Yan Sang jumped, and as he did, the oiler Jose Marti, in tears from fright, was pushed from the deck above by his well-meaning colleagues. Yan Sang, with limited skills in English, gave image-filled evidence:

"I see other ordinary seaman. He near me, jump over guard [rail]. He can't swim, jump into seas. He make noise and cry and everything. I can't save. I take one hand and start to swim. I see something out there coming, one dog hollering, little dog from passenger. Little dog come at me. So I catch dog and I want to try to take dog too. At that time I had two hands can't move no more. Start to go down. I think too bad. I can't help it no more. I let go of the dog. Man I let go and then start swimming with hand. I let go dog. Dog go down; finish, gone."

Essentially, Yan Sang saw that Marti couldn't swim, went to save him, and took Marti's hand in the water. He also tried to save the dog and almost went down himself. A few feet away from him, Mr. Bunjakowski, now torn between his money and the little life-jacketed dog, let go of any lingering self-protective instincts he still felt and the sea smashed him against the hull of the ship that had been taking him to a new life.

From the deck above, Ross Thomas watched Mr. Bunjakowski. "I said to him, 'Swim away from the ship.' He was swimming, I could see his hands moving and the dog was going along also. The last I seen of him where he was, he turned by the stern of the ship there and the lifeboat was off probably, I can't say how many yards it was to be exact, but between the end of that ship and the lifeboat. That is where something happened. I don't know if it was his heart or drowned or what."

Out in the **Greely** lifeboat, Robert Husband swung in and picked up all four passengers, who, he found, due to exhaustion "were unable to help themselves at all. One man as we approached him was lying on his back with his eyes open giving the appearance of being dead. We hauled him on board and at that time I feel certain he was dead." This was Mr. Bunja-kowzski.

Husband and his crew also saw the dog, who was trying desperately to keep his head above water. But the weight of the life jacket kept pulling him this way and that, and soon the dog vanished. "At the time I saw him we had our hands full pulling men out of the water and were unable to save this dog."

Carlsen never took his eyes off Husband's rescue efforts, and Husband became aware of the captain's vigilance. When he had the four men in the boat, three safe, one dead or dying, Husband waved to Carlsen and began to point toward **Flying Enterprise**'s stern; he seemed to be advising this as the point of optimum safety for anyone trying to jump clear.

The young naval officer had confirmed Carlsen's own instincts. Given how the weather had come up again so severely, and given his fresh experience of people having jumped from the boat deck rail, and now confirmed in his judgment by this evidently competent rescuer, Carlsen changed his mind and sent all his crewmen and the two remaining passengers to the stern of the ship. To get there, each person still on board had to crawl some sixty yards on his hands and knees.

Three more men jumped; Husband picked them up and took them to **Greely,** where cargo nets had been lowered. Each of the seven **Flying Enterprise** jumpers now in Husband's boat was hauled aboard **Greely** by means of a line passed over their heads and fastened under their armpits. On board they were taken straight to the ship's hospital, where doctors and nurses had been standing by. Nikolai Bunjakowski was unconscious on arrival and was certified dead shortly afterward.

HIS FIRST JOURNEY safely completed, Husband pulled away from **Greely**—and immediately found himself in a swell so great that he rose level with the troopship's decks. The time now was a quarter to two. The rescue operation had begun at half past eight that morning, and the majority of people still had to be taken off **Flying Enterprise**—twenty-eight, not counting Carlsen and including two passengers: Curt Müller, husband and father, and the elderly Frederic Niederbrüning. As Husband headed toward **Flying Enterprise,** he had to circumnavigate **Westfal Larsen,** which had come between **Greely** and Carlsen to pick up her own lifeboat crew.

Alongside the crippled freighter again, Husband made "three or four passes" and picked up ten men, one man at a time. He missed one, Balthazar Gavilian, but he followed him in the water until **Westfal Larsen** picked him up safely. Husband went back to his own ship, unloaded his ten survivors, and came back for more. And now there were seventeen.

THAT IS HOW THE **Flying Enterprise** passenger-and-crew rescue operation concluded: through the expertise of a young seaman working hand in hand with a captain who perceived that expertise. No further serious incidents occurred. One man, the oiler Georgy Miterko, was picked up by the German ship **Arion.** David Greene, the radio officer, was in the last boat—as was Richard Cosaro from the Black Gang, who, after all, had been among those offering to stay until a tug could be found.

"The captain said, 'No, get off the ship. That's an order,'" Cosaro recalled. "We asked him, 'How about yourself? You coming?' He said, 'I'll make my decision when you are all safe in the water.' Well, more of the crew had already jumped back aft. I was in the last group to leave the ship. There were about fourteen of us at the time, and when we were in the lifeboat, all in the lifeboat, we kept waving to the captain saying, 'Come on, Captain! Come on!' And he didn't say anything."

As Robert Husband told it, he asked the chief mate, Frank Bartak, where the captain was. Bartak told him that "the captain would not leave his ship." Husband pressed Bartak on this point, Bartak repeated his answer, and Husband "had no choice but to head back to the **Greely.**"

None of them knew—poetic coincidence— that all the clocks on **Flying Enterprise** stopped at that moment, just before three o'clock.

THE **GREELY** LIFEBOAT disappeared into the spray and reached the mother ship in safety, leaving Carlsen behind, alone. "To windward of the **Enterprise,**" reported Husband, "I saw the captain standing on the boat deck aft and we all waved to him." Husband got all his remaining survivors up onto the decks of **Greely** "with no accidents in the transfer." He then headed for **Southland** to pick up his shipmates who had been on the damaged lifeboat. By now his own boat was "taking increasing amounts of water over the bow and in danger of breaching."

Back on board **Greely,** "at this time being covered from head to foot with black oil along with everyone else," Second Officer Husband discussed with his captain the wisdom of trying to recover **Greely**'s foundered lifeboat from **Southland.** Olsen decided against it and stood **Greely** by. **Flying Enterprise** lay seven hundred yards distant, the closest Olsen had ever dared come to her.

Alone now, with dusk closing in fast and the sea still bombarding him, Carlsen wrestled his way back to the radio shack, shining his flashlight. In order to ascertain that all his crew and passengers had indeed been rescued, he had one more task: a "round-robin" of calls to each participating ship. The radio auxiliary batteries had almost died; in the listing of the ship, the battery acid had drained out. He had just enough power to build the roll call.

Greely's crew told him that they had thirty-three people—all of them saved by Robert Husband, who had simply shuttled his lifeboat over and back, over and back again, in seas that most ships would never have attempted to sail. **Southland** had rescued a total of fifteen, thereby reuniting Elsa Müller with her two children. The German ship **Arion** had taken one man, Georgy Miterko, who eventually fetched up in a Liverpool hospital with a broken leg. **Westfal Larsen** had picked up Balthazar Gavilian, who had been drifting unnoticed in the swell until Robert Husband saw and policed him to safety.

Ship by ship, Carlsen added the numbers, thirty-three plus fifteen plus one plus one, until he could tell the rescue ships that he had reached the magic number of fifty. Each passenger and every seaman had been taken from the storm.

On board **Greely,** the radio officer received the signal from **Flying Enterprise's** radio room and reported the number of people his ship had taken safely on board. He had as yet no knowledge that Mr. Bunjakowski had died and therefore transmitted a "full" number of survivors. As he signed out, he asked the man who, he thought, was his opposite sparks, "When do you come off?" He didn't know he was speaking to Carlsen, who replied, "I'm staying."

Greely's man radioed back, "What about the captain? When is he leaving the ship?"

Carlsen replied, "I'm the captain and I'm not leaving."

PART TWO

16.

CARLSEN SENT ONE MORE MESSAGE
that Saturday evening—to his ship's owner,
Hans Isbrandtsen, in New York: "All passengers and crew now saved as far as I know STOP
I will remain until tug Ocana [**sic**] arrives
please notify wife." The message was relayed at
six o'clock. Then, for the time being, soaked to
the skin and exhausted, he ceased talking to
the world.

All Carlsen's shipboard norms had disappeared. With alarming kicks and heaves, his
freighter continued to wallow. The severe tilting meant that he couldn't walk anywhere simply, couldn't get dry, couldn't feel safe, couldn't
assume anything. Fore and aft of him stretched
this long, desperate ship, a huge, helpless metal
whale that sometimes bucked up from the
prow, and sometimes rolled hard at the stern.
Nothing in her movements allowed any prediction of any kind; she could go down at any
moment or she could settle like a floating
plank if the sea grew calm.

In the meantime, she could hurt him with a sudden lurch; she could knock him unconscious. Or she could trap him in her innards by slamming a door shut behind him and then take him down in a sucking dive, and only his stripped bones would be found—and then only if the ship was ever found. He was the last man standing in a wintry, violent, and inundated prison, and he was master of nothing that he surveyed. And the elements that had first begun to attack **Flying Enterprise** continued their wrecking. Winds tore up and down and in and out; waves surged across the decks and poured down stairways, along corridors, into cabins.

But Carlsen had formed his strategy, a tough-minded, stubborn intent: "I will remain." If he stayed on board and took charge of a tow, he would not lose his ship and he might even recover some cargo. He had been convinced—if he needed convincing—by Isbrandtsen's cable telling him that the tug had been chartered: "on way to you, 700 miles distant noon today."

Both men understood what was needed: a vessel robust enough to broach those seas in that weather and assured enough to tow a loaded, listing ship a distance of several hundred miles. The leading towage and tugs company in northwestern Europe was, and still is, L. Smit, out of Rotterdam, with representatives all over the world. Isbrandtsen knew L. Smit well. When he contacted his nearest tugboat experts, the New York office of the Salvage Association (who had affiliations with the marine insurance underwriters Lloyd's of London), he would have assumed that Smit would be the company of choice in those seas.

Sure enough, Isbrandtsen was told that one of the Smit vessels, **Oceaan,** had overheard **Flying Enterprise**'s Friday afternoon Mayday. It had already acted on the emergency call— tugboats hunt for opportunity—and was even now steaming to Carlsen's aid. That was how Isbrandtsen knew about **Oceaan** as early as Friday night, while the passengers and crew were still aboard **Flying Enterprise.**

Carlsen had had a double stroke of luck. First, and of the utmost importance, he was lucky to be getting a tug at all. The waters of northwestern Europe had other, richer pickings that weekend; few tugs might want to take on a ship that seemed about to sink and whose cargo was almost certainly somewhat compromised. Second, **Oceaan** should get to him on Monday—giving the sea less time to wreak total havoc.

This excellent news about **Oceaan** intensified Carlsen's sense of purpose. He was exhausted, he was soaked to the skin, he was chilled numb, but he went to work. To begin with, he needed a secure communications system. He would need it for the towing—and, more crucially, he had better be no more than a radio signal away if he felt the ship going down. Once he could easily talk to the outside world, he could start to rebuild his own strength. Towing was hard work for the towed as well as the tug, and he hadn't slept a full night or eaten a hot meal for seventy-two hours—not since Wednesday, the night before the fracture.

It was in Carlsen's nature to draw on every competence in his repertoire all the time. His merchant seaman training had included radio officer certification. After the postrescue roll call of survivors, he knew that all David Greene's power supplies—the main batteries, the emergencies, and the reliable auxiliaries— had now, finally, expired. The backup of the backup of the backup was gone.

Carlsen went back to his cabin, where he opened up his own source: the transmitter on his ham shortwave. He kept it spread all along the bulkhead across from his bunk. The moment he looked at it, he knew that it, too, had died. All its battery acid had spilled in the storm; W2ZXM/MM was off the air.

But he had on board a small shortwave set, as a gift for his father, Martin, who had recently built a small cabin cruiser. Carlsen had specifically brought the apparatus on this trip so that he could set it to the European coastal frequencies that his father would need in the waters off Denmark.

This transmitter worked by voice, not telegraphy key. A virtual radiotelephone, it had dry batteries, and thus no acid to spill. Not only that, but if the battery ran down, he knew that he could probably hook it up to the old Zündapp and recharge it by running the motorbike's engine.

Carlsen set up the little radio. The power worked, but it needed a local antenna. So he ran a simple wire out on deck. He tested the rig, and the startled radio room crew on the **Greely,** still standing by, said they heard him perfectly.

In tinny exchanges across half a mile of ocean, they worked out a system. **Greely** would become Carlsen's mailbox for the world. They would receive and transmit all his messages and, until the tug arrived, Carlsen would call through to them every two hours—except, he said, during the night when he was asleep. His amiable matter-of-factness about sleeping astounded the **Greely**'s radio crew, especially when they looked across the sea at the slumped old ship on which he was proposing to get a night's rest. They concealed their astonishment, noted his general cheerfulness, and bade him good night.

On the C1-B freighters, the captain lived in two rooms: an outer office and a bedroom, near the wheelhouse, not far from the radio shack. Everyone who sailed with Carlsen knew his clinical sense of order. He inspected the crew cabins once a week, and his visit was always preceded by a mad scramble to tidy up— the seamen knew how scathingly he disliked chaos. Now, though, the storm had trashed his own space. The drawers in his bulkhead cabinets had fallen out; his possessions lay strewn.

Also, his rooms sat on the starboard side, which had become the highest part of the ship; if he suddenly had to jump, he couldn't go off over that rail—he'd simply be slammed back against the side of the freighter. Given the condition of the vessel and the continuing rage of the weather, he might need swift egress should **Flying Enterprise** suddenly decide—especially at night—that she had had enough.

He counted his requirements—safe haven,

speedy escape, and a means to communicate—
and then reversed the usual order. To keep the
little shortwave apparatus dry he would make
his own cabin the radio room—but he would
sleep in the radio shack, which lay on the port
side and therefore nearest the water. And it had
a door to the outside world, through which he
could drop straight into the sea.

It also had a "foundation" on which to set up
a makeshift bed. All radio rooms in C1 and
C1-B ships contained a leather couch. Large
enough to seat two people, fixed to the angle of
the wall and the floor, this one had never
moved in the storm, and the leather upholstery
would wipe dry. Carlsen lifted bedding from
his own quarters and from other dry cabins
and built them into a bed on this leather
couch. Everything sat at a new angle; the tilt of
the ship meant that the wall had become
the floor.

When he had as firm a rampart as he could
manage, he changed into his pajamas and
donned extra outer clothing, including a
sheepskin coat. Warm enough, dry enough,
perfectly calm, he settled down to a form of
sleep that can, when needed, prove watchful as
well as restful. He laid his hand on the floor in
the mouth of the open doorway, so that the
sea's cold claw would wake him should she de-

cide to take **Flying Enterprise** during the night.

The last crewman had jumped hours before. Darkness had closed in shortly afterward. All these simple tasks—final radio transmissions, a survey of possibilities, making his bed—had taken several hours, and had been performed by flashlight.

Carlsen knew that, beneath him, the holds had taken on water; he knew that his cargoes had shifted. The Volkswagens had almost certainly crashed down; the steel container vans had surely keeled over, wrecking their fine art and splintering the works of Stradivarius; the sacks of coffee and grass seed and U.S. Mail had been rag-dolled and soaked through. And he knew that the pig iron pyramid had toppled over and that the ingots weighed the ship down on her port side.

Elsewhere, behind the other walls in the other cabins, lay the sad detritus of threatened and fleeing people. The sea had annihilated those few possessions that the passengers had needed in their cabins for the voyage. And those crewmen who'd expected to sign on with this ship again—they had lost their kit bags and their tender family photographs, their favorite razors, and the books they were reading; John Crowder had lost his typewriter.

Which of them, passengers and crew, had not been terrified when they knew they had to jump? Some had had to be virtually thrown overboard. At least the seamen had homes to which they could return. The ten passengers, all of them emigrants, possessed not a stitch of clothing, other than what they were wearing.

But by now they all had eaten hot meals and they all rested safely in warm, dry bunks, these people whose lives Carlsen had saved. And by noon Monday, or thereabouts, less than forty hours away, the oncoming tug would arrive alongside and he would complete the second half of his rescue mission: he would save his ship. Then he would also be safe—and satisfied. So fell to sleep Captain Kurt Carlsen on the night of Saturday, December 29, 1951.

PAUSE FOR A moment and see the picture: this small, lone human, his arm outflung as an early warning system, lying fast asleep inside this vast, mostly wrecked ship. The proportion of man to ship takes the breath away.

In the port of Baltimore lives S.S. **John W. Brown.** Preserved as a heritage vessel, she's run as a museum by local volunteers, some of whom love this lady as much as they ever loved their mothers. The C1-B freighter, **Flying En-**

terprise's class, has long been extinct. Perhaps there's the hulk of one plying somewhere in the world; perhaps some coastal trader still keeps such a freighter going. Aficionados of cargo shipping doubt it—and they point to **John W. Brown** as an extant vessel from that period and style nearest in size to the C1-B.

Stand on **John W. Brown**'s deck. Walk its length. "Feel" the ship. Even if he presumed that a tug was about to come and tow him to port, how could Carlsen have stayed on alone to handle something of this size? How could he even have **conceived** of doing so? Obviously, rowboats and dinghies do not come near Carlsen's equation. And for single-handed, around-the-world sailors, nothing on their boat is typically more than paces away. But on **John W. Brown,** and therefore on **Flying Enterprise** (which was only one-eighth smaller), the size, compared to a human scale, is huge.

When he found himself alone on **Flying Enterprise,** Carlsen didn't sail her single-handedly; nor could he have. And he had worked out his own measure of how to approach his environment. But to think about him, five feet six, with his bandy-legged walk, standing on these decks, looking around him and taking this thing on by himself—the mind balks.

Then factor in the freezing, blinding weather and the seas that kept pouring over the entire ship—all the time. In terms of proportion and physical magnitude, it's like imagining a child by himself in charge of a huge, swaying old barn, where the walls are falling down and the floors are heaving and splintering and the pipes bursting and great objects that you can't see are crashing down everywhere.

17.

CARLSEN SLEPT LONG AND WELL— and dry—and on Sunday morning, not long after nine o'clock, he woke up hungry. Before he opened his eyes, he knew that the sea hadn't calmed. Not too far beneath him he could hear the waves still ramming into the hull. The wind had dropped a few points, but it plucked at anything that stood in its way; and the temperature had fallen noticeably.

He climbed out of his pajamas, put the outer clothing back on, and hauled himself along the sloping corridors to his own quarters, for his first radio transmission. When he tried to call in **Greely,** his new apparatus refused to work.

During the night the wind had knocked down the makeshift aerial and ripped away his antenna, and now he had to rig it up all over again.

Again he improvised. The desk lamp in his cabin had been ruined in the storm, so Carlsen ripped the cable from the lamp and stripped it a little, to expose a foot or so of bare wire. Then he wound it around the blade of an oar, pushed the oar out of a porthole's side and jammed the porthole as shut as he could get it. He was helped in his ad-hoc engineering by one of the few advantages of the ship's tilt: the porthole in his cabin wall had become a skylight. This also meant that the makeshift antenna sat on the highest point of the ship—and the radio worked clear as a bell.

He impressed the **Greely** men again with the normality and vigor in his tone of voice—and then he asked them to send a signal to Isbrandtsen in New York. This message openly set out his range of concerns, and it stands as perhaps his most revealing communication in the entire calamity:

Understand tug Oceana [**sic**] will be here tomorrow STOP Please dictate me terms in plain language as no contracts available here STOP Will of course stay with vessel until port is reached or she goes down STOP Weather forecast promising but under towing hatches will be exposed to heavy seas STOP Have you calmed my wife STOP Am still able to communicate through General Greeley.

In that signal lay the attitude that brought Captain Carlsen to the attention of the world—and in it lay the codes to the intrigue that settled around his name. Not always a pleasant mystery, it began slowly enough and intensified over the years. At its deepest, it formed a cloud around Carlsen; it even took on political dimensions in the Cold War. And over time, it became one of those bizarre questions that continued to reverberate, no matter how often or kindly answers were offered. The question remains to this day: Why did Carlsen elect to stay on board such a damaged ship in such appalling weather?

Clues abound in the message to Isbrandtsen, a signal that consisted of six sentences, each a major component. First, judging from the previous night's signal from Isbrandtsen, **Oceaan** would now arrive within twenty-four hours. Second, in anticipation of the tug's arrival, Carlsen asked to be put in a strong position. He needed to know what terms had been negotiated with the tug skipper: a flat fee, a commission of the cargo's value, whatever.

If none of this had already been agreed on, he should know whether—or what—he might be expected to negotiate. More important, the contract, if already negotiated by Isbrandtsen, would tell Carlsen how much the tug would be prepared to do for him. Was this salvage or rescue towing?

Not only that: in the remark "as no contracts available here," he reveals a matter-of-factness about his position, saying, in effect, "I don't have the documents here to get this contract formalized." As if he could expect to effect the papers on a ship in that condition and in that weather?

Third, there's "Will of course stay with vessel until port is reached or she goes down"—a simple declaration of intent. Nobody leaving the ship grasped the depth of Carlsen's determination—until his stay on board actually began. The departing crewmen in Robert Husband's lifeboat had beckoned and called to Carlsen. He had waved them away. There had also been that moment when four crewmen offered to stay on and help when the tug came. Carlsen rejected their offer, too. Even though the tug had been hired and had already set out, he still didn't want to risk anybody else's life.

But who could guess how long the ship would last and what his own chances might be of surviving?

The fourth sentence in his message shows how well he understood the risks: "Weather forecast promising but under towing hatches will be exposed to heavy seas." Had he been saving his own skin, Carlsen could have left the ship on the rescue boat's last detail. He could have waited and jumped off dramatically, the captain the last to leave his ship, and so on—a valuable gesture. Robert Husband would have picked him out of the sea, and obviously expected to do so.

No; his ship was still afloat and Carlsen unequivocally elected to stay on board in order to get the tow under way, even though it put him in heightened danger. He knew the snags, the risks. For example, no matter how slow a speed **Oceaan** could be persuaded to adopt, any extra wash across **Flying Enterprise** could sink her fast, and he would not be able to anticipate that adequately from the deck of a watching vessel.

In the fifth sentence of his message to Isbrandtsen resides one of the most overlooked and important details in the entire saga. Never taken up by the world at large, or by the conspiracy theorists, it justifies, when analyzed, the entire set of actions that Carlsen took. "Have you calmed my wife?" he asked Isbrandtsen.

As I was about to find out, the saga of **Flying Enterprise** turned out to be, in a serious dimension, a story of familial love.

Finally, he showed how he had prepared for anything that would now happen by indicating that he had set up a communications base: the radio contact with **Greely** and its commander.

Essentially, Carlsen showed Isbrandtsen and **Greely** (and the world—there are few secrets in a disaster at sea) that he had decided to test the situation until the best or worst solutions had played out. No one possessed the power or authority to order him otherwise; Carlsen made this decision by himself, for himself. He made it on informed grounds as a seafarer with twenty-three years of experience, fifteen of them as a certificated ship's master.

Yes, his ship was listing severely, and yes, she had suffered grievous damage. But the wounds had not yet proved fatal and he believed—as he had done since the morning three days ago when she cracked—that he had a chance of getting her to a haven. If **Oceaan** proved worth her salt; if the right contract had been, or could be, made with her; if Carlsen could then get a line aboard from that tug; and if the weather then calmed down, even a little, he would win. A lot of ifs to ride—but he had had a little time to contemplate them, and he still had time to change his mind.

He was also driven by another, overriding if: if he quit the ship yet she continued to float, then she and her contents could fall into the paws of any salvage vessel, any tug or treasure hunter—**Oceaan** included—who would, Carlsen knew, want a hard bargain from Isbrandtsen and the underwriters. They were roaming the seas already, searching for the flotsam of this great storm—that was their living. By staying aboard, he became part of the negotiations over his own ship. Every shipmaster had a store of nightmare stories about ships abandoned that don't sink and are then picked up and towed to port. Carlsen was not going to give that dread a foothold.

HIS DECISION, THOUGH, exposed him to a new storm, one that never registered on Beaufort's scale. It wouldn't hit him for a few days—but he would never forget it.

Southland was heading for Rotterdam, **Arion** for Liverpool; **Greely** would depart soon. When they all reached their different ports, reporters would be waiting as the gangway came down. The passengers and the crewmen would

certainly talk, have their brief twirl in the lime-
light. They'd been saved from a shipwreck after
all, and who could deny them that shot of romance?

Once they told their thrilling stories, the
beam would switch to Carlsen, "out there on
the mad Atlantic," they would cry, alone on his
"keeled-over ship"; they would portray him as
"this crazy hero, this dedicated skipper"—Isbrandtsen, brilliant at manipulating the press,
knew what they would write. Isbrandtsen also
knew that the coastal relay stations would
either leak information or be eavesdropped
upon and that every detail of this event, every
word in every signal, could soon become public. If this possibility had crossed Carlsen's
mind, he would have recoiled at the thought.

Luckily, the season also bought him some
time. Post-Christmas torpor had blunted the
general antennae. Some newspapers, as a result
of the radio traffic, carried word of **Flying Enterprise**'s calamity and Carlsen's decision to
stay aboard, but only in their shipping pages.
For the moment, Carlsen could get on with
making some kind of life on board and Isbrandtsen could oversee the arrangements to
have him towed.

18.

ON SUNDAY MORNING, WHEN HE had finished his first bout of radio work, Carlsen went looking for food. On the radio a few days later, he said how he made sure to eat to strengthen his body and to sleep to strengthen his mind. He headed for the kitchen and the stewards' quarters. No matter where he went, no matter what route he chose, he faced problems.

Out on deck, the only way to get from place to place was by half-wedging himself in the angle of the teeming scuppers, using the side of the ship to lever his body along. The metals skinned his knees, his shins, and his ankles; his boots, socks, and feet became sodden and frozen—the temperature had dropped even further during the night. Snapped wires whipped through the air like random weapons.

Inside the accommodation block, he found all kinds of damage. In the swilling waters along the corridors, bits of debris swished past his legs like nervy rats. Many of the inside doors would no longer open easily—they had been forced permanently open or blocked by objects fallen across and behind them. Door frames had bent in the storm; such handles as remained workable proved too wet to grip and turn. Furniture and fittings rattled about, clanging off the walls.

Much of his ship had all the characteristics of a wreck on the bottom of the sea. Indeed, Carlsen had to behave like a diver: scarcely able to see his way forward, avoiding loose and dangerous fitments, and needing both hands to feel his way, hang on, and propel himself forward. His intimate knowledge of every rivet meant that he could largely get by without using his flashlight—for which he had no spare batteries.

He found no food in the pantry. It had been cleaned out, and understandably so, by the crew in their last hours on board. The empty refrigerator had warmed since the power had failed and offered only the dashed hopes of unclean water. Carlsen then clambered from the saloon to the permanent stores. Here, the angle of the ship had tilted the coldroom, so that the door handle met Carlsen's feet.

He tried to haul the door up. He eased it open a chink, caught the odor of rotting food, and let it drop shut. Along the corridor, where they kept the dry stores, he met another heavy and jammed door. It tilted slightly forward, and because its handle sat reachably above his head, he had a better chance of levering it ajar. He judged that he could probably ease the door outward a little. Yet he also understood that, given the angle, he would then have to prop it open. He went out on deck and kicked some heavy wooden wedges away from a hatch coaming; these wooden slices pinned the broad canvas straps holding down the four tarpaulins on each hatch.

Back inside, he opened the door of the dry goods locker and dragged it out far enough to let his body squeeze into the opening. He stood half inside the huge closet, propping the-door open with his shoulders. Then, with the back of an axhead that he had also collected on deck, he tapped the four wedges at intervals into the inside jamb of the quarter-open door.

This operation took almost half an hour, and he tested it rigorously to make sure that the door would stay open. Its own weight kept it pressing inward; and he could not press the door back any wider, because the wedges could have fallen out.

Now he had given himself a gap of almost two feet to squeeze through. He had to do it slowly, gently. If, in one of the ship's lurches, he was thrown against the door, the force could

knock out a wedge or two—or three, or four—
and the weighty door, on which he would not
then be able to get a purchase, would close
hard enough to pin him there, half in, half out.
Or if the wedges fell out once he had climbed
inside the store, the door could slam shut and
incarcerate him.

At last, he climbed in through the narrow
angle and shone his flashlight around: no food,
nothing, on the front of any shelf. He reasoned
that everything had slid to the rear in the
room's tilt, so he got himself onto one of the
large shelves sloping down and backward and
then ventured into the interior.

Thin pickings: he found some tea, some coffee, and, still in its circular tin mold, a large
cake like a giant doughnut with raisins, baked
in anticipation of New Year's Eve. He hooked
this confection around his wrist, turned
around carefully, crawled back up the sloping
shelf, and started to emerge. At that moment,
Flying Enterprise bucked in the swell and
dipped forward several degrees. Carlsen was
thrust out and down from his shelf but did not
fall. As his head stuck out, a large, catering-size
can of tomato juice fell from a shelf high above
and hit him on the skull like a hammer.

His consciousness flickered like a failing

light bulb, but he had the presence of mind not to react, not to take sudden action. He hunched there, keeping himself still, waiting—hoping—for his dizziness to pass. His flashlight had fallen from his hand—but in the recovering heave of the ship it slid down to him again. He dared to shine it at the door: with great good fortune, the incident had not loosened any of the wedges and he was not trapped.

Minutes later, out and free, Carlsen braved the decks again. Braced by the weather, which blew away the concussion's blear, he wore the cake like a comical giant bracelet and nudged the gallon of tomato juice ahead of him in the scuppers like a boy kicking a stone along a lane. Back in his own quarters, he entered in the ship's record an account of the stores he had just taken, then sat down to consume some of them.

BY NOON ON that first day alone, Sunday, December 30, Carlsen had adjusted his focus. He took on his new life as though nothing unusual marked his circumstances, as though nothing remarkable had taken place in the previous two days. With a satisfying anticipation of the tug about to arrive the next day, and his optimism for getting a successful tow under way, his exhaustion passed quickly.

Now his concentration moved forward to the business of reasserting himself. Sooner or later the freighter would start to become an active creature again. He would have to organize her behavior as best he could when establishing and maintaining the tow. And if she got to port, he would have to supervise the recovery of such cargo as had survived, and he would have to oversee the establishment of a repair contract. A master pays close attention to his ship's records. From their official home in the chartroom, Carlsen extracted the logs. As did most shipmasters, he kept two logbooks: the daily, or "rough," log, into which any officer could make an entry, and the more serious official, or "smooth," log. Into this, the captain or one voyage officer of his appointment transcribed the contents of the daily log, a task central to the running of any ship—because the official log has the status of legal record and belongs to the U.S. government, specifically the United States Coast Guard.

Carlsen found the daily, "rough" log water-damaged beyond use, but the official, "smooth" log had been preserved dry and intact. Due to the impossibility of writing during the storm and the ensuing crises, he had made no entries in the smooth log since December 24, the day when the weather had first begun to cut up the sea.

Wishing, as always, to observe protocol and avoid entering primary records in the official log, he cast around for usable paper but found none. With one of the chartroom pencils usually reserved for plotting courses, he began to write a record on the wall of his cabin—never was a rough log rougher. Obviously, if matters became more settled, he could transcribe that record into the smooth log; he would then, to his own satisfaction, have kept the ship "legal." When he had done his first stint of paper-work—wallwork—he settled down to reading a book on maritime law, taken from his own well-stocked bookshelf. And he apparently saw nothing extraordinary in anything he had done.

19.

AS CARLSEN SETTLED HIMSELF, events of which he knew nothing were about to have a direct bearing on his life. On **Greely,**

Commander Olsen cabled his superiors requesting new orders. Having reported the slightly marred success of the rescue operation ("1 of survivors dead on arrival here") he signaled, "We continue stand by ship as captain remaining aboard until arrival tug X All other ships released X Please advise if should continue stand by X Due to weather conditions please expedite reply." He also gave his position. Because of the survivors he carried, Olsen had a natural desire to get to port, where they could be more adequately examined and tended to.

Unbeknownst to him, a signal had already gone out from the U.S. Navy Atlantic headquarters in London dispatching U.S.S. **John W. Weeks** to relieve **Greely.** This seven-year-old destroyer, two months older than **Flying Enterprise,** had seen distinguished service in the Pacific theater, not least at Iwo Jima. The original John Wingate Weeks, a former naval officer, Boston banker, and Republican senator from Massachusetts, had served as U.S. secretary of war under Presidents Warren Harding and Calvin Coolidge.

Weeks had just arrived in Bordeaux after a journey through the Bay of Biscay in weather so ferocious that her commander reckoned it would take a week to fix the storm damage. He gave shore leave to most of his crew and took his officers to a cocktail party in the U.S. consulate—where he then received a message to get under way again as fast as possible.

On her voyage back up along Europe's flank, **Weeks** immediately ran into the same heavy weather that had now been hammering the western coasts of the continent since the night of Christmas Eve—seven days and nights of unrelenting gales and monumental waters. In his signals, her captain repeatedly updated his estimated time of arrival, saying that at best he was going to make no more than sixteen knots in a Force 8 that was blowing straight into his face.

The Atlantic command in London, knowing **Greely**'s anxiety to get the survivors to New York, diverted another American ship: the stores transporter **Golden Eagle,** under Captain William Donahue. In a real sense, because the sea was slowing up **Weeks** so much, this left Carlsen with a shepherd of less power, less speed, and fewer resources, though just as much good intent. And then the sea caused him another problem, also in the Bay of Biscay. This one proved much more threatening to Carlsen's interests.

. . .

ONCE L. SMIT & CO. had confirmed that
Oceaan was headed for **Flying Enterprise,**
Hans Isbrandtsen believed that he need do
nothing else but wait—just as Carlsen did.
Both men felt grateful that nobody thought
their ship beyond hope—and that some other
piece of the Atlantic carnage hadn't proven
more enticing. More than a dozen ships had
asked for urgent assistance in that storm; by
and large, they received it. Now, though, and
to the great detriment of Carlsen's and Isbrandtsen's interests, one of the helpers needed
help herself.

As a sister vessel to **Oceaan,** the heavy tug
Zwarte Zee, Isbrandtsen's first choice, was also
owned by Smit. But she had gone to save a
Danish cargo ship heading for the rocks on the
French coast. **Zwarte Zee** (the name translates
to "Black Sea"), built in 1933 and tough as
nails from nearly two decades of salt swells, did
manage to take the Danish ship under tow. But
in mountainous seas, she failed to get fully
clear of the coast, and in her maneuvering,
Zwarte Zee collided with her dependent.

Oceaan, which by now had made excellent
time, seemed about to get to **Flying Enterprise** well ahead of her own ETA and might
have Carlsen under tow perhaps even by Mon-

day noon, but calamitously for Carlsen, the Smit head office diverted her to help **Zwarte Zee**—she would not be coming to tow **Flying Enterprise** after all. Carlsen learned this news in his next communication with **Greely.**

For the rest of the day, through **Greely**'s radio shack, Carlsen's voice messages and Isbrandtsen's cables debated their next move. In the two hours between each of the communications, Carlsen continued his administration of the ship's business—while hoping that Isbrandtsen could find a tug.

Isbrandtsen came back to say that the Salvage Association had turned up **Abeille 25,** out of Calais, through the French company Compagnie de Remorque et de Sauvetage. And again, he found the operators a move ahead of him. On Saturday, responding as **Oceaan** had done to Carlsen's Friday morning Mayday, **Abeille 25** had edged out of the harbor at Calais and ventured west along the Channel to look for **Flying Enterprise.** When she saw the face of the Atlantic, **Abeille 25** turned back, intending to try again when the weather abated.

It didn't matter; when Isbrandtsen told Carlsen the details of **Abeille 25,** he also said that he doubted that she had the pulling power to haul his ship. When Carlsen heard her specifications, he agreed—had she reached **Flying Enterprise,** he might have had to turn down **Abeille 25** as underpowered. If they could use her, she would have to come into play as a second tug, but they had grave doubts about putting a second towline to a cracked ship. This rejection meant that they still had no tug.

THUS CARLSEN'S FIRST full day alone proceeded: from establishing successful communications, to a brush with death, to achieving a kind of food supply, to reaching a degree of contentment—and then to bitter disappointment. Now he had no idea whether he stood any chance at all of getting towed. He knew how a salvage company would add up the task: a powerless freighter lying on her side and taking on water more than three hundred miles from a good port, in weather with a bad forecast. Tough call, especially with so many more viable jobs on the water.

Carlsen did have the comfort of knowing that Isbrandtsen possessed the same understanding—and sufficient knowledge of Atlantic and northern European shipping to understand all the options and possibilities. If some salvage company did come to the table, the contract ramifications needed to be worked through by somebody who understood the arena. Carlsen himself would have preferred a say in addressing them; on the waters of the North Atlantic, he would have been quite prepared to negotiate fees, tables of commission, and ports of destiny.

Furthermore, if he didn't, would Isbrandtsen hammer out an agreement that didn't necessarily have the right shape for these peculiar circumstances? A deal that would put terms above results? At the very least, Carlsen knew that he would be able, when the time came, to discuss methods of towing and speeds under tow, and fight for the best rather than the most economic option. Given that he could communicate his wishes only through Isbrandtsen and the head office, that would probably be his only say in the matter.

After the debate over **Abeille 25,** Isbrandtsen went back to looking for a tug as big as **Oceaan** and **Zwarte Zee.** He found one. Out of Falmouth in Cornwall, she was "the strongest tug in the world," her owners claimed; she even had the perfect name for the occasion: **Turmoil.** But when Isbrandtsen sought to book her, **Turmoil** already had a ship in tow, a Shell oil tanker named **Mactra** that had been in trouble off Ireland since December 26; she had lost her propeller.

THAT WAS HOW Sunday, December 30, began to wind down—with one disappointment after another. And there was another uncontrollable challenge to come. This one reached deep into millions of lives.

The ship, like Prospero's isle, was "full of noises," many of them sudden, unexplained, and alarming. Through all the moanings and clangings, Carlsen now heard a new sound, different from any of the "thousand twangling instruments" that the wind and the weather were orchestrating, a sound never heard in Shakespeare's tempest. He went out on deck to check.

Coasts all over the world click with chatter—it saves lives. Much of the maritime radio traffic had already broadcast the **Flying Enterprise**'s misfortunes to the shipping world. Many of those signals came ashore into the nearest English relay station—at the Land's End, in Cornwall, a promontory whose cliffs form the front teeth in the upper jaw of the English Channel.

For centuries, Britain's south and southwest

coasts have watched for marauders from France and Spain. From the shores of the Channel to the mouth of the Atlantic, the counties of Kent, Sussex, Hampshire, Dorset, Devon, and Cornwall guard the island. That Sunday afternoon, a navy observation aircraft took off from one of the southwestern bases to search for **Flying Enterprise.** An abandoned drifting wreck has multiple ramifications, from life endangered or lost to insurance considerations to ownership of property in international waters to the dangers of a floating hulk.

When he found her, the navy pilot flew in a low circle above, seeking traces of life. Carlsen heard the aircraft engines, came out on deck, and, in heavy rain, waved up from his listing ship. One of the aircrew took a photograph.

That night, somebody looking to pick up a little moonlight sent the indistinct snapshot to London, where it came in on the wires of the **Daily Graphic** (later the **Daily Sketch**), one of Fleet Street's most popular newspapers. The picture desk puzzled over it: a freighter off the southwest coast, wallowing dramatically on her side, and a large ship standing idly by?

The editors called in naval and maritime experts, saying, What is this? See this speck here on the afterdeck? Could that be a man on this wrecked and sinking ship? Where are the crew?

Is this some kind of latter-day **Flying Dutchman**? They telephoned the navy base. How much do you know of this ship? There's a speck in this photograph, a detail that's puzzling us—could it be a man? Aboard alone? You mean a lone sailor against the elements?! This is a headline: "Trying to Save His Crippled Ship"! You mean you **know** about it? Who **is** he? Are you intending to fly above the ship again? Can we send a reporter? There's a night train to Penzance.

20.

THE YEAR 1951 CAME TO A QUIET close. nonetheless, growing—and significant—political issues materialized and marked the end of the beginning of the West's postwar change. For six years the cleanup operation had gone on. Food rationing persisted in parts of Europe, where myriad towns, villages, and cities had to be rebuilt, some from the ground up. (Even today, in Berlin, you gasp at the sheer intensity of the destruction.) For two years, the four major Allied powers had governed quadripartite Berlin—Britain, France, and the United States in the west of the city, and Stalin taking the lion's share in the east.

Now politicians' thoughts had shifted to structures that might—that should—prevent a European war from ever breaking out again. Just in time for New Year's Eve, the foreign ministers of Belgium, Italy, France, Luxembourg, West Germany, and the Netherlands reached a milestone agreement. Their countries would form what they, in part, described as a single parliament. In time, they insisted, Europe would federate. Dean Acheson, the American secretary of state, had high praise for this "historic decision."

The Cold War, that "horribly stable" era feared and defined by George Orwell, had been up and running almost since the German and Japanese surrenders. India's Prime Minister Nehru had now given the term "Third World" to the countries unaligned with either side in the Korean War, which had just begun to draw copious blood.

Those same First and Second Worlds had already traded their capitalist and Communist gibes and had long been at daggers drawn. Even though it would be ten years before the Soviet Union drew a line between the First and Second Worlds by building the Berlin Wall, sabers rattled everywhere that capitalism met

communism. Eugenio Pacelli, the highly political Pope Pius XII, got in on the act with his
Christmas message of "especial affection" for
prisoners held in Communist bloc jails because
of their Catholicism.

Meanwhile, America boomed at home, with
the highest national production figures ever
recorded. Within cautionary memory of two
world wars and the horrible Wall Street crash,
prudence climbed high; people saved more and
spent less.

But 1951 also left a bitter aftertaste in
America. Julius and Ethel Rosenberg were sen-
tenced to death for spying; the great national
figure of General Douglas MacArthur fell from
the president's grace. The nation could do with
a new hero and was already making suggestions. A man in an old tub of a boat had won
an Oscar: Humphrey Bogart in **The African
Queen.** Another man-and-ship story topped
the best-seller lists and took a Pulitzer Prize:
The Caine Mutiny, by Herman Wouk; and a
biography of Herman Melville won a National
Book Award. A man-against-the-sea theme was
rising—small human nature against great
odds, mortal versus cosmos.

In Ireland, we knew nothing of this zeitgeist;
we had only the spirit of our own time in our
own place. Like every half-developed island

people, we thought we looked out from the world's center. We had had our own busy year of mixed feelings. The godfather of the twenty-eight-year-old Free State (now a Republic), Éamon de Valera, had been returned to power in a minority government. A ferocious divisiveness was still attached to his name. The country had a volatile memory of the rancid civil war a generation earlier—a war that de Valera, some said, "didn't start but could have stopped." Such talk I picked up only in neighbors' houses because my pillars-of-the-community schoolteacher parents kept their political opinions to themselves.

Not that they seemed unaware of the world; a local newspaper in the southwest, **The Skibbereen Eagle,** whose circulation probably numbered in the hundreds, had famously stated half a century earlier that it was "keeping its eye on the Czar." My father's watchfulness may not have had the same grandiose scope, but he tracked the world not dissimilarly. Now the weather in the Atlantic had delayed Winston Churchill's visit to President Truman; my father rolled that kind of fact around every mealtime.

My own world went on turning in its usual orbit: school and escape, school and escape. I had to have such a routine. My primary education took place at the hands of my parents; if I didn't get into the fields and the woods, among the pheasants and the steaming horses and the crows in their gaunt trees, I'd have been in my father's presence between home and school, twenty-four hours a day. To this day, I have difficulty doing such uninterrupted duty with any human.

Our family Christmas in 1951 lived out its usual merriments, squalls, and terrors, lulled by engrossing books, card games with neighbors, and amiable visits. With never a white Christmas in those latitudes, we saw no more than the usual rain and mildness, occasional frost and brilliant starry skies. I can still reach back and hold each light gray day and each clear night in my hand.

IN VERY DIFFERENT weather out on the sea, Captain Carlsen, of whom I had not yet heard, spent New Year's Eve alone. The book that he had selected, **The Seaman and the Law,** was perhaps of limited use to him: international conventions had long pushed shipmasters out from under the umbrella term "seaman." Carlsen's practicality, though, never slept, and there might have been something in the book that he could use one day. Nothing would have kept him from viewing his position with anything but "business as usual" pragmatism.

Yet he had landed in a circumstance of great tradition: the lone sailor on the wide and storm-tossed sea. Admittedly, in Carlsen's case, it had a unique twist, but the world had long taken a romantic view of such figures. Coleridge's Ancient Mariner probably remains the most famous—except that, out of common with the events in the poem, Carlsen cheated Death when Death came looking for the souls on his ship. Solo yachtsmen or oarsmen, taking on the Capes of Horn and Good Hope, had not yet become the vogue that would give them a regular slot in the world's headlines. Four years earlier, though, another individual Scandinavian had conquered the ocean—and our imaginations.

That explorer, Thor Heyerdahl, built a balsawood raft and named it **Kon-Tiki,** after an Inca god of the sun. With a crew of five he then made a journey of four thousand miles across the Pacific. He did it to prove ancient migration routes, based on ocean currents between South America and the Polynesian archipelagoes.

Heyerdahl's journey took the world by storm. In the dog days after the awful revelations of war, from the skeletons of Germany's death camps to the ashes of Hiroshima and Nagasaki, he reminded people of "clean" adventure, where humans did not have to die hideously. Heyerdahl, being a Norwegian, had the good fortune to bear no stains of war. And he looked like a hero—a blond, clear-eyed outdoorsman, slim as a whip, firm as a rock, and evidently possessing superb ability.

He also reminded people of a romantic history—of the Vikings in their longboats and their legendary seamanship. Out of this history, Heyerdahl paved the way for Carlsen; the world was about to hail another Viking hero— one whose heralds arrived that morning.

Every two hours, Carlsen turned from his reading and his tasks to keep faith with his radio. During one hiatus he again heard the sound of aircraft engines. Twice in twenty-four hours? Nevertheless, he again went out and waved; he never failed to remember that he did, after all, represent the Isbrandtsen Line. This time, the photographs would have a more professional clarity.

CARLSEN'S RADIO CONTACTS with **Greely** followed a pattern. First he gave a reassurance that he continued to fare perfectly well. Then he asked for their weather forecasts, essential in that volatile sea. Next, he took collection of any messages for him. Tug news took priority. **Turmoil** had indeed been engaged to come to him; her owners had confirmed with Isbrandtsen. But they didn't know when she might reach **Flying Enterprise**—she still had to bring in the limping Shell tanker.

The last phase in each of Carlsen's radio contacts concerned his family. He asked repeatedly that Isbrandtsen keep them apprised of events and that his three dependents in Woodbridge be informed not only of his safety but of his cheerful spirits, and he sent them greetings for a "Happy New Year."

THEY NEEDED HIS reassurances. Just after Christmas, a neighbor in New Jersey had telephoned and asked Mrs. Carlsen whether she had heard of the storms.

"What storms?"

On December 23, when Carlsen—from the English Channel—had wished "Happy Christmas" to Agnes and the two girls, the foul weather had not quite reared its head. From the friend who now called, Agnes learned that in the great and violent cyclone pounding the

North Atlantic, the name of **Flying Enterprise** had been mentioned as one of the many ships in the area.

Soon, a bush telegraph began to throb. Neighbors telephoned solicitously; close friends began to drop by. Bit by bit, the pieces jigsawed into a disturbing picture: one had heard a mention on the radio; there had been a report in some shipping columns two days earlier that an American freighter named **Flying Enterprise** had encountered difficulties in an Atlantic hurricane.

The full harsh light shone on New Year's Eve, when **The New York Times** ran a front-page story about the European gales. On the inside pages, the newspaper printed a map showing the seas of distress, with accounts of ship after ship in trouble and vessels splitting in two. It mentioned **Flying Enterprise** as being "in serious danger."

Responding to Carlsen's message—"Have you calmed my wife?"—Hans Isbrandtsen called the family. He told Agnes of Carlsen's success in evacuating his passengers and crew, and of his refusal to leave the ship on account of his conviction that, with the right tug, he could save it. By and large his news sounded good; Carlsen had received no injuries and seemed to be in excellent spirits. Whatever her anxiety, Agnes declared herself unfazed.

"I knew his quality. I knew Kurt would not take on such a task if he didn't think he would succeed at it," she said.

All her days, Agnes Carlsen professed two great faiths in her life: in her God and in her husband.

AFTER THE VIVID diversion of the rescue operation, S.S. **Southland** resumed her interrupted voyage from Savannah. On the night of New Year's Eve, Captain William Lawton took her through the Rotterdam docklands, still devastated from the bombs of the war. **Southland** tied up at twenty minutes past eleven.

On the cold, dark quay stood representatives from the United States consulate—and Lieutenant Commander William Sayer of the U.S. Coast Guard at the consulate general's office in Antwerp. These officials already knew that an American ship called **Flying Enterprise** had foundered in the Atlantic; was "now," said the BBC, "reported adrift with only her Master aboard"; and they also knew from naval sources that there had been one fatality, a middle-aged male, and that **Southland** carried fifteen survivors of the accident—seven passengers and eight crewmen. These survivors wore clothes borrowed from **Southland**'s crew and most of them had, since being rescued, stayed in their bunks, too shattered to do more than eat or sleep.

WHILE **SOUTHLAND** WAS settling down for the night, a number of young men shared a compartment on a train that rode the southern slopes of England from London to Cornwall. One of them, age twenty-seven, had been visiting friends that day in the capital. His parents ran the post office in Hook Green, on the borders of Kent and East Sussex, south of London, near the town of Lamberhurst. This countryside has many such picture-postcard hamlets, with their patch of village common ground where the men play cricket in the summertime: Sparrow's Green, Bells Yew Green, Shover's Green.

During a telephone call to his home, the young man, Kenneth Roger Dancy, heard that he had received a telegram. His parents read it out to him; it meant work, and he went immediately to the City, the oldest commercial part of London, to the offices of the Overseas Towage and Salvage Company. They had connections to the coastal tanker on which Dancy had just been working and that had since been sold. Another of their vessels, however, needed a mate because the regular man, they told him, had gone to give evidence at an inquiry into the events surrounding the loss of a ship. Dancy needed the job, they needed Dancy, and they sent him to Falmouth—to join **Turmoil,** the tug Isbrandtsen had hired.

The other young men in the train compartment had also been hired as replacement crew—on the Shell tanker **Mactra,** which was, at that moment, being towed up the estuary into Falmouth harbor—by **Turmoil.**

When Dancy arrived in Falmouth, that tow had still not been completed. On account of the bad weather, the **Mactra** skipper wanted the comfort of the big tug standing by until it felt safe for the little local tugs to take him and his tanker up to a mooring; Falmouth claims to be one of the five or six largest—that is also to say, longest—natural harbors in the world. Dancy, on a night that was still blowing a gale, booked a room in a seafarers' pub, the Chain Locker, by Customs House Quay.

21.

IN THE FIRST FEW MINUTES OF NEW year's day 1952, Carlsen jumped awake. He heard sirens: Was Olsen trying to wake him? Did the men on **Greely**'s watch know something? He clambered up to his own cabin and called them. They told him that the sirens represented a hail and farewell; **Greely** had received orders to sail for New York, and another United States Navy ship would now stand by: **Golden Eagle,** under Captain William Donahue.

Like a cranky neighbor, Carlsen complained that it was after midnight, and the sirens had awakened him. Before he went back to bed, he checked again—any negative messages from **Turmoil** or Isbrandtsen? No, just the confirmation that **Turmoil** hadn't left Falmouth yet; she expected to arrive sometime on Thursday.

Thursday? Anything could happen in those forty-eight hours. The wind had backed up to northwesterly again; it was ricocheting between Force 7 and Force 9, seas heaping up into white foam, chimneys crashing off houses.

Thursday seemed a long way off. There's no doubt that Carlsen saw the odds stacking up against him. In one of his many radio transmissions, he described the seas being "all over" **Flying Enterprise.** How could they not be? The wind that howled through his ship stayed in the upper register hour after hour after hour, as though something had enraged it.

UNDER UNITED STATES LAW, the loss of a life from an American ship demanded a U.S. Coast Guard inquiry. Coast Guard officers began investigating **Flying Enterprise** while she was still at sea. At just after eight o'clock on the morning of New Year's Day, aboard the **Southland** at her mooring in Rotterdam, the first notes were sounded, overture to the main event, which would open nine days later in New York.

"With the exception of Mrs. Dannheiser," said the U.S. consulate report to the State Department in Washington, "the passengers were reasonably well on arrival in Rotterdam. The doctor who examined Mrs. Dannheiser after her arrival stated that her condition did not appear serious."

Lieutenant Commander Sayer, under orders from New York, interviewed fourteen people that day. They included eleven of the saved fifteen—three passengers and eight crewmen—as well as three of **Southland's** personnel. The four **Flying Enterprise** rescuees whom he did not interrogate were Nina Dannheiser, Maria Duttenhofer, Lothar Müller, and Leonore Von Klenau.

It seems possible that Mr. Sayer skipped the questioning of these passengers on humanitarian grounds, although I have found no such evidence. In demeanor and well-judged brevity, his examination of all the others—while missing no essence—suggests a belief that they had already had enough; they needed to move on.

The Rotterdam inquiry was designated "In the Matter of the Listing of S.S. **Flying Enterprise** 28 December 1951"—not in the matter of the death of a passenger; no inquest had yet been held. In any case, the issue of "listing" opened many pathways. It could ask whether Carlsen had acted responsibly; and it could also raise the question of what had happened to cause the listing, whether blame should be ascribed. Blame could touch interesting sensitivities—blame of a man who had already done so much and who was still at sea, trying to save his ship.

Mr. Sayer began with Leanne Müller, who was lucid and brief. He touched on the matter

of a boat drill and heard that it had not happened; nobody had shown her or anybody else
how to put on a life jacket until they knew they
would have to abandon ship. Her testimony
feels almost more powerful and atmospheric
between the lines.

> Q. Did you hear any sounds of the ship
>   cracking or anything like that?
> A. Yes. All the time.
> Q. That was just creaking and cracking?
> A. Yes, sir.

Her most telling evidence described how
they sat on the floor of the ship "for twenty-
two or twenty-four hours."

> Q. Did they tell you to get dressed
>   warmly?
> A. Oh, yes they did, but we weren't able
>   to because our suitcases were closed
>   and we weren't able to open them. I
>   told you that we were seasick and we
>   stayed in bed for five or six days.

She had no complaints about the crew of
Flying Enterprise—or the crew of **Southland.**
Her mother testified next, with Leanne
translating.

Q. How did you leave the ship?
A. I jumped with a line in my hand.
Q. It wasn't tied to you?
A. No, I held the rope in one hand, then
   I got the rope with two hands.

After not much more than two to three minutes of such exchange, Mr. Sayer asked Elsa
Müller, "Do you feel all right now?" and she
replied, "Tired, but very happy to be saved."

No other passenger spoke at greater length.
Rolf Kastenholz was asked, "Where were you
going in America?" He answered touchingly,
"To my father."

Not surprisingly, the crew spoke longest, and
George Brown, the chief engineer, longest of
all. He took Mr. Sayer carefully through the
voyage, from the fog on the Elbe through the
events of the fracture, and then to the final listing. In length, the Rotterdam inquiry runs to a
twentieth of the U.S. Coast Guard inquiry that
later took place in New York, but Brown nevertheless managed to give comprehensive evidence, often speaking for several minutes at a
time, with the practical eloquence of a man
who knows what he's talking about.

His loyalty to his duty, never mentioned by
him, comes across with strength and presence.
At one moment, he shows the pain of a deeply

felt failure. When water was pouring through the crack into Hold 3, "faster than we could pump it out," he had to choose between trying to pump out the water or trying to pump fuel oil. "So the only thing I could think of to do was to pump fuel oil," he said. "But I never would have gained on that damn water."

Mr. Sayer asked Brown and others about Carlsen, about Carlsen's performance under fire.

Brown testified, "I never saw him excited at all."

Harold Gleaves, the pantryman, when his turn came, said the same: "I have been through other procedures where the Captain was panicky, excited, nervous, but this Captain was calm, very calm and very efficient."

Nobody singled out Carlsen for praise; nobody volunteered compliments to his handling of their rescue. Carlsen engendered respect rather than warmth in his crew; he kept them at a distance. On the other hand, more than one of the Black Gang singled out George Brown with remarks such as "I never see a young man like that do such a wonderful job" or, as John Crowder, Brown's second assistant engineer, put it, "I never saw a man stand up as well as he did."

The questioning ended at just before half

past four on the afternoon of New Year's Day. In a preliminary report to his superiors in Paris, Lieutenant Commander Sayer principally observed some formalities of fact: the broad details of the incident at sea, the number and nature (passengers and crew) of survivors, the cracking of the ship's plates; and the permanent listing. His final points swung between querulous inquiry and plain commendation: "All information indicates no panic or undue confusion, and in several instances of unusual devotion to duty, particularly Chief Engineer, who kept plant operating despite list until generator burned out, presumably because unable to retain lube oil. Boat crew of S.S. **Southland** also praiseworthy."

While Mr. Sayer pursued his inquiries, the consulate officials also talked to each survivor and then began to slice through the immigration red tape. Early the next day, Hans Isbrandtsen cabled his Dutch shipping agents, Vinke & Co.—still operating vigorously out of Rotterdam and still "specializing in handling tramp vessels." Vinke was instructed to make sure that all the survivors from **Flying Enterprise** were fed, clothed, and safely accommodated in Rotterdam until they could be flown onward to New York.

22.

JAKOB ISBRANDTSEN LIVES IN A SALT-white house in norwalk, Connecticut, within a stone's throw of the Atlantic where it flows through Long Island Sound. A stocky man with bright, strong white hair, he looks like a weathered sailor. He has been close to the water, one way and another, since he was born. If the human body is seventy percent water, Jakob Isbrandtsen's must have been brine from birth; he is the sole natural son (there was also an adopted brother) of Hans Isbrandtsen— known to all as "H.I."

Jakob (who came to be called "J.I.") seeks balance when describing his father; he calls him "tough—and compassionate, very compassionate" and he tells a story: "The Mayor, La Guardia, put all the organ-grinders out of business and we had an organ-grinder near our office and my father went and got the man back to play again. That's the kind of thing he liked to do."

Hans Jeppesen Isbrandtsen turned sixty a few months before **Flying Enterprise**'s accident, having been born in 1891 at Dragør (pronounced "Drauer") in Denmark—a small and orderly cobbled town on a droplet of an island that produces vegetables for Copenhagen, less than a dozen miles away. Here, Hans Isbrandtsen grew up, the middle child of a sea captain and a shipping merchant's daughter.

He grew tall early, and quite fierce, with a muscular personality and immense energy. Every feature of his face would always speak strength and endeavor, aggression and suspicion. He ruled his companies like an overlord; he faced his opponents like a warlord. By 1951, he had reached the heights of the shipping trade. From that vantage point he irritated, galvanized, annoyed, and provoked whomever he encountered—his shipping rivals; trade authorities and associations; the governments of many nations; his own agents, executives, and captains; the White House; the world at large.

With eyes blue as ice (the name Isbrandtsen means "the son of ice and fire"), and fit as a fiddle, he kept his body as hard as his spirit. From regular workouts, and from farming his land and his pedigreed dairy herd on Long Island, he had developed muscles on his arms like small hawsers. Where other men found that the simple act of walking worked quite adequately, he hammered his way across the city and the universe, using his physique as his engine.

In his company's most successful period, the Isbrandtsen Line had as many as 120 ships at sea—a dozen of its own, the rest chartered. H.I. tracked them all with models on a board, like a desk admiral at war. The other half of his business included oil and gas and such diverse retail interests as his own brand of coffee— called "26," for his New York office address at 26 Broadway. A year before the **Flying Enterprise** affair, his rivals (who were many and outspoken) had reckoned him worth in excess of thirty million dollars.

As he expected his captains to, Isbrandtsen led from the front. He peppered his employees with instructions, ranging from the trivial to the policy-making. Few stood up to him, and many left—they became known as "Wasbrandtsens." Only the grizzled and experienced lasted; more than one contemporary profiler noted that Isbrandtsen's personal assistant had been an aide to the imperious General George Patton.

Isbrandtsen's office served as his mountaintop. From it poured a steady stream of his views on the world in general, and marine commerce in particular. He published a magazine, a handsome and large-format publication called (with no respect for superstition) **Albatross.** This appeared at the intervals of his whims, and he used it to pound and expound. It contained manifold opinions never shyly uttered, and its content had about as much predictability as the winds that buffeted the ships of the Isbrandtsen Line.

On Jakob Isbrandtsen's bookshelves, the dark brown, leatherbound volumes of his father's magazine stand out with an energy of their own. A kind of encyclopedia of one man's ego, the tall and glossy pages of **Albatross** offer no predictable lines of thought or editorial direction. No set pattern of desired influence seems to operate here—except that the collected editions do embody a philosophy: a belief in the power of marine commerce and its right to trade freely across the world.

Across Western literature, figures of ambiguous magnetism such as Isbrandtsen make immortal characters. The Scandinavians defined them sharply—in Ibsen's plays, such as **An Enemy of the People, John Gabriel Borkman,** and **The Master Builder.** In England, they towered in the novels of Charles Dickens, Anthony Trollope, William Makepeace Thackeray, and John Galsworthy—repellently dominant but arrestingly vulnerable men at the core of developing society. American writers gloried in them; Henry James's millionaire Adam Verver, in **The Golden Bowl,** traveled through Europe in search of culture, objets d'art, and love.

Isbrandtsen could have been the star of such a novel. Along with the Morgans, Vanderbilts, and Fricks of New York, he would have gratified those who define the complex, domineering personality system that they call "alpha male." He was direct and ungovernable, a merchant king, a medieval baron.

Nobody who met him ever forgot him; he had a certainty about him that infused everything he did, and it came out of a family shape as complete as a cube. Uncles and great-uncles, grandfathers and great-grandfathers, cousins and kinsmen, had captained ships, owned sail, generation after generation—and had been swept overboard, sucked down, frozen to death, drowned, destroyed. Isbrandtsen's father, a shipmaster, had died of pneumonia when Hans was two; Captain Isbrandtsen had gone to check on his ship, which had been trapped in port by the winter ice.

The widow decided that her son should not join the ranks of the iced and fallen. She apprenticed H.I. to a local ship's chandler, a large retail establishment that supplied every vessel

up and down that coast with every kind of required provision. Nicoline Jeppesen had an ex-
ceptional spirit, and the teenager, whatever his
bitter disappointment, dared not go against
her. Instead, he found ways of loosening her
straitjacket by working within it.

Already trained to do all manner of tasks—
he could smoke fish and salt meat, make
sausages, bake bread—the teenage Hans persuaded his employer to let him start a small
offshore retail service. In this, he intended to
sell needles and anchors to passing ships, even
if the physical operation of getting the goods
on board vessels under way proved dangerous.

After understanding the risks, Isbrandtsen
adjusted the operation. He still sailed out to in-
tercept the passing trade, but he no longer carried goods. Now he gambled on the fact that
many of the vessels were freighting to and from
factories up and down the shore, so he printed
out competitive prices on a big board, which
he held up from his rowboat. Then he took orders from the seamen, and raced his deliveries
over by bicycle when their ships docked a few
miles away.

Within that background and experience was
born everything Hans Isbrandtsen became.
From his own DNA and from boyhood experience, he had an innate knowledge of the sea,

its vessels, and their risks; he knew what ships needed in order to function; he had a natural, nearly atavistic understanding of how the oceans figured in commerce.

His mother saw to it that he achieved an education in marine commerce, one that specialized in steamship trading. He went to Paris as a chartering clerk and came home to Denmark at the outset of the Great War, in 1914. Through a cousin, he became involved with a Scandinavian steamship line that tried to make a living by running the shipping blockades set up by England and Germany in their war. As all of Europe was drawn into the conflict, the American flag, still neutral, soon offered safer registry, and Isbrandtsen went to New York to manage ships there in a company called American TransAtlantic.

His natural daring paid off, and by squaring up to, facing down, or dodging any navy that still sought to block supplies to their enemies, he kept his ships moving and made handsome profits. In the three major years of his wartime operation, 1915, 1916, and 1917, he took the American TransAtlantic Company from an opening thousand dollars in the bank to a balance of nine million. For this, he received one of commerce's typical rewards: he lost his job and his directorship in a takeover.

Isbrandtsen's next incarnation roughed him up some more. He tried to develop docklands in New York but, coming from a land of Calvinistic rectitude, he first failed to perceive, and then refused to acknowledge, that New York had graft and bribery the way he had veins and arteries. The unscrupulous ones were given sight of his plans, and they beat him to the punch every time.

Not only that but when he did hire someone to go down there and bring some gold up out of the dirt, Isbrandtsen chose a man who went down too far. At this glimpse of the underworld, H.I. ended up buying a gun, and in time he canceled all his ambitions to build new docks on New York's waterfront.

He had always been destined for shipping, however, and in the 1920s, after marrying a widow, adopting her children, fathering his own son, Jakob, and building a house and farm on Long Island, he went into business with a cousin who owned a shipping line. Maersk remains one of the most powerful names in ocean freight; when he joined forces with it, H.I. was thirty-seven.

Thus did Hans Isbrandtsen arrive on the major plateau of his life. With his huge and flamboyant presence he had no choice but to try to influence the world. To the New World he brought great tranches of his young European life and, as with all domineering men, this sometimes appeared capriciously. For instance, he knew from growing up in Denmark how much Europeans liked music in public places—from big-city events to local bands playing in the squares of small towns. In New York, down on Wall Street, within earshot of his office, he hired a thirty-five-piece regimental band to play at lunchtime. He hoped that other local firms would contribute to the cost; when they refused, Isbrandtsen went ahead anyway, and the bands played on for a decade, to general delight. And he ended the concerts the first day a band played jazz.

Another musical experiment also ran aground. He loved that Italian dockworkers seemed more energetic when singing snatches of opera, so he arranged for Puccini, Verdi, and the other usual suspects to be piped to them. The workers took this as an insult to their own singing. When the union threatened action, Isbrandtsen disconnected the speakers.

Isbrandtsen ran 26 Broadway like a ship. His floor, the "Maindeck," connected by a ship's ladder to a balcony above named the "Bridge." He never had a visitor's chair in his office, and he conducted all meetings standing up—he even stood at his own desk, a harking back to the younger days of Danish countinghouses and clerks at tall desks.

None of his employees, captains excepted, received a rich wage (yet he had a reputation for handouts to strays, especially wandering Danes). At 26 Broadway, his word was not only law, it was holy writ; he sounded off about this, that, and the other, left, right, and center. Using his great height to great effect, he descended on his employees, loomed over them, and berated them about the untidiness of their desks; he then returned to his own desk and wrote them coruscating memos.

As with all such breathtakingly dominant men, he could respond unexpectedly well to a touching remark. Sonia Carlsen, visiting her father at the office one day, met Isbrandtsen—she was barely ten at the time—and told him that he looked dashing in his linen suit. He warmed to the compliment and told her that when she was "of age," she could have a world tour on one of his ships. When the time came, she remembered and reminded him—and he honored his promise.

Her father had a good psychological handle on Isbrandtsen. Early in his service with H.I., Carlsen asked for radar. Isbrandtsen cheapskated down as far as pencils for the office, and on the radar issue he repeatedly brushed off

Carlsen—and the other captains. But Carlsen knew his man and watched for a chink. He found it.

Isbrandtsen loved his sister, Emma. When she was returning from a trip to Europe on Carlsen's ship, Carlsen went to work on her. He told her that not having radar was now dangerous, and that it also slowed them down; Maersk, her cousin's line, had radar and was beating the Isbrandtsen ships by days. Soon after Carlsen delivered the sister to New York, Isbrandtsen ordered radar for his entire fleet.

Whatever his aggressions and transgressions, no matter how much he gritted people's teeth, Hans Isbrandtsen had all the instincts and experience for dealing with a crisis at sea. He knew the right thing to do, and he showed it when he told Carlsen to put his own safety first. Yet he also knew that he had no control over a captain at sea—and, with Carlsen, little power to influence a man so fixed.

He also knew his man; he had given Carlsen his first master's command four years earlier. Carlsen, like all master's ticket holders, had served time as a mate of different standings, and much of that time on ships in which Isbrandtsen had an interest. And like so many Scandinavian—and other—mariners in the United States, he wanted to go on working for

Isbrandtsen, because no matter how controversial the circumstances, Isbrandtsen always supported his captains against his crews and unions, often risking trouble to do so.

The two men got on comfortably, with occasional gusts of rancor. Isbrandtsen chose his skippers carefully and paid them well; Carlsen earned more than the average freight skipper's thousand dollars a month in 1951. As Carlsen admired H.I.'s policy of backing the ship's master, Isbrandtsen received from Carlsen the firm loyalty he demanded. Whatever Carlsen's forthrightness to Isbrandtsen in their own dealings, he defended his owner's interests tooth and nail. Each knew how the other operated; each perceived the other's limits.

In the **Flying Enterprise** fracas, Isbrandtsen not only had to know his man, he also had to review his own position. Jakob Isbrandtsen remembers a newspaper advertisement that "really impressed" his father: "It showed two trapeze artists in whites, swinging on a black page, and one going to catch the other, and the caption on this is—the question is, 'When to Let Go?' "

Jakob recalled the observation in reference to Carlsen's stay-on-board decision. Yet it also had to apply to Hans Isbrandtsen, who could try to influence Carlsen but—no small difficulty for such an emperor—could not tell him what to do. Which explains why Isbrandtsen was able to say, when the newspapers questioned him about Carlsen, "He will either take the ship in, or he'll see her down."

23.

GOLDEN EAGLE, THOUGH A LARGER vessel, had much in common with **Flying Enterprise.** Also built in California, she too had been commissioned as a wartime freighter and delivered to the War Shipping Administration early in 1943. After 1945, she had a brief civilian life and then returned to military duty with a run remarkably similar to **Flying Enterprise's**—out of the eastern United States to European ports such as Bremerhaven and Rotterdam.

At eight o'clock on New Year's Day, just as Lieutenant Commander Sayer in Rotterdam had begun to ask the first questions about **Flying Enterprise,** and as Kenneth Dancy still had the liberty to sleep late in Falmouth, Carlsen fulfilled his first two-hourly radio routine with **Golden Eagle.** He spoke to Captain

Donahue, who introduced himself and engaged Carlsen in conversation.

They talked about the rescue effort. Carlsen revealed his pride in his crew and how touched he was to see how his "boys took it on the chin. I saw only one man crying and that was either through pain or fear because he had fallen down and hurt his arm." (Think of twenty-two-year-old Matias Moraes, blown off his feet when the rogue wave hit him inside the wheelhouse.)

Captain Donahue suggested that while awaiting the tug, Carlsen might like to come over to **Golden Eagle.** Before he could specify how they would fetch him, Carlsen politely refused, with this observation: "We shipmasters are entrusted with people's lives, with a ship and its cargo and it is a responsibility we cannot let go. I have very valuable cargo aboard here, I have five hundred tons of United States mail." He thanked Captain Donahue for the offer and signed off to have his breakfast—of beer and pound cake.

Once more, Carlsen began his daily rounds. First, he needed to remedy an increasingly urgent deficiency: he had nothing to drink but beer. (His daughter Karen recalls a jibe from a schoolteacher: "Of course we know why your father stayed on board the ship. He's a sailor—all that beer.") Due to the ship's internal damage, there was no fresh water. When George Brown found the ship's own water supply spilling across the floors of the engine room, he turned off such taps as he could reach. Carlsen recovered a little water to drink (most of it stale) by searching crew and passenger cabins for night-table water flasks.

With this quest behind him, he became his ship's master again. Every captain tracks the condition of his vessel during a voyage, and Carlsen had a lot to inspect. He checked for new depredations—too many to count. He looked at the cracked plates—who could say whether they had opened wider? He saw that the wind had pulverized his deck cargo—the sacks of naphthalene had become an obstacle course; they lay strewn like large garbage bags around the main deck, blown off the breakwater that was sheltering the repairs on the fracture. Carlsen visited, scrutinized, and noted, as though observing a normal routine.

Some routine: to avoid being swept overboard, he again traveled to most points on his hands and knees, or half-standing in a kind of monkey walk, one hand on the deck, the other grabbing what he could by way of rail or fit-ment, and always drenched to the skin by the sea and the rain, and always frozen to the bone by the chill of the wind.

Back inside, he resumed his paperwork: crewmen's food and drink debits, wages lists, the rough log that he was keeping on the wall. He pressed on with the general daily administration of a ship, and he even granted overtime awards to those who had come back on watch three days earlier to help repair the cracked plates.

OUT IN THE WORLD, other than Winston Churchill's **Queen Mary** voyage to the United States, not much else was happening. Therefore, on one of the slowest news days of the year, the photographs England saw that morning in the **Daily Graphic** made history. The newspaper had scooped the world with some of the most dramatic shots ever taken of a ship at sea. They showed the freighter listing alarmingly—the wonder being that she still floated. And then they highlighted the greater marvel: that a lone man, the captain, had remained aboard and that he meant to get his ship to port under tow.

New Year's Day has always been a silent day in Europe, a still day in the Irish countryside, marked only by Mass for Catholics, a church holy day, the feast of the Circumcision of Christ. (To my certain knowledge, the term **circumcision** was never explained or defined to us. It was glossed over and when I inquired, my mother's answer had an uneasy, fobbing-off tone. Nor did she come forward any further when I asked, "Aren't we supposed to learn **every**thing about Jesus's life?") Weather permitting, I roamed the fields as usual on New Year's Day, hoping to see a fox; otherwise, the books received as Christmas gifts were there to be read.

Our household had a rule (one of thousands): only my father listened, and always alone, to the six-thirty news from the sole national station, Radio Eireann. He limited strictly our access to the "wireless," which lived, hooded like a parrot's cage, in the parlor, a chintz-and-lace place usually kept for receiving guests or for special family occasions. To listen, my father lifted the fringed brocade cloth and tuned the dial through the whistles and hisses of Hanover, Hilversum, and Luxembourg and settled to the BBC in London—or to Ireland's transmitter, in the very center of the country, Athlone.

When he sat in there alone, under the soft yellow light of an oil lamp (we had no electricity in 1952, and the radio operated on huge batteries), we could hear, from the kitchen, the gentle froth of the static and the distant hint of sonorous, announcing tones; that was as close as we got to the news at half past six.

But on that first evening of 1952, he— astonishingly—summoned the family in a rush to the door of the parlor. Standing there, looking over his spectacles, he said, in a thrilled voice, "There is an incident happening at sea"—this from a man in whom the stir of excitement never broke cover.

Soon we heard the frying hiss of static around Carlsen's radio messages, the flat, strong Danish voice and the concerned twang of his American shepherds. Then my father switched to the BBC, where grave commentators further hailed this man whom the daily newspapers had begun calling "Captain Courageous."

The entire family switched into a mode of wonder. That very night, and for the next two weeks, a new and powerful topic of conversation flowed around the household, more vital than a circus come to town. And that night too, as we sat down to supper at the long table in the kitchen, the sea poured in across our threshold and washed words up at our feet, words that lay there glittering like a trawler's catch.

Teachers teach, unstoppably, involuntarily—
and, in my father's formal, churchy intonation,
we were now taught every word that arose
from this news report.

Captain comes from **caput,** the Latin word
for **head;** the word **skipper** descended from
"the sound of the Dutch and northern European pronunciation of **ship** as **schip.**" The
Greeks supplied **ocean,** from their god
Oceanus; Oceanus was the "river of life" encir-
cling the globe. **Sea,** however, came down from
the north of the world as a sound-word, the
hissing of waters meeting to form a marsh or a
tide. **Deck** was a word the Dutch used for the
cloak or blanket covering a horse—the nautical
extension of it portrayed the deck not as something sailors walk on but as a shelter for the
cargo below.

Log and **knot** also came along a practical
road. To measure their speed, the mariners of
old pitched a log into the sea, to which they attached a string. The string had been calibrated
with knots tied at regular intervals, a foot or a
meter, and then wound around a reel, which
was set beside an hourglass. The speed at which
the string unwound from the reel—that is, the
number of knots sent through in an hour—
told them the speed of the ship. The captain's
"log," therefore, recorded the information

given to the ship by the log to which the string was tied.

I had been in such territory before—with my grandfather, though with no sense of obligation to remember all I was hearing. Now I knew that I would be questioned on these teachings the next day and, dear God, I knew I had better remember them. My father even defined the word **duty**—and delivered it as a lecture, all of which I can recall almost verbatim, because he repeated it so many times.

"It comes from an old French term, **du tout,** meaning 'of all' or 'of the total'—in which consequence it represented that portion 'of everything' a man earned which he has given to the church or state. **Are you listening, sir? Duty,** as in Customs and Excise"—my father used a great number of capital letters in his little orations—"also means a proportionate charge. Thereby, **duty** stretched its meaning to embrace moral obligation—and a sea captain's moral obligation is to women and children first and the safe homecoming of his ship. **Duty** in that sense comes to represent how large a proportion of himself a man gives to his employer. **Are you taking this in?**"

If I had not taken it in, if I failed to answer tomorrow's questions, I knew without a morsel of doubt what would happen. Whereas my grandfather's stories of the sea danced into my mind through the door named "Delight," my father's lessons strode through the door marked "Fear." Did fear teach more effectively than delight? I recall both men's lessons with equal clarity.

Even more clearly do I remember that my devout mother, that very evening, added "the safety of Captain Carlsen and the **Flying Enterprise**" to our nightly family prayers. And now that we knew, the world knew.

24.

AT TWENTY MINUTES BEFORE NINE the next morning, comnaveastlant, the United States Navy command for the eastern Atlantic, received the following message from **John W. Weeks:**

> Relieved **Golden Eagle** as standby vessel for disabled S.S. **Flying Enterprise** at 020330Z [three-thirty in the morning of January 2] X Radio Voice Communications established with master X Baro 29pt62 dropping steadily X Wind WSW

Force 8 sea very rough swells heavy sky partly cloudy visibility unlimited X **Flying Enterprise** on southerly heading drifting east at 2 knots X Captain Carlsen in good spirits X No apparent change in condition of ship X All messages have been relayed to Captain Carlsen.

Now Carlsen sent a punchy message through **Golden Eagle** to Isbrandtsen: "Situation morning of the 2nd: Number Three Hold full of water. Engine Room taking some water however not much. Decks awash to hatch coamings port side but chances are good that she will stay afloat. List about 65 degrees. Otherwise conditions unchanged. Will transfer to tug when contract is signed satisfactorily and lines are fast."

When he had finished his signal, Carlsen spoke to Captain Donahue on **Golden Eagle** and thanked him for the care and attention. During their exchanges, and for the first and only time during his catastrophe, Carlsen revealed some emotion. He told Captain Donahue, "I am sorry this has upset your schedule—you have lost a couple of days." And then he said, "I'm getting a little lonesome."

From a man of Carlsen's rigid and shipmas-

SIMPLE COURAGE   *217*

terly demeanor, this equaled a diva's fit of wild
weeping. He buttoned himself back up immediately. Later that day he made a request of
John W. Weeks: "I wouldn't mind some hot
coffee and meat sandwiches, and some magazines." This was the first time he had asked for
anything for himself; up to then he had sub-
sisted without comment or complaint on his
beer and pound cake.

AT 376 FEET long and 40 feet wide, the destroyer **John W. Weeks** was slightly shorter
and narrower than **Flying Enterprise,** one-
third of the weight, and over twice as fast. And
fuller: she had a typical complement of 330 officers and men. Under Commander William
Thompson, a Texan from McKinney, north of
Dallas, she arrived while the seas remained
heavy and the wind at gale force. After his first
sight of the distressed freighter, Thompson said
to one of his officers that she looked as though
she were "about to go down at any moment
now"; he remarked later that he spent the
whole day catching his breath while looking at
Flying Enterprise.

Early in the morning, Carlsen opened radio
contact with **Weeks,** the third standby vessel
with whom he would maintain his two-hourly

spoken vigils. They discussed the arrival of **Turmoil** the next day and the management of the situation until then. Carlsen introduced a new decision: if **Flying Enterprise** started to sink fast, he would set off the ship's blue emergency flares. The men on **Weeks** would know that by the time the flares hit the sky, Carlsen would have jumped off the ship on the listing, port side and would at that moment be swimming toward **Weeks**—wearing a life vest, of course. He then announced that he was going back to sleep.

In a conversation with Carlsen at noon that day, Commander Thompson tried, as had Captain Donahue, to persuade him to come across to **Weeks**—at least until **Turmoil** arrived. When Carlsen refused, they then had the conversation about food. Thompson's chefs had prepared an enormous bag of provisions of all kinds, including flasks of coffee and packets of cigarettes. Carlsen, by arrangement, went to the aft starboard rail of the main deck, the nearest point that they all considered safe for accepting a line.

Who **were** those seamen? They had warmth, skill, and daring; handling a ship the size of **Weeks** in those seas tested everybody. Thompson timed his approach to the rhythm of the swell, hoping to get in step with the rise and fall of **Flying Enterprise.** If they could get a line over to Carlsen, he could make it fast to the rail and they could then slide the sack of food across. When he had taken it on board, he could release the line again.

It took ages. The men on **Weeks** got hammered over and over by the waves and weather; Carlsen had become used to these conditions. Finally, across not much more than thirty feet of sea, dangerously close, a line reached Carlsen and he caught it. Too thin—if he started maneuvering a heavy weight of food along this rope, the cord would cut him to the bone.

He dropped the line, and the food fell into the sea. Carlsen left the deck, went to his radio, and called **Weeks,** telling them to abandon the attempt because they were taking a greater pounding than he was. He also lost to the sea the shell casing they'd tried to send over, containing a thermos of coffee.

JOURNALISM OFFERS not so much "the first draft of history" as the first snapshots—and snap judgments. In New York next day, the **Daily News** reported, "The skipper of the **Flying Enterprise** held out in his lone and heroic stand against the sea for the sixth day today, despite gale force winds and two failures by the U.S. Navy to get a line aboard the freighter." The report suggested that "further attempts were postponed" and that it didn't seem to matter because, according to "a New York spokesman for the Isbrandtsen Line," Carlsen had "emergency electricity apparatus lights and plenty of canned food and water."

Sharper and more accurate details were about to emerge—because the news story began to pick up speed. After those first photographs from the **Daily Graphic** had been flashed around the world, the media began a two-pronged attack. They reported on the survivors and they zeroed in on Carlsen, because by now they knew that he intended to stay aboard until the British tug—already on its way—hauled him to safety.

This story bulged with glorious ingredients. It had a hero in impossible conditions. There were survivors about to arrive. And it was wholly transatlantic, the Old World coming to the aid of the New. The New York **Daily News:** "A British tug raced tonight to the rescue of Captain Courageous as his ship, **The Flying Enterprise,** wallowed in strong new gales. . . . The tug, **Turmoil,** one of Britain's fastest and largest, set out from Falmouth, bucking 60-mile winds and heavy hail showers." Plus—the journalists were coming back to work after their Christmas and New Year break.

An old newspaper adage says, "People want to read about people"—and this story had so much and such quotable human interest. There was Leanne Müller, who said, "When the steward came rushing into our cabin and told us to quickly, to get out of bed and put on our life jackets and then when we went out in the gangway we saw that the sea was like a terrific mountain, I've never seen anything like that, all covered with foam."

Danish Leonore Von Klenau, described as "39 and Viennese," had "saved her camera but was unable to take pictures because the camera got wet"—the tiny detail that is often the only thing remembered by the newspaper reader.

One by one, the survivors stepped forward. "Rolf Kastenholz, an accountant, was greeted by his father Joseph who lived on 94th Street—they had been separated for 20 years." And "Mrs. Nina Dannheiser, 55, from Hamburg, credits the saving of her life to a bracelet and to an officer who held her above the water by grasping the bracelet. [She was] greeted by her daughter Yolanda Wolkonski of 35 Hamilton Place." Readers marveled at and for them.

News editors goggled with pleasure as "eyewitness accounts" told how "the passengers had been gathered together and huddled in the upper passageway in preparations for rescue. At daybreak the rescue efforts began, the passengers were put on the deck and one passenger was allowed to jump over with each crew member."

The interviews given in Rotterdam had primed the New York reporters. They now hurried to Idlewild Airport. One by one they pieced the stories together and highlighted the eyewitness experience—such as Leanne Müller saying, "Everybody was so excited you really didn't realize how dangerous it was."

ASK SOMEONE, "What is the first news event you recall?" and the answer will define the generation: the death of Diana, Princess of Wales, and her universal funeral in the golden late summer of 1997; or Nelson Mandela walking to freedom in February 1990; or the crowds dancing in the streets as the Berlin Wall started to come down in November 1989; or the sidewalk huddles weeping over John Lennon's death at just before midnight in December 1980; or Neil Armstrong's giant steps on the moon in July 1969; or President Kennedy's assassination in November 1963; or Victory Day at the end of World War II or Pearl Harbor in December 1941.

Carlsen's drama played in that theater. In the baritone of radio, in the black slabs of the headlines, he made all of us who watched feel important to ourselves. He gave us a chance to share in a world event.

Everybody felt the visceral need to express a reaction. As we wished for his safety, we belonged to the action; we wanted to help, and we could see ourselves as people who would and could help. Through him, we had a safe opportunity to display great emotion. It had nothing to do with us, but we could show that we cared. And through our views of his crisis, we could get known and perceived for the quality we had and were.

Carlsen also made us feel better—because he was doing this wonderful, noble thing. He was trying to save his ship, his livelihood, his owner's property, without regard for his own safety. Everybody talked about it. Politicians spoke of Carlsen's example and hoped, thereby, to be associated with him—they could show that they at least knew the word **honor.** Preachers found a text in the man alone under God. Women loved his bravery; men discussed his reasons.

In our parish, people who had never seen the

sea tried to grasp its wonder. Large farmers with large hands asked my parents what it was like out there. They, teachers to the marrow, spoke with the authority of mariners who had come back from the deep—yet in none of their generations had anyone ever been to sea, not even Steve the stevedore.

To a small boy it felt better than Robin Hood or Cowboys and Indians—it was real, it was new, and with every morning's newspaper, every evening's radio bulletins it supplied its own breathtaking variations. Above all, it showed a man who had reason to be afraid but who braved it out.

Day by day, Carlsen grew larger than everything, greater than the other news that had at first run normally alongside him. At first, he shared the pages with a Mormon gentleman who, with his six wives, had been indicted for bigamy; with a killer sent to the electric chair for murdering his parents with a hammer; and with the statistic of thirty-five thousand road deaths the previous year in the United States.

"Captain Courageous" soon began to rise above all the others. Within days, he became the greatest one-man news story since Lindbergh flew over the same ocean. After New Year's Day, once the public of the Atlantic seaboards caught **Flying Enterprise** frenzy, the newspapers, the broadcasting organizations, and the nightly film newsreels made Carlsen and his family and the Isbrandtsen shipping line the focus of unprecedented attention.

The spirit of the time had spoken, and people now got what they suspected they had needed: a clean and gallant hero. No blood, no one being killed, no doubtful morality, no unbearable loss, but a dignity born of straightforward duty and uncomplicated courage. Consequently, every manager in every significant news outlet on the northern Atlantic seaboard scrambled to cover this story. Flights and hotels booked, planes and boats and trains ascertained, big-name reporters landing like princes—the world descended on this drenched, windswept speck in the Atlantic, fifty degrees north and fifteen degrees west.

In New York, the Isbrandtsen Line employees, besieged by the media and the public, had to move out of their offices. The pressure of goodwill made work impossible as Americans by the thousands telephoned at all hours, jamming the switchboards.

When Jakob Isbrandtsen worked there with his father, the company, he told me, employed two telephonists. "In the ordinary day's business," he said, "a call came in and those women plugged a line into a hole in the wall to put the call through. When Carlsen became news we didn't have enough of those holes in the wall. We couldn't do any business, we couldn't take orders for freight, our business was being eclipsed by the public response. And to my father the point was, this wasn't some romantic hero all the women should be swooning for, this was a calamity. Carlsen wasn't told to sink the **Flying Enterprise.** He wasn't even told when he left Hamburg—what ship's master is told such a thing?—to bring it safely back. It was **assumed** that was what he was doing."

25.

THE REPORTERS FOUND AGNES CARLsen early in the saga. They called her "a slim, tense little woman" who was "waiting tensely for news of the man on the slanting ship." She and the two girls had no protection from inquiries, because they continued to answer the phone in case Carlsen himself, with his ham radio ingenuity, called from the ship. However, things got to be too much, they all felt, when a French reporter telephoned and asked Sonia what they ate for breakfast and whether "the family dog was missing the captain."

After a few days, they left their house in Woodbridge. Hans Isbrandtsen had them driven away, which lifted the siege of cars and cameramen on Alwat Street. According to the press reports, they had gone to "a secret destination." Karen recollects, "My sister and I first went out to our friends', Edith and Herman Hansen's house, in Perth Amboy, New Jersey, to avoid the reporters. Unfortunately, they found us there. [The Hansens] were distant cousins of ours." According to Sonia, their mother went to another friend in Metuchen.

After this, the Carlsens next went, according to Jakob Isbrandtsen, to the Margaret Hotel in Brooklyn—but were discovered too. H.I. finally brought them to his house and then, by means of a connecting passageway not visible to the public, they moved in with Isbrandtsen's sister, who lived next door to him. There they stayed, undetected.

Until the early 1990s, Agnes continued to live in Woodbridge, where Carlsen had taken her some years earlier, when he had been advised by her doctors that she needed "a small house with a garden." In the later reaches of her life, when she was almost eighty years old, she moved to Rochester Hills, Michigan, where her daughters, now Mrs. Fedak and Mrs. Mueller, lived within easy reach.

Agnes Sorensen, born in the middle of a family of nine children (all of whom she outlived), met Kurt Carlsen, one of five, in the west of Denmark. In the rural norm of the day, she ended her education when she finished primary school, in her early teens. Trained as a gymnast, she competed for her country against the other Scandinavian nations.

She then got a job as a governess and formal-dining-room maid for a prosperous meat-packing tycoon and his wife. They owned a house on the "Danish Riviera"—the country's resort strip, a twenty-mile slice of Zealand's coast north from Elsinore. Kurt had begun his merchant marine studies nearby, and a neighboring mansion owner had asked the sharp young naval student to keep an eye on his yacht.

The meat packer's wife saw this winning and confident boy from Bagsvaerd village. She thought he already showed signs of remarkable character, and she embarked on a little matchmaking.

One day, while they were watching the yachts anchored just offshore, she drew Agnes's attention to "that boy" as he handled some load or other, and told her to go and help him.

Agnes, obedient to the letter, rowed out to the yacht. They had different dialects—with Bagsvaerd so close to the capital, he spoke an urban Danish; she, from the country, spoke "mainland."

Kurt Carlsen emerged from the academy with distinction, continued to pursue every qualification and certification available to a professional seaman, and married Agnes in Maryland on Sunday, July 24, 1938, when he was twenty-four and she twenty-seven. After his distinguished graduation, he had emigrated to the United States and had sent for her.

Agnes found America difficult, mostly because of the language barrier. All her life she spoke with a Danish accent more pronounced than her husband's, and she achieved less control of English grammar and syntax. When his great crisis began, it could have been a risky trigger point for a woman who had once been hospitalized seriously with what we now identify as postpartum depression—from which she had suffered severely after Karen's birth, in 1944. As **Flying Enterprise** foundered, although rigid with fear at her husband's circumstances, she navigated her way through it in a number of different ways. A devout woman, she prayed a great deal, and her unquestioning faith gave her great comfort. She also had an

uncomplicated common sense, which transmitted itself supportively to her daughters.
They, aged eleven and seven, simply believed
that their father would come home safely because he had always done so before.

However admirable, neither of these positions had roots in the hard facts of a man
whose ship was being torn apart by the Atlantic. So, as a third level of psychological de-
fense, Agnes turned to something that she
knew about the man to whom she had been
married for thirteen years. Her husband, she
thought, would have made his decisions levelly
and logically; he would have measured his situation according to the possibilities he saw
available to him.

She told me that as she saw it, Carlsen had
three options. He could have gone with the
passengers and crew—but the ship was still
afloat and therefore still his responsibility. Or
he could have transferred to the ship standing
by, and in a more comfortable way awaited the
tug. But that had its risks; if the ship sank
without him, he would, in effect, have abandoned what she called "the old freighter."

Carlsen had taken the third option—because he thought he could make it work. Not
only that, but when he'd decided to stay on
board and supervise the towing, he had made a

plain statement to the owner: that he was staying on board to save his ship.

When I asked, as I would many times, "Why
do you think your husband took that course of
action? I mean, he took the most difficult option," her eyes filled with tears. She was sitting
in an armchair in her senior-community suite
in Michigan.

Mrs. Carlsen didn't answer immediately;
then she said, her Danish accent a touch more
pronounced, "He did it for me." On that November Sunday afternoon, the weak sun lit the
pretty room; on a shelf by Agnes's chair sat a
photograph of the younger Captain Carlsen in
his cap and gold-braided uniform.

Both daughters stood nearby, and the sunlight caught the tears in their eyes too. Each of
them would later, when away from their
mother, divulge the private reason for this un-
heralded and very moving surge in emotion.

Before I met Agnes Carlsen, I had spoken to
her many times on the telephone. Always hes-
itant until the conversation settled down, she
had no cunning that I ever detected, and at
heart she held little suspicion of people—she
assumed them to be as open and well-meaning
as herself. In our first telephone conversation, I
introduced myself and broached the subject of
my interest.

"I've been interested in him since—well, since I was a small boy."

This was her immediate response: "I loved my husband. I still love him. He was a wonderful husband and father. He was a wonderful man."

At first I thought she was making a preemptive remark, her way of saying, "I don't care what you write about my husband, I don't care what you think about him—this is what I thought of him." Or, maybe, "Be careful where you tread with me—be careful not to denigrate my husband in any way."

In our next telephone conversation, though, she said the same thing. She used slightly different words, but only because, as I would soon establish from her demeanor, she was not speaking to a formula. "Kurt," she said, "was wonderful. He looked after me and the girls so well. We could not have had a better husband and father."

These conversations, six or seven in all, took place over a period of about ten months, and by the time we had arranged that I could come and see her, she had eased considerably, and her relaxation seemed to reduce the Scandinavian pressure on her accent.

She was tiny, not much above five feet tall, and still attractive in her nineties. Her history of physical agility showed; she moved as easily as a bird or a dancer. And she was still, after nearly sixty years in America, very "Scandinavian"—that is to say, her demeanor straightaway reminded me of people I had met in Norway, Sweden, and her own Denmark, countryside people, farmers, fisherfolk. She appeared as fragile as some of her medical history had suggested, yet less frail than I had expected, and she immediately made me want to protect her—that was one of her main psychological attributes. It also showed in the way she was regarded by the personnel of the building, who came and went during the afternoon.

Impeccably groomed, instantly hospitable, she still seemed uncomfortable talking about **Flying Enterprise.** Again, as she had done when speaking to the press almost fifty years earlier, she spoke of "the old ship" and "the old freighter."

During the visit, she referred many of my questions to her daughters. The three women worked as a team, supporting one another, amplifying an answer, contributing a detail here, an embellishment there. Agnes's first response to the news of the catastrophe had been one of dismay. This dissolved—somewhat—when she heard his "calm" voice on the news bulletins, relayed from the standby ships. She felt then that her husband would come through; sometimes she called him "Kurt," sometimes "my husband," and sometimes, "Captain Carlsen."

Again and again, with her daughters corroborating, she said that her greatest pressure came from the press. She must have known perfectly well that they wanted as much drama as they could get—whereas all she wanted was her husband safe.

Soon, the core point of the entire story began to surface—even though it did not take shape for some time. Mrs. Carlsen told me that the reporters asked her if she thought her husband would stay with the ship, and she replied, "I think so, because if you lose your ship you don't get another one. So I thought he would do his best and I prayed for him. I thought he would do all right."

"How anxious were you?" I asked.

"I prayed a lot; that I know."

A few minutes later she again said, "If you lose your ship you lose your cap, you know—because he had always said that." At least three more times that afternoon and often on the telephone, before and after our meeting, she repeated the point: "If you lose your ship you don't get another one."

That afternoon, the straightforward "hero" view that I had held of Carlsen down through the years began to change. Other motivations began to surface; yet others would soon become plain and assemble into a picture; Carlsen had been fighting for more than his ship.

From the outside, the Carlsen family appears to have been a simple and straightforward, well-conducted arrangement. And so it was, in many ways. At core lay the husband-and-wife relationship, with its clear demarcations. Married to a seaman, Agnes Carlsen accepted none of the stereotypes—no salty language, nothing off-color. Together, the couple established a values system that accommodated—as it had to—his long absences. Into this, they incorporated attitudes in which he followed as much as he led. "He ruled the sea, she ruled the land," her daughters like to joke.

Their father had always run his ships along tough behavioral lines, and a bunch of seafaring men needed a lot more by way of handling than a couple of preteen daughters. Agnes, for all her simplicity and fragility, had more than a little of the matriarch about her. As part of their marriage's nature, when Carlsen came home from a voyage, he fell into the way of life in which she controlled the household.

Both daughters, who saw more of their mother than their father, grew up with this rigid system of discipline and behavior. Duty and obligation became all-important—as their mother stated and repeated daily. They would have done in their lives—if called to—what their father was doing at sea.

These standards had come down through generations of northern European Protestantism. In a world where Agnes found it difficult to believe that wrongdoing could take place, no wrongdoing could be countenanced. She expected her daughters not only to do as she said but to do as she did. Find good in everyone. Expect the best from everyone, including yourself. Each daughter has repeated a phrase to me: "the highest standards of behavior"; each daughter learned very young, according to Karen, "never to do anything that would embarrass anyone."

This family, therefore, had no innate, instinctive protection from the press. As far as they could see, "Captain Carlsen," as his daughters still sometimes refer to him, was doing a job. As he always did. They felt amazed that the world should even ask; didn't everyone have these values? Both Carlsen parents belonged to the "Greatest Generation"—that breed of immigrants who never stopped working to build the country in which they came to live. If Agnes and the two girls had dread after fear, alarm after shock to address in the early days of 1952, they were supposed to take it in their stride.

As did Captain Carlsen. One day before they left the house in Woodbridge, in a desperate bid to hold on to normality—"Why shouldn't we answer our own phone?"—Sonia picked up the receiver.

She spoke not to a reporter; this time, on the other end of the line, from his wind-howling, rattling ship, she heard the voice of the experienced radio ham himself. Carlsen's words comforted them, the perfectly ordinary sentiments of a husband and father: he was safe and in no danger, they must look after one another until he got home, and they mustn't worry; he expected everything to go off just fine.

26.

SINCE SHE WENT TO FIND THE SHELL tanker at Christmas, **Turmoil,** by now out seven days and seven nights, had been listening to all the frequencies. As did every such rescue tug; and when they alerted their owners ashore to distress signals (in London, Rotterdam, Calais, wherever), those head offices made—or responded to—the calls that secured the contracts. Now, at last, Captain Dan Parker sailed from Falmouth on Thursday morning, January 3, in pursuit of this latest "casualty," as tugs referred to a troubled vessel.

During the night, the landlord of the Chain Locker had tapped on Kenneth Dancy's door and told him to wake up; it was time to find his ship.

When clear of Falmouth, Captain Parker signaled ahead and got the radio shack on **John W. Weeks.** He said it would take him between thirty-six and forty-eight hours to get there—he was making twelve knots—and although the weather encouraged him for the moment, he'd have liked a better forecast. For Carlsen's sake, he still regretted the fourteen hours he had spent with **Mactra,** standing idle at Falmouth's edge.

They called Captain Parker "Father" because he looked paternal, priestly and venerable. He had black eyebrows and shocking white hair, and in shape he somewhat resembled the tug he commanded—not very high but solidly wide, with a low center of gravity, built for the job. Photographs show a trustworthy, watchful man of—like Carlsen—natural authority; he would have made perfect casting in a 1950s television commercial for tinned salmon.

The young Parker had worked on family trawlers from the age of twelve, served in the Royal Navy during World War I, then went as a skipper for hire on luxury yachts all over the world—out of the Riviera, the Caribbean, settings with the glamour of Hollywood. Part of his legend hints that he might have captained a sloop that stood off Philadelphia during Prohibition, one of the ships from which people could buy liquor.

When World War II came, he served on a British minesweeper—not the safest post in the world, although with appealing English understatement he said it "bored" him. At the end of the war, he tried to leave the sea. Like so many other sailors, he failed; sea legs don't work that well on land. He ended up on tugs and finally found his natural home on **Turmoil**. Everyone in the salvage business on those Channel and Atlantic shorelines knew Father Parker and knew **Turmoil.**

Oceangoing and low in the water, **Turmoil** was hard as a cliff—she needed to be for the work she did. She had all the beauty of a bulldog and, with the specification "rescue tug," she had been designed longer and tougher than the busy little pilots who delight us like puppies in the harbors of today.

During World War II, the British Admiralty

built eight such rescue tugs to help those wartime Atlantic convoy vessels that had been crippled, torpedoed but not sunk, or were simply victims of the weather. Each of the tugs in this class was supposed capable of taking any ship in the world under tow. They looked like something that only a mother could love, and the Admiralty named the first one—and thus the entire class of tug—**Bustler,** because she bustled off the drawing board and onto the sea.

They built **Turmoil** in Leith, outside Edinburgh, in 1944, and she came into the world with the name **W 169,** an armory of eight guns, and twin diesel engines giving 3,200 horses, almost as strong as **Flying Enterprise.** She was also classified as a "bollard" tug, her pulling power measured by simulated towing against a quayside bollard.

The Admiralty still owned **Turmoil** (they took her guns away after the war) and had chartered her to Overseas Towage and Salvage, now in partnership with one of the tug owners whom Isbrandtsen had earlier approached, Compagnie de Remorque et de Sauvetage (which called all their vessels **Abeille** and merely numbered them for identification).

Turmoil measured 205 feet long, just over half **Flying Enterprise's** length, and 41 feet across at her broadest point. She weighed

1,600 tons when fully loaded, could travel 17,000 miles without refueling, and had a top speed of 16 knots, over 18 land miles an hour. She had crewed forty-two men in the navy and in peacetime between twenty-five and thirty, depending on the job. A crew of twenty-seven, as she had that morning, was a customary average. Some were regulars; some, like Mr. Dancy, jobbing seamen with their appropriate tickets.

Her special breeding for war service had already identified her; she looked different in the family photograph, neither perky nor endearing. Certainly she had the agility of the little ones, who could turn on a coin, who could spin a circle within their own length. And certainly she had the same capacity to kiss up to the suave liners and the other big ships as they patronized their ports of call. But **Turmoil**'s extra size and punch gave her a more serious air appropriate to the high stakes and the risky, complex game she was often asked to play.

THE TOWAGE INDUSTRY now divides broadly into the relatively uncomplicated hauling of barges, as it once towed people in their houseboats along canal banks; the guiding of great ships into small harbors or difficult spaces; and the moving of massive installations into final positions, sometimes halfway across the world. But the business also involves the rescue of vessels in trouble—which steers them into the turbulent waters of salvage. Here, the tug's work gets opportunistic. On the one hand, she's a helper of men and ships; on the other hand, she's picking up what she can, when she can, because she can, giving the tug an almost piratical air. That's what the public learned to think when looking at what might happen to Carlsen.

But this is not the tugboat's fault. Few areas of international dealings have such complexity as maritime law, which is as variable as the sea itself. And few areas of maritime or admiralty law pose such awkward questions as the business of salvage.

AROUND THE STORY of Carlsen, the word **salvage** came up every hour of every day. It has connotations of treasure, of a haul, of people bringing an abandoned ship to shore and then owning all its cargo. No matter what the world thought about Captain Carlsen, they believed he was staying on board because he didn't want his ship to become prey to marine jackals.

Not so. If he had come to a different decision, if he had chosen, say, to leave **Flying Enterprise** when everyone else went, because in his judgment she might sink at any minute, the ship would not automatically have been the property of the first tug to reach her and take her in tow.

Those circumstances would not have granted Hans Isbrandtsen much joy. At the very least he would then have had to fight a sharp and complicated legal battle over what percentage of the recovered value the freelance towing company should receive. For the salvors to gain any substantial reward for their risk, Isbrandtsen would have had to announce publicly, "I no longer wish to have any claim to this ship. I'm calling in my insurance." And then the insurers would have had a thing or two to say.

Therein lies one clear point of salvage: until an owner has declared that he considers his ship "gone," he still has proprietary interest in it. Just because his employees on board were forced by wind or rain or fire to give up their places on the ship on the sea, that does not mean that the man who owns the ship has relinquished his property. If a bus driver runs out of gas and walks away, the company still owns the bus—even if a garage has to tow it in. A ship gets viewed differently from a bus because if the ship goes down, the loss to the owner is big and total. Therefore, the laws of salvage tend to look favorably on the tug that came in, took the risk, and towed a derelict vessel into port.

The salvor doesn't even have to be a tug or a dedicated salvage company holding the rope. Any ship can tow—and often will. The example that crossed the heart of every skipper in Carlsen's generation was a freighter called **American Farmer.** She was abandoned by her crew on a voyage to Spain; she didn't sink; a British merchant ship towed her to safety and gained hugely. Such an example heightened the scavenger connotations of the word **salvage.**

Few skippers would ever leave a ship derelict. In **Lord Jim,** one of the greatest books ever written about the sea and seafaring men, Joseph Conrad built his entire plot and moral inquiry on the fact that the officers of a ship called **Patna**—"a local steamer as old as the hills, lean like a greyhound, and eaten up with rust worse than a condemned water-tank"— abandoned her and her passengers after a collision. And then the ship didn't sink. The cowardice, the opprobrium, that attached itself to those fleeing officers and ruined their lives sears the reader's heart.

In wide outline, therefore, a salvage mission rewards the tug (or whoever tows) under any or (ideally) all of three conditions: if the tug company had no obligation of any kind to go out and rescue that vessel; if the vessel couldn't have been recovered without the tow; and if the tug succeeded in bringing all or part of the ship or its cargo home safe.

TURMOIL AND DAN PARKER went out to **Flying Enterprise** under a question mark that absorbed the entire shipping industry on that day: what kind of contract or agreement would the tug owner and the ship's owner forge? Isbrandtsen's charter had behind it the weight of a man who owned a shipping line; H.I. also had about him the same hint of gunslinger that attaches to bounty-hunting salvage tugs. The contract negotiations could have been worth overhearing.

If it had been strictly a rescue job, Isbrandtsen would have been hiring a vessel—in this case, an oceangoing tug powerful enough to do a tough job—with the intention of getting the stricken ship to shore and with no intention of paying it anything other than a fee. Yet when news of the tug hiring broke, word had it that

Isbrandtsen had specified to **Turmoil** "no cure, no pay"—if she didn't bring the ship to shore, she didn't get paid.

"No cure, no pay," the harshest of salvage agreements, surfaced in the press. Under the heading, "Salvage Experts Become Popular," **The New York Times** reported, "Newspapers, admiralty law firms, and other sources of information have been besieged in the last few days with inquiries on the subject and more specifically on the question why the determined shipmaster has stayed aboard his vessel."

Patiently, the story went on to quote the expert distinction "between a distressed ship, which the Enterprise is, and a derelict, which she has never been." Gently deploring the discoloration of the public opinion by "Hollywood and fiction," the reporter helpfully searched for the essential phrase that determined a ship's qualification to be salvaged, and summed up the multifaceted and bewildering salvage puzzle neatly. He reached for a "standard work in maritime law" and from it quoted the pointed and satisfying phrase "without hope or expectation of return."

If Carlsen had departed his vessel "without hope or expectation of return," admiralty law would have defined the vessel as "derelict."

More fascinating is the comment (never expanded upon but chillingly arresting) that had he left his ship and gone merely to rest for a time on **Golden Eagle** or, now, **John W. Weeks,** "Captain Carlsen's position would not have been a particularly strong one, since he would lack complete assurance that the destroyer would not pull away with him, leaving the **Flying Enterprise** a derelict."

Would Isbrandtsen then have sued **Golden Eagle**—or the U.S. Navy? For taking his captain away from his ship? That's a case that would have lingered in the courts.

The newspaper goes on to say that from what it can judge, the contract asked a "professional salvage tug operator to haul the distressed freighter to port. Hans Isbrandtsen, head of the company, has not disclosed the terms of the operation. The tug could be hired on a per diem basis, for example, just as one hires a tractor for plowing."

On January 8, however, a source identified only as "London" (in security communiqués, a euphemism for the U.S. embassy) sent a confidential telegram to the secretary of state and marked it "PRIORITY." Copies went to, among others, the navy and the fledgling CIA (then four years old). It began: "SS FLYING EN-

TERPRISE salvage operations performed under Lloyd's standard form salvage agreement 'no cure no pay' by arrangement between United States Salvage Association and Overseas Towage and Salvage Co managers tug TURMOIL. Agreement will be signed by Captain of ENTERPRISE upon arrival Falmouth."

Isbrandtsen, as a member of the United States Salvage Association, had won a tough deal: if Parker didn't bring home **Flying Enterprise,** he didn't get paid. As to the United States government's involvement, U.S. Navy ships were standing by under orders and a U.S. citizen was in trouble in international waters— and, as it would transpire, Carlson was carrying freight with a security implication.

27.

As **TURMOIL** SAILED ON TOWARD **Flying Enterprise,** the men on **Weeks** finally fed Carlsen—for whom they now had such respect. Every crewman would have gone over to help him, had their captain asked. Instead, on Thursday morning, January 3, they went out on deck for another attempt to get some food to him. This time, they followed his directions: they packed only what he asked for and in the way he dictated. The package had to be light enough for Carlsen to haul in, and portable enough for him to manage.

Into a long cylinder they packed a flask of coffee; next came some hot food—steak—wrapped in a napkin; on top of this they folded a newspaper and a magazine, on top of which they put a packet of sandwiches, some "candy" (unspecified—though Carlsen loved licorice), and a long rectangular box of two hundred cigarettes, the kind sold in duty-free ports. (Carlsen had asked only for "a smoke" and in any case, he was a pipe man.)

The radio shack made the arrangements with Carlsen, and this time the **Weeks** crew got a rope to him, a line so light that Carlsen could easily make it fast to the ship's rail, aft on the main deck. Across this sagging line, swinging like a baby from the stork's beak, went the cylinder wrapped in a canvas sack.

They chose a moment when the sea had relented enough for them to close to a narrow gap between **Weeks** and **Flying Enterprise.** Notwithstanding the fact that they had a degree of relative calm to ease the way, the seamen on **Weeks** must have handled the big destroyer like a dinghy in order to get her as close as they did. Carlsen waited at the rail; the gentler weight of the parcel made it easier for him to haul the line in slowly; he swung the food aboard. Wednesday of the previous week was the last time he had eaten anything half decent; never was a man so pleased to give up his cakes and ale.

Soon, Commander Thompson sent a signal to his control center. "He is in excellent spirits," observed the message, "and is certain **Flying Enterprise** will ride it out if weather does not deteriorate again."

Earlier in the text Thompson had remarked, "Weather greatly improved wind northwest force 5 sea moderate to rough with long swells baro 2990 rising steadily"—and he had disclosed that he had established voice contact with **Turmoil.** On his signal also appeared the first hints of the decisions that lay ahead: "She should be towed by stern to protect weather decks and deck house from wind and seas."

ABOARD **TURMOIL,** Father Dan Parker and his twenty-seven men plowed on. Some slept, according to their turn on watch. Some merely rested, reading or occupied with other pastimes; they had forty-eight hours to fill.

When Kenneth Dancy's name hit the newspapers, they listed his hobbies as "classical music and knitting." The knitting caused some buzz—at which oceangoing seamen laughed. Sailors were always knitters—of sweaters, of their own socks. They had to do something to fill those long-horizoned days, those uneventful nights. They also made models and ships in bottles, they whittled, they carved—my grandfather told me all about it. With one shipboard pastime they added significantly and uniquely to vernacular expression.

You'll find in every New England shoreline town a curio of the seaman's free time—a piece of "scrimshaw," a carving or etching, often quite elaborate, on the tooth of a whale or the tusk of a walrus. I own a long narrow box, ideal for pencils, that carries on its lid a delicate line drawing of a ship under sail. It has all the feeling of ivory, and the "scrimshander" or "scrimshoner" who etched it had plenty of time. (My grandfather might have told him—and my father certainly would have—that the word climbed out from an old Dutch term that meant "to avoid work.")

Those not knitting or whittling or scrimshoning on **Turmoil** that Thursday checked the equipment. Heavy work lay ahead. A tug

looks buxom, because her wheelhouse has to
be pushed forward in order to make room for
a broad, deep afterdeck. Her power will be determined by the size of the machinery that can
be fitted in this space—in which, as far forward
as it can be accommodated, squats the tug's
muscle, the enormous towing winch that has
to take a thousand yards of steel cable thick as
Popeye's forearm.

Turmoil had a huge winch, more than six
feet across, and, when it was engaged, her cables flowed out a portal not in the stern but in
the side of the tug, almost halfway up her
length. This allowed her as much play as possible for the huge fish on the end of her line.

ON THURSDAY AFTERNOON, Carlsen
thanked the men on **Weeks** for the food and
provisions. One major weight had now been
removed from his shoulders: he no longer had
to be a hunter-gatherer on his own ship. Another problem, however, moved swiftly in, a
tougher consideration. Carlsen could see that
his ship's ailments had been intensifying.

It had already been determined that **Flying
Enterprise** would be towed from her stern,
and that had to be, in great part, Carlsen's

voice speaking. During the afternoon, he took part in a three-way conversation with Parker and Commander Thompson. Parker said he didn't want the man overseeing the hawser on the towed vessel—that would be Carlsen—too much at the mercy of the sea; towing from the higher stern would protect him. Carlsen reinforced this, adding that towing from the bow would more forcefully shoot the wash back into the accommodation block—and into the crack just aft of the housing. Nor did Carlsen want the brunt of the sea hitting his hatches as the ship moved forward on the tow rope.

Also, he now knew something else. He knew that the cargo shift had indeed been serious and permanent and more or less total, and he knew that the ship was dipping ever lower in the water. This newly intensified listing seemed slight at first. She'd dip into a heavy lurch and not come the whole way back up to where she had been. This meant that the holds had begun to take on deeper and deeper water—which raised a vicious question. Assuming they got the tow on board, assuming that Parker's skill got them moving, assuming that the tow held and they reached, say, a manageable two to four knots—at what point would the journey to port become a race against time? Could they get to Falmouth before **Flying Enterprise** became so waterlogged that she just gave up and went down?

CONTRAST THIS REALITY of Carlsen's with an announcement made about him that very day. One of the lighter movies of 1951 had been **That's My Boy,** starring Dean Martin and Jerry Lewis, produced by the renowned Hal B. Wallis, who, later in 1952, would release **Sailor Beware,** starring the same pair.

Nautical themes had obviously been on his mind. While America had its heart in its mouth following Carlsen, **The New York Times,** as part of its daily Carlsen coverage, reported that "Hal Wallis has the jump on his fellow-producers." He had registered the title **The Flying Enterprise** with the Title Registration Bureau of the Motion Picture Association of America, "thus effectively blocking its use by others." Later he said he had a new title: **It's Hell to Be a Hero.** Mr. Wallis said that he wanted Burt Lancaster to play the heroic captain.

This merry squib added to the happenings ashore—of which Carlsen had been getting hints in his radio calls. Now his new fame arrived in his face. When the weather finally produced a relatively calm, sunny day, the reporters arrived in droves. Commander Thompson, on **Weeks,** watched this onslaught—plane after plane, swooping in low, coming back again and again. Concerned that one of them might actually crash into Carlsen, he spoke to his navy base in London.

COMNAVEASTLANT set in motion a series of inquiries and suggestions that brought in the authorities. That was when they introduced an air corridor over Carlsen's part of the Atlantic; the reporters' pilots now had to observe the same regulations as they did at an airport.

Carlsen could see what was taking place: the men with their cameras and notebooks were hanging out of aircraft windows; small ships of all shapes were tramping the sea beside him. As he already knew from his conversations with Commander Thompson that his story had hit the big-time news, Carlsen went out on deck. In a spirit of hospitality—and knowing Isbrandtsen's penchant for publicity—he gave the lensmen the great shot they wanted: he clung to the rail where the cameras could get a clear look at him.

One plane came right in low, almost too low. As Carlsen looked up, more than a touch alarmed, the pilot dropped an object. Carlsen scurried to reach it—he had to make the usual monkey struggle across the slippery, tilting decks. When he opened the packet, he found a silver cigarette case from a Canadian beer tycoon offering him thirty thousand dollars to endorse a brand when he came ashore. Enough: Carlsen went back inside and carried on with his day's work.

28.

THURSDAY NIGHT CLOSED IN. AT least Carlsen had eaten well and had tasted good, naval coffee, a wonderful improvement on beer and brackish water. He also knew that in the early evening, before all the light had gone from the sky, **Turmoil** had come within the horizon's reach. Just after ten o'clock Greenwich mean time that night, she reached the destroyer.

Dan Parker's contract may not have considered **Flying Enterprise** "derelict"—but that is certainly what the rolling, yawing freighter looked like, especially when the racing clouds released the moon to glint on her poor hull. Parker went in for a closer look under his own and **Weeks**'s searchlights. Knowing the dangers and complications of rescue towing, he never rushed a job. When he came to a casualty, Parker first of all surveyed the task in hand and then decided and announced his course of action. He did this without fuss or drama, and this thoughtfulness also contributed to the nickname "Father."

Carlsen had asked **Weeks** to wake him up the moment **Turmoil** arrived, so that they could begin towing no matter what time of day or night. He had arranged to stand at the rail on the highest part of the stern and signal the ships—the **Weeks** supply drop had sent him an extra flashlight. Customarily, the tug would then fire over a rocket. At this point, **Turmoil** did not know of Carlsen's deck cargo: the scattered sacks of volatile naphthalene.

Towing at this level of strength followed a system. The rocket carried a strong rope, the "messenger" line, and the crew of the receiving ship would grab it and haul it in. This was heavy, heavy work, usually needing at least four crewmen, because at the end of the messenger came the five-inch steel hawser, spooling from the giant drum of the winch on the tug.

Father Parker had looked ahead. This procedure might not work for **Flying Enterprise,** because there was only one man on the ship and that man could use only one hand—he would need the other hand to hold on to something.

So Parker decided to send over, to begin with, a much lighter rope, to which a slightly heavier line would be attached in a bowline knot, and then a slightly heavier line knotted or cleated to that—and then, likewise, the messenger line would come. Furthermore, as Carlsen by himself could have no chance of securing the heavy steel hawser to anything, **Turmoil** would send the earlier lines doubled back into a noose. Carlsen could then take this loop and slip it over the head of one of the bitts, the thick, three-foot-high iron bollards far back on the stern of the freighter, around which the hawser would have to wind in order for the tow to hitch.

When this loop ran like a loose necktie around the bitt, **Turmoil** could then begin to haul. The long line of thinner ropes and then the messenger line would slide around the bollard and be hauled back to **Turmoil**—which held the other end of the loop. Then, lumbering along behind, would follow the attached hawser.

Carlsen could then make sure that the cable was indeed guiding itself around the bitt and continuing its journey back to the tug, all one mighty string after the little lines and the messenger. Instead of looking like one end of a huge rope made fast to the freighter's bitts, it would look, as it left **Flying Enterprise,** like a looped rope—from which they could then tow. Parker and Carlsen, with contributions from Commander Thompson, agreed all this in advance.

Weeks and **Turmoil** sounded their sirens and woke Carlsen to tell him that the tug had arrived. Out on deck he looked across and saw the blaze of lights on **Turmoil** and the men busy around the winch. Across the high swell, **Weeks** turned on her searchlights. When the men on **Turmoil** saw Carlsen position himself on the stern, they set up and fired over the first rocket. Carlsen immediately flashed an urgent signal—"No rockets!" and then, to drive the point home, yelled at them. If a rocket landed on one of those sacks, the naphthalene would explode like a bomb.

Change of plan: they regrouped on **Turmoil.** If they couldn't fire a rocket, what could they do? They could only try to throw—by hand—the first, very light line to Carlsen. And they did so. Dan Parker brought off what one of his crew later described as "a feat of considerable seamanship" and got **Turmoil** to within yards of **Flying Enterprise.** Such a risk—the freighter was by now an even greater danger to others than she had been before.

To free both hands, Carlsen jammed his knees and hips in the bars and stanchions of the rail; he reached out and he caught the light thrown line as it flew past him in the air. Still wedged at hip and knee, he contrived to clip this rope to the rail.

Then he freed himself, moved across the afterdeck, edging the cleat on the rope with him along the rail, until he got level with the bitt around which he needed to secure any tow rope. Over this bollard he looped the light line and watched as **Turmoil** hauled. The line began to slip smoothly around the bollard and head back, through the rails, toward **Turmoil.** Good: all going according to plan.

Next, knotted to that line, came the slightly heavier line, then a third, heavier still—and then came the messenger, a three-inch rope of manila hemp, not light even when dry, and now carrying ice from the cold sea.

He got it on; those small hands still had the sailmaker's power, and Carlsen steered these ropes accurately on their way around the ship's bollard. During this part of the job, he used only one hand; with the other he kept himself from sliding down the sixty-degree deck. **Fly-**

ing Enterprise bucked and reared slowly like a wallowing horse and Carlsen thought of lashing himself to the deck fittings, but he concluded that the wind and the sea would rip him away.

Just after the three-inch manila rope started its journey around the fat neck of the bitt and back to **Turmoil,** the thick, steel serpent of the hawser arrived behind it. Also icy, it came with a heavy metal shackle attached, and Carlsen even managed to ease that around the bollard and send it back to **Turmoil.** Moving the hawser at all should have required a minimum of two men working in tight concert; he did it alone, flicking the twenty-five-pound shackle around as he needed to. What did Carlsen weigh? Not more than a hundred and sixty pounds.

But when the shackle got back to **Turmoil,** it split from the cable, which went whizzing back from **Flying Enterprise,** lighting sparks with its speed at the bitt. Carlsen jumped out of the way. Slowly, the tug's crew reeled it in. The operation had collapsed. They had been within inches of setting the tow; it would now take some time to reset the winch. They called it a day.

29.

Early on the morning of Friday, January 4, Commander Thompson signaled to his base in London, "**Turmoil** alongside **Flying Enterprise** at 11 P.M. last night. [He was reading from a new time zone.] Preparations now under way for taking **Flying Enterprise** in tow." His text included details such as "listing 60 to 65 degrees, is down slightly by the head. Rudder and screws are clear of the water and rudder swinging free. Ship will be towed by the stern to prevent further flooding."

Two days earlier, he and Carlsen had had a conversation designed to anticipate any measures Carlsen might take to help **Turmoil**'s efforts. Carlsen asked Commander Thompson to tell Parker, when they next spoke, "My wheel is hard right"—meaning that he still intended to handle this ship as much as he possibly could.

The commander said to Carlsen, "Captain, do you realize that your rudder is swinging free?"

Then and only then did Carlsen know that

his steering gear had been bent away from the ship. He was able to identify the moment when it had happened: in the second wave, when George Brown had told him that, yes, the rudder was answering. Now Carlsen knew that only the rudder gauges had been answering—that the machinery had been disconnected in the great wave. So this was the reason why the ship had never answered his commands of hard to port or to starboard—the blade of his rudder had been sheared off.

THEY TRIED AGAIN at first light. After the night's disappointment, it had taken them two hours to rerig for this morning's effort. Carlsen pressed everyone, anxious to get on—as though he truly believed that his ailing, unruly metal horse might somehow be subdued by a lunge line. He had the direct aid of a skilled towing captain and twenty-seven crew members; he had the standby presence of 330 U.S. Navy sailors and their strong commander; and he had the good wishes of the whole world. We all willed this rescue to succeed.

The ship seemed sometimes a little crazy in the water. One minute placid and somewhat up and hopeful, she was then buffeted down to a list of eighty degrees by some random wave delivering a passing kick. Carlsen was, as ever, drenched to the skin; within minutes of going out on deck in the earliest light, the **Turmoil** crew took on water too—in their eyes, their faces, their clothes, their boots.

They had to hurry; given the clouds, their best light might not last for more than five or six hours. The weather forecast proved accurate. Lashing showers came in, bigger than squalls, smaller and shorter than storms, but vicious and unpredictable; the crew could see them coming, hurtling across the surface of the sea.

Everyone knew his job. **Weeks** manned the airwaves, warning off all other ships, keeping the sea clear for **Turmoil**'s efforts. Parker had every movement of every rope, every knot of every bight, every snap of every shackle reported to him on the bridge of **Turmoil.** Carlsen picked his spot again—same as last night—and hoped that his footwear, now in shambles, and his feet, raw as fire, would give him a half-decent purchase when he moved the first loop of rope across to the bollard.

At eight o'clock, they made their move. The gusts came over the sea at up to thirty-five miles an hour, making twenty-foot-high waves. When the wind was quiescent for a few minutes, **Flying Enterprise** still listed on average to sixty degrees; Carlsen had found this manageable last night. If she slipped and stayed a lot farther down, his chances of getting any footing anywhere would diminish proportionately. And would anyone around him still think that a ship at such an angle could survive being towed a few hundred miles through the ocean?

They threw the first line. The wind took it, the ship lurched—Carlsen reached but didn't catch it. He offered a small target for the man on **Turmoil** throwing the line; Carlsen perforce had to wedge himself in one position and, being only five feet six, did not have gorilla-length arms. The line fell into the sea.

Carlsen repositioned himself and **Turmoil** pulled back. The light rope, now trailing in the water and with all those other, heavier ropes attached backward on it, might foul **Turmoil's** twin propellers—or snag on Carlsen's damaged rudder, which bent up at an angle away from the red hull.

Again, resetting for the next try took a long time. First, Parker had to make sure that the throwing line and those ropes attached to it had all been safely hauled aboard his afterdeck. Then the men had to tend the winch like the seconds in a boxer's corner. When everything was ready, Parker had to back off, then come back in order to get **Turmoil** lined up for the next throw. As his crewmen worked on, he watched, and it struck him that one of the problems seemed to be the lifting of the stern—and, he noted, **Flying Enterprise**'s bow rode lower in the water.

Therefore, on the radio with **Weeks,** Parker now discussed whether throwing to the bow might not have more success. Commander Thompson agreed and **Weeks,** on the bullhorn across the water, asked Carlsen to go forward. Not a simple request; with his elbows, knees, and feet in raw condition, Carlsen had to get himself along the whole 396 feet of the freighter. When he got there, he wedged himself beside the most forward bitts and waited for **Turmoil** to get into position. Carlsen had avoided being as exposed and weather-lashed as this since standing the long hours beneath the lifeboats on the afternoon of the rescue.

Parker's crew again waited for the optimum moment, an instant when the swell of the water and the swirl of the wind abated at the same time. From the very edge of their afterdeck they threw the line over to Carlsen on the bow of his ship. It missed again. They hauled back as fast as they could, got the lines up out of the water, came back in, and threw the light nylon loop to Carlsen for the third time that morning. Once again, the effort failed—unfortunate but hardly surprising. They had been trying to toss a ribbon from the back of a rocking horse to a man twenty yards away on a bucking bronco.

THE MORNING PAPERS in New York that same day, Friday, January 4, carried banner headlines: "TUG REACHES HERO SKIPPER" and "FAIL IN 3 TRIES TO PUT LINE ON SHIP" and "MAN-AGAINST-SEA FAILS 3 TIMES TO CATCH TUG'S LINE." That last story went on to say, "Three times Carlsen, clinging to a support with one hand and trying to catch the line with the other, failed because of the 60-degree list and the lurching of the freighter."

On account of the time difference, the newspapers in New York now had the drop on everyone in Europe; eight o'clock where Carlsen struggled translated into four o'clock in New York, so there was still time to print a fresh story for the breakfast tables.

The news desks got their reports in terrifically direct routes. During all the efforts between **Turmoil** and Carlsen, Parker had kept up a running commentary on the radio with Commander Thompson. Thompson, in turn, relayed this to his base in London. And those conversations had eavesdroppers, even though the nearest relay stations, especially at Land's End, conscientiously kept everybody off their air except the parties concerned.

In fact, all the radio traffic had the ham community listening across it, because one of their own had hit trouble in the Atlantic. The whispers on the ether proved loud enough, the word got out, and America woke up to discover that the British tug hadn't brought much joy to "Captain Stay-Put."

THE TIME MOVED ON; in New York by now the presses had begun rolling, slamming out the big "FAIL IN 3 TRIES" black headlines. Parker tried one more throw to the bows; it failed. So he went back to Plan A, towing from **Flying Enterprise**'s stern. Carlsen made the painful journey back to the fantail. They threw—and they threw—and they threw. Carlsen caught the line and it snapped. Or it fled his hands and slipped away. Or he missed it again.

Commander Thompson watched Carlsen through binoculars from his bridge. On **Turmoil,** they watched from closer range—almost face-to-face at times; that's how near they came. And every time Carlsen, from his impossibly limited position, gamely snatched at the flying rope, the **Turmoil** men cheered him. They all saw, though, how he was tiring, and they broke to give him a chance to recover. He went back to his home in the radio shack, where he still had warm coffee, sandwiches, and a smoke.

30.

O N   FRIDAY   AFTERNOON,   THE weather dropped noticeably—still cold, but with fewer wild gusts. **Turmoil** and Carlsen had now made seven efforts to get a line aboard—frustrating though the failure had been, they could see that it might work. After all, in last night's attempt the lines had actually taken around the bollard, but the pressure of the sea had ripped the shackle from the hawser. Parker could also see that Carlsen put himself at high risk every time he tried to grab the line. Nevertheless, Carlsen was the man driving this; he was asking for more attempts. And Parker's contract didn't pay if he didn't cure the problem.

In the early afternoon, with new men on the

winch and Carlsen refreshed and a little rested, they set up again—still aiming at the stern. On **Turmoil,** the stand-in first mate, Mr. Dancy, had been directly or supervisorily involved in all of the efforts so far. Captain Parker, from the moment he had accepted the **Flying Enterprise** job, had figured that Carlsen would need help, though he had never shared that thought. But should they ever attempt to get help over to the listing freighter, he had already singled out this new fellow, Dancy, as the best candidate—young, fit, intelligent.

However, once Parker was standing beside **Flying Enterprise,** he concluded that they had no chance whatsoever of getting anyone over to help Carlsen. How could they do it? A breeches buoy? They couldn't get a light nylon line to Carlsen at the moment, let alone a heavy contraption with a man sitting in it. A breeches buoy needed to be anchored heavily on the receiving vessel, but they could not fire the essential rocket. Nor could they guarantee that Carlsen—even if he caught a line that eventually hauled in the breeches buoy— would get enough footing to help aboard his ship the man sitting in the buoy. Parker dismissed the idea and went back to waiting and watching.

At around half past three, a moment came

again when the swell briefly died down. A crewman, standing as far aft as he could on the tug, threw the thin leader line to Carlsen— who caught it and began to haul it in successfully. Loud, loud cheers on **Turmoil;** the entire crew, even those off duty and supposed to be sleeping, had come out on deck.

Slowly, Carlsen drew the light line in hand over hand, then looped a valid length over the neck of the bitt. He waved a signal and, on the deck of **Turmoil,** they started hauling. First they saw the leader line go fully aboard; Carlsen shepherded it through, until it wound around the bitt and left the ship on its journey back to **Turmoil.** Still they winched and still the lines kept coming—the second, slightly thicker line after the light nylon line, then the third, and then the messenger rope.

On **Turmoil**, every man held his breath as the hemp rope went through to Carlsen—and they saw it come back to them. With one hand Carlsen was steering these lines through the guiding chocks and around the bollard.

Then came the steel hawser. It lumbered through to Carlsen. He fed it—that heavy, icy cable—one-handed through the guides. It began to wind around the bollard. It wound farther around it and began its return journey to the tug.

Turmoil had a gearing system on its winch that automatically adjusted the strength of the tow. If the sea dragged a ship hard, the automatic system told the winch to slacken. If the rope sagged unsafely, the winch got a message to tighten. At the moment the hawser left Carlsen's care, **Turmoil** lifted on the swell; the winch responded to a signal from its dynamometer and tightened the tow. Too soon: the lighter messenger line was first stretched, and then snapped asunder from the hawser. Sparks flying metal to metal, the cable slammed backward around the bollard and snaked backward off the freighter into the sea.

Bizarrely, his ship's listing condition had saved Carlsen from loss of limb and possible loss of life. Since he was gripping a stanchion, trying to hold on to some kind of efficient balance, he was kept back from the path of the rampant cable. At that weight, at that tension and that speed, it would have cut his leg off— or sliced his body in two.

Once again, the **Turmoil** crew started over. They assembled the series of lines, each one attached to the one behind by a bowline knot or a figure-eight bight. And they weighed each length of line in their hands, and they gauged whether it was too heavy or too light. And they attached the messenger line, to which they then shackled the hawser, so tight you could loop it around a mountaintop and haul off the peak. And they looked at the ominous sky and they thought they had better make this one work.

And it did work, with Carlsen again risking every piece of skin on his hands to slide these ropes, these skinny and fat and unremittingly harsh snakes, to ease them around the thick bollard that looked like a huge collar stud. But when the hawser got back toward **Turmoil** and seemed ready to take to the drum of the winch, the sea came after it and a bitch of a wave snapped it like a pencil. In the stunned moment, Parker's men leapt out of the way in case the hawser backlashed. Over on **Flying Enterprise,** Carlsen did something extraordinarily out of character—he swore the air blue.

Then, a very fast movement took place in the corner of **Turmoil'**s eye.

The night before, as he'd watched Carlsen's difficulty in accepting or controlling the towrope, Kenneth Dancy had already reached the same conclusion as his skipper: Carlsen would need help. But how could they make it happen? During the last effort, Mr. Dancy stood on the bridge of **Turmoil** and watched every motion of the freighter and the tug. The swells of the waves kept shoving them to and from each other, like great lumbering dancing partners.

There came a moment when everything suddenly appeared to simplify. **Flying Enterprise** was still listing to about sixty degrees, as well behaved as she had been all day. **Turmoil,** down in a trough, began to rise and in a few seconds would likely ride high above **Flying Enterprise**—or level with her decks.

Kenneth Dancy sprinted from the bridge. When he reached the farthest aft point on **Turmoil,** the vessels actually touched. He stretched out, climbed on **Turmoil's** rail—nobody quite realized what he was doing—and half-stepped, half-jumped toward **Flying Enterprise.**

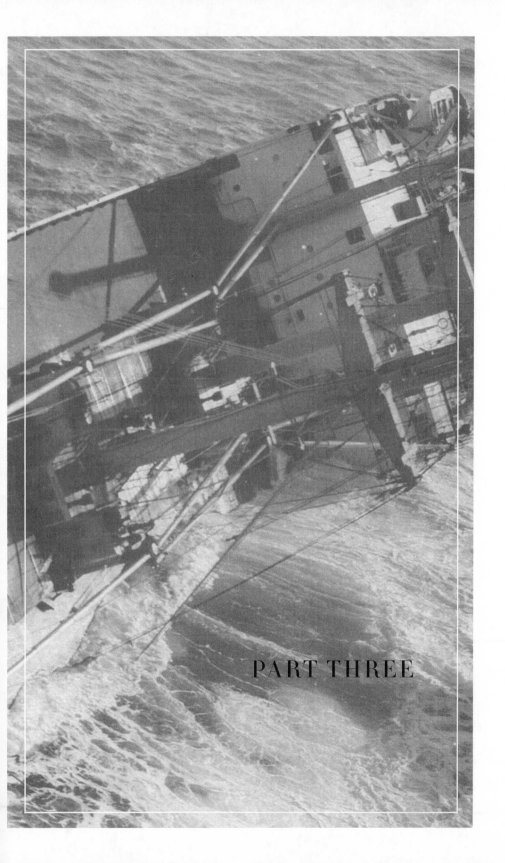

PART THREE

31.

IN HIS EARLY EIGHTIES NOW, KENNETH Roger Dancy offers no flamboyance when discussing that hectic and famous moment. A pleasant man, warmhearted and ready to laugh, he and his wife live outside Amsterdam in a neat, sweet, and, well, shipshape house.

When I call he answers the telephone with the words "Mate Dancy." As he greets me at his door, he hides any of the irritation that he must surely feel; he's about to be asked yet another bunch of questions on this old topic by someone who, irritatingly, remembers the story from childhood. Mr. Dancy may feel a reticence on the subject, but his good manners never crack, not even when the word "hero" creeps into the conversation.

"So you're the man who jumped from one ship to another in the raging Atlantic."

"No, no," he says. "It wasn't a jump. More of a step really."

His voice has lost none of a burr that can still be heard in the south of England countryside.

Wearing a blue open-necked shirt with a cravat and blade-sharp creases in his gray slacks, he sits large-framed in his armchair, and his hands move all the time, as though he might flutter this visitor away and have done with all these questions. But when asked to, he has almost always contributed generously—as he does now—to the **Flying Enterprise** record.

DANCY CAUGHT THE lowest spar of the taffrail, where it curves to the right on its journey around the stern. At that precise moment the sea pulled the tug away from the freighter, leaving him stranded. None of his shipmates could reach him now. He wore deck working clothes—and no life jacket. His hands gripped the rail, and every thumping movement of **Flying Enterprise** yanked him high in the air or dipped him close to the water.

Carlsen had seen him run from **Turmoil** and, to help Dancy, he started to quit his own rope-handling position on the freighter. At that moment, a crewman on **Turmoil** threw across the line they had been preparing for another tow attempt. The line sailed through the air close to Dancy and he grabbed it with one hand, hanging on to the taffrail with the other.

Focused on the purpose of his giant "step"—

to help get a tow under way—Dancy began to
climb the rail with the line in one hand. He got
near enough to Carlsen to hand him the light
rope; Carlsen, crouching on the deck, crabbed
his way back to the bollard, pulling the line
with him.

Dancy, one-handed, on the taffrail, fed the
first stretch of line through to Carlsen and then
wedged his own feet into a crevice on the outside of the ship. He wrapped an arm around
the rail, so that he could use both hands, and
he hung there, hauling all the time on the line
from **Turmoil** and watching Carlsen take it
through on board and loop the noose around
the neck of the mooring bitt.

When the lines began to pour through
steadily from **Turmoil,** Dancy looked behind
him. The tug had now pulled right off and
would never get near enough again to take him
back. In any case, his presence alongside Carlsen could make all the difference. De facto,
Kenneth Dancy had joined the crew of **Flying
Enterprise.** Still on the outside, he clambered
sideways along the taffrail. This brought him
nearer to where Carlsen crouched.

Carlsen was trying to steer the early lines
through the chocks and around the bollard.
Now he grabbed some of the many handholds
with which he had familiarized himself every-

where and got over to the taffrail. On his knees, he shook hands through the rails with Dancy, who said, "Congratulations, Captain Carlsen."

Carlsen beamed the first smile he had been able to show another human being for almost a week and said, "Welcome to the **Flying Enterprise,**" and helped Dancy aboard.

Then came an utterly typical Carlsen remark: "Did the tug cause any damage when she bumped me just now?"

Dancy thought for us all: "You're on a ship in this condition and you're worrying about a little bump?"

He got to work beside Carlsen, and they secured the looped tow to the bollard. It failed. Over the sea between the two vessels, the early ropes snapped asunder. Parker pulled back and away, leaving the two men on the freighter under no doubt that there would be no further attempts that day. Night drew in; the wind climbed. Everyone had been working hard, and Dancy needed to get acclimatized. Besides, some question had arisen as to whether the winch on **Turmoil** had developed a fault.

Carlsen led his new mate to the radio shack, showing Dancy how to negotiate the tilting decks—the monkey walk, bent forward from the waist, palms flat on the wet, oily surface.

The men reached the gloom. Carlsen entered as though into a normal living room, Dancy into circumstances he had never seen in his life and had difficulty addressing: the havoc, the damage, the water everywhere.

As the captain cleared the remains of his early meals and his feasts from **John W. Weeks,** Dancy surveyed in astonishment how Carlsen had slept. He now had to work out some kind of similar arrangement for himself. Carlsen's "bed" depended upon the angle of the ship; when the wall of the radio shack had become, in great part, the floor, it had made the radio shack's leather banquette into a deep V, into which Carlsen had piled his bedding to make a large seamless pad, a kind of hollow nest. But there wasn't another such nook on board.

Now Dancy began to learn how long it took to do everything on a listing ship. With Carlsen showing the way by flashlight, they fetched mattresses from other cabins. As Carlsen went off to make a last radio contact for the night, Dancy picked his own place to sleep at the foot of the leather settee and tried to make himself warm despite his soaked clothes and the winds whistling through the open door.

Carlsen returned, climbed into "bed," and fell asleep as fast as a child. Dancy took longer, listening in the dark to the appalling noises that came from everywhere in the ship. **Flying Enterprise** trembled like a bad fever—all the time. When a heavy sea hit her, she shook worse than an earthquake. Everything loose shifted and slammed and clanged and rattled and rolled.

And still, he said, that ice-white sea rolled on—strong enough to bounce the freighter up and down, up and down, like a child's rubber ring in a pool. He heard the wind hissing and whistling through every opening on the ship, including the gashes in the plates. Rivers of brine coursed along the slanting decks, and he could hear the waters sloshing into the cabins beneath him. And then another wave would come rearing through, shoving the ship in a different direction.

The loudest and most insistent banging came from the stern, and Dancy later identified it as the great broken rudder swinging free. Every thirty seconds or so, it pounded against the hull—a massive, slow, clanging **tock!** like some dreadful timepiece. Carlsen slept through this and all the other noise. The chill breezes whistled around their heads, and Dancy scarcely closed his eyes until near morning.

He awoke to the sounds of Carlsen's pottering. "Would you like a cup of tea, Mr. Dancy?"

Carlsen had put some of the tea he had found in the dry stores closet into a can that used to contain Isbrandtsen's 26 brand of coffee, into which he poured some of the stale drinking water that he had scavenged from various flasks around and about the ship. He also had some candles from a Christmas wreath. Carlsen had been given this traditional decoration by his radio ham dockside visitors, Wolfgang and Liselotte Wichman, when they came aboard for a seasonal drink on sailing day at Hamburg. Kurt Carlsen, Boy Scout of the high seas, having poured water into the old coffee can, held the lighted candle underneath it, and sat there until the water boiled.

When they had breakfasted (Dancy had the privilege of tasting the big, now elderly, doughnut-shaped pound cake), Carlsen went off to his radio duty and confirmed the next phase of towing attempts with Captain Parker.

WHILE CARLSEN AND Dancy had been eating, Commander Thompson and **John W. Weeks** had prepared to steam away to Plymouth for urgent refueling and some shore leave. They were relieved at just after eight o'clock by another destroyer from the United States northern European force. **Willard Keith** had been named after a young officer who'd died on Guadalcanal in 1942. One-third the weight of **Flying Enterprise,** she had a complement of nearly 350 men; a greyhound of the sea, she could reach a top speed of thirty-five knots, and she'd sailed in from Brittany under Commander Leslie O'Brien from Arkansas.

Carlsen, on his radiotelephone, used his time economically. He thanked Commander Thompson and his men for all the food and care; he introduced himself to **Willard Keith** and explained his emergency system of sending up blue flares if he—and, now, Mr. Dancy— had to leave the ship suddenly; and he arranged the next moves with Captain Parker.

At nine o'clock, the full crew of **Flying Enterprise**—that is, Captain Carlsen with his new (and unexpected) first mate, Mr. Dancy— made its way to the bow of the freighter. Out on deck, the wind had dropped, as though Dancy had been an angel bringing calm on his wings. A mixture of sporadic fog and light drizzle drifted over the sea. The waters had not been calmer since **Flying Enterprise** had entered the English Channel at Christmas.

Turmoil came by and stood off the starboard bow; her crew had prepared the light line, the leader of all the other, heavier ropes. This time, they got the line aboard, where Carlsen and Dancy threaded it, and all the lines that followed, through the "fairleads," the metal guides that Carlsen could never have managed single-handedly. These fixtures steer and stay the ropes on a ship, and give added control. In due course, as Carlsen and Dancy hauled each successive advance line out of the way, the three-inch-thick manila hemp rope arrived, the messenger.

Carlsen and Dancy worked ferociously. No longer was a loop being attempted; with the extra pair of hands, Parker had suggested, they might try to get the cable on as it should be— shackled to the bollard. **Turmoil** now attached the necessary steel shackle to the messenger rope, and it dragged the heavy hemp farther down to the water. But it got across to **Flying Enterprise,** where the two men grabbed it, hauled it in, got it off the hemp rope, and set it into place. Then the steel hawser appeared, and they hauled it aboard.

With their bare hands, Carlsen and Dancy fitted the hawser around the bollard to the U-shaped shackle. They cinched the shackle closed with the thick cotter pin at its mouth. The danger, of course, had now doubled. With two pairs of hands in play, both men could get right to the bitts. But they still had to crouch; they were still being forced to move awkwardly because of the ship's condition. If anything snapped now, and the cable began its screaming retreat, both men would be dangerously vulnerable to its backlash.

With the shackle closed, the noose seemed adequately tight, secure around the bollard, a massive four-in-hand knot on the steel necktie. The two men on the freighter's bow stood back and waved; **Turmoil** slipped into forward gear. As Carlsen and Dancy watched, the cable played out from the winch—and played out, and played out. The engines on **Turmoil** ramped up their growl as Parker on the bridge gave a "Slow ahead" order. **Turmoil** began to move; Carlsen and Dancy watched the small wake from her stern several hundred yards away—and still the winch played out the cable. It would always sag a little, to allow play on the line; now it began to dip deeper and deeper into the sea.

Both Carlsen and Dancy understood what Parker was doing: he intended to make this an unusually long towline, to keep the pressure as slack as possible; he was playing a big, wounded fish. Slowly, the gap of the sea

widened between the tug's stern and the
ship's bow.

AT LAST, no wind to speak of; a gray morning; some faded sunlight tried to break through
the halfhearted fog. When Parker had gone
some distance the winch stopped. It started
again, but this time it reversed its paying-out
mode and began to reel the cable in, to wind it
around the giant drum. Within the next few
seconds, as the winch gripped harder and its
machinery took over the tow, they would all
know whether they had prevailed.

The winch tightened and tightened—and
then Carlsen and Dancy felt the slight movement beneath their feet, saw the water slipping
slowly past the battered hull beneath them. A
delicate tow had begun. **Flying Enterprise** was
no longer out of control.

THE TWO MEN on the freighter stepped back
from the bollard; that shackle seemed as normal as a shackle should be—firm and immov-
ing, holding fast. They went to the starboard
rail, the ship's higher side, and from there
watched the tow begin: all seemed to be in or-

der. And so, a small convoy—the stout, slowly thrusting tug, the lopsided steamer, and the gray, rakish destroyer—set off in a northeasterly direction, on a journey of nearly four hundred miles, across the unpredictable Atlantic.

In the convoy steamed another tug, the **Abeille 25;** she had come along to provide a countering tow, if needed. If she applied a towrope at another angle to **Flying Enterprise**'s starboard, or higher, side, she could adjust the freighter, drag her a little more upright in the water. So said towing theory.

Carlsen and Dancy watched over the tow for some time. **Flying Enterprise** seemed to have settled. Nothing major had worked loose; as far as they could judge, the sea hadn't ripped any new fissures in the metal. Now all they needed was luck—luck with winds, luck with waves. If the weather stayed like this or got better—and it couldn't get much better—this agreed pace of three knots would continue night and day until perhaps early Wednesday; at the very latest, Thursday morning's dawn should show them the mouth of the Fal River estuary.

HIS SPIRITS BUOYED, Carlsen led Dancy on a tour of the ship—with another man's help, he could now reach supplies previously denied him. Most of the stores from which he wanted to draw needed one pair of hands to hold the doors open while the other pair searched behind them.

First came a life vest for Dancy. Since the previous night, he had been making do with a child's—undoubtedly one that had been worn by a Carlsen girl on a voyage with her father. Next, Carlsen said he wanted some butter, because he could not reach the grease supplies down in the engine room and they needed to lubricate the shackle, the fairleads, and all the chocks and guides, to keep the hawser free of chafing. On a long tow, and especially if the weather came up again, an unoiled cable, even five inches of thick steel, could start to fray where it rubbed. Carlsen also wanted to find some dry clothing for Dancy and himself.

More than all that, though, he wanted to make sure that they could establish a pattern of retrieval. This first exploration proved one of many such "excursions." Carlsen suggested each day to Dancy "an excursion" to the upper deck to get a ladder, or "an excursion" belowdecks to find some tools.

When they reached the slop chest, the store that contained the clothing, Dancy received another lesson in how to live aboard a listing ship. They had to open—and hold open—a heavy steel door that now tilted sharply upward. Carlsen had brought along the key. Dancy sat down on the wet floor of the corridor and wedged his feet into the skewed angle of the floor and the wall. This gave Carlsen a stepladder. He stood on Dancy's shoulders and turned the key in the lock above him. After a few attempts, his feet pressing down hard into Dancy's collarbones, he wrestled the steel door open. Once the door had been secured back against the wall, Carlsen climbed up into the store and began handing down clothing for Dancy and himself. As he did so, he kept a record; he itemized and signed out everything they took.

Carlsen concluded his business in the slop chest, came out, stood on Dancy's shoulders again, closed the steel door—and locked it. Dancy, since the moment he came aboard, had grasped that no relaxation of discipline or formality would ever take place on board this ship, whatever the circumstances. He would be, as long as they were together, "Mr." Dancy; and his shipmate, "Captain" Carlsen. Thus when he saw the door being locked so diligently, Mr. Dancy thought better of asking Captain Carlsen whether he feared burglars.

Out on deck again, Dancy saw Carlsen eyeing the American flag, still flying, though now with its edges much raveled from having been lashed by the storm. In none of the hot photographs in the newspapers do we see any trace of the flag flying upside down, the traditional distress signal. Nor, in ordinary practice, would the freighter have been flying any flag at sea, unless special signals had been called for. Flag etiquette more commonly applies to port display and special occasions.

On **Flying Enterprise,** Carlsen had raised his banner as a mark of defiance, as a celebration of resistance, a tribute to his ship's fight for survival. Were she to sink, he would see to it that she went down with her colors flying. Remarking to Dancy that the ship carried a spare Stars and Stripes, he went looking for it. When he returned with the folded flag, Dancy suggested that they not fly it now, that instead they hoist it triumphantly when coming into Falmouth Harbor, an idea that delighted Carlsen.

Forward, they checked everything again. They looked ahead along the towrope to **Turmoil;** they examined the cable and shackle; they smeared the butter on the shackle and the hawser. All serene: the convoy was making the agreed three to four knots. This would remain their speed to Falmouth; they would not increase it, even were the days temptingly fair.

Back in their "suite," as Dancy changed into warm, dry clothing, Carlsen opened up the folded flag and spread it out across the wall so that the creases would ease out. Then he went to his cabin and his jerry-rigged radio.

He ran a "so far, so good" check with Parker and with **Willard Keith,** who discussed with him the viability of delivering food. Then he sent two messages. The first went to Isbrandt-sen: "Now under tow by Turmoil. Carlsen." The second read, "Dear Agnes and children. Will contact you on telephone as soon as possible. Love, Kurt."

32.

AS HE SIGNED OFF, CARLSEN RE-ceived a message of his own, relayed to him by the departing **Weeks:** "This is Father speaking, Kurt. We are proud of you, Kurt, and I have special greetings from your Mother who is sleeping now. We are all with you in our thoughts, Kurt. Good luck. We know you will get the ship in safely."

London's **Daily Express** newspaper had

found Martin Carlsen in Denmark, and it quoted him at length in the story it ran on Friday morning, January 4. The banner headline read, "THIS MAN, CARLSEN" with a strap headline: "Each hour fills in the portrait of a man who has got the world excited—as it always will be by the spectacle of one man alone fighting against tremendous odds."

A touch of nationalism flashes across the story's introduction: "It has taken Britain with its own seafaring traditions to make Carlsen a hero for the Americans (cables the **Express** New York office). British papers are themselves making news in the American Press and now Carlsen's 'private island' competes on front pages there with world news."

When the story finally gets under way, it shows a photograph of Carlsen dining with Agnes and the girls, all prim and disciplined on board **Flying Enterprise** during a previous trip. The copy brings in the castle of Shakespeare's **Hamlet:** "The way of 'this man, Carlsen,' who has roused the world by sticking to his ship like a fly on a windowpane for the best part of a week, began at Elsinore." It continues with Carlsen's father telling the story of the sailor who asked the boy to keep an eye on the ship for a few minutes, and it quotes Martin:

" 'Do you think we could keep him at school after 14? Not likely. The sea! Only the sea mattered.' "

The newspaper advances on the story from all sides: "Three sketches—show LIFE . . . at 60 degrees." A group of line drawings portray, first, a little man in a dark suit up on a high bunk beneath tiny portholes—this was labeled "Sleeping." In the next sketch, the same little man (presumably) sat with his behind wedged in the angle between the wall and the floor, his hands curved to his mouth; it was titled "Eating." The third drawing was captioned "Walking"—beneath two portholes, the little fellow toiled in a crouching position, hauling himself along an upward slope by means of a rope fast to a ship's rail.

Below that feature, under the headline "Way Back in New Jersey by His Wife, Agnes," ran the sentence "We spent our honeymoon on board a freighter hit by a cyclone off Panama in 1938, so I have some idea of how my husband is looking and behaving."

Under this: "**Sydney Smith cables:** 'Mrs. Agnes Carlsen and her two daughters were pictured last night by TV in a million American homes. They live in a pleasant colonial-style bungalow in the seaside suburb of Woodbridge, outside [**sic**] New Jersey. There is only

one corner of the house which so far has not
been pictured. That is the small hobby room
where the captain keeps his own amateur radio
equipment. Says Mrs. Carlsen: "I couldn't possibly let anyone in there without the skipper's
permission—he's skipper at home as well as at
sea." ' "

The **Express** also ran an interview with
Karin, Carlsen's mother, known in the family
as even more timid than Agnes. "I have not
had much sleep this week," she said. "I have
just been sitting and waiting. I know Kurt is so
stubborn, and when he sets his mind to do a
thing he will go through with it."

When the other London newspapers saw the
scope of the **Daily Express** story, they guessed
what had happened: the **Express** had secured
the Carlsen parents and would keep them in
luxurious captivity as the story played through.
Other papers now threw their hats in the ring.
One secured Dancy's brother, another approached Dancy's parents for "exclusives."

And so the choir grew. When Dancy made
his move, it reached full throat—as with the
London **Evening News,** which sang out,
"SHE'S IN TOW!" Both sides of the Atlantic had
the story, at eleven in the morning in New
York, ideal for the lunchtime radio bulletins,
and four o'clock in the afternoon for London.

I heard it on the six-thirty Irish radio news, and my mother added to the rosary that night, "Pray for the safety of Captain Carlsen—**and** Mr. Dancy."

New York's time difference again worked in its favor. After the **Daily News** headline of January 3—"LONE CAP'N COURAGEOUS BUCKS GALE 6TH DAY"—and the reported failures to get the line aboard, the breakfast tables of Manhattan on January 4 got "TUG PUTS MAN, LINE ABOARD HERO'S VESSEL," underscored by "PRAYERS ANSWERED, SIGHS MRS. DON'T-GIVE-UP-SHIP" with a photograph of Agnes Carlsen waving and smiling.

In **The New York Times,** the story had long climbed above the fold and joined the front-page news that most people would first see when they picked up the paper. In the dead center of the page, underneath the masthead, appeared a snappy little strap: "Tug Turmoil Puts Her Mate Aboard the Flying Enterprise— Everything Now Is Said to Depend upon Weather." The **Times** then observed the standard reporter's dictum: give the full story in the first sentence—let the embellishments follow: "A strong pair of hands joined Capt. Henrik Kurt Carlsen on board the Flying Enterprise yesterday afternoon when Kenneth R. Dancy, 27-year-old mate of the British salvage tug,

Turmoil, climbed over the stricken American freighter's taffrail after several attempts to get a towline aboard had failed."

Over at the **Daily News,** different shades of color appeared: "A rope about the thickness of sashcord became a lifeline today for the courageous captain of the disabled **Flying Enterprise** and a Scotsman [**sic**] riding the listing vessel with him in the stormy Atlantic." The "Scotsman," it transpired, "was Harry Davies, 27, of Aberdeen, who was vacationing from duty on another tug when he was pressed into service as mate of the Turmoil." The telephone lines must have been thick with static when that copy was taken down.

By the later editions, and by Sunday's pages and pages of features, all corrections had come through. "Harry Davies," though still twenty-seven, had revealed his true identity as "Kenneth Dancy," and, an Englishman now, he had "moved" to "Hook Green"—which, after all, rhymes with "Aberdeen."

News of Carlsen's latest adventures roared like a high, warm wind across the world for thirty-five hours. The accounts of **Turmoil**'s arrival on Thursday night included the first unsatisfactory towing attempts. The successive failures all day on Friday raised the tempo of the story; Dancy's move on Friday afternoon cranked it up several more notches—and then came the climax of the tow on Saturday morning at nine o'clock.

This pattern, thrilling in itself, threatened to have its downside. Once the excitement of the efforts had passed, the gentle and steady procession of the convoy to Falmouth could more or less kill the story. Nothing much would need to be heard from Carlsen and Dancy until they got to Falmouth.

Meanwhile, the Sundays took wide spreads, with more angles than a geometry book. They had maps and diagrams and towage and salvage; they had cargo men and tug men and captains and mates; they had wives and winchmen and wave levels and weather. **The New York Times,** still running the story as a lead, and still high on the front page, prepared its readers "for at least four dangerous days of the haul to Falmouth, some 300 miles away."

And the newspaper quoted one oddity, from a most reliable source: "Observing Royal Air Force aircraft reported that at one stage the Abeille had a line attached to the bow of the freighter and was steaming away from the starboard side at a 90-degree angle to the course of the Turmoil. The purpose of this apparently was to reduce the Enterprise's 60-degree list to port, which allowed the seas to sweep up the main deck from that side."

Did Carlsen change his mind? No. He had considered such a possibility when **Abeille 25** showed up, but had dismissed it as too risky. Handling one towline from one tug embodied enough problems, and what effect would a transverse or differently angled tug have on the fractured plates? So **Abeille 25** sat in behind **Flying Enterprise** and, presently, **Dexterous,** another tug from **Turmoil**'s own company, joined the parade astern. There was no second towline.

Weather forecasts became crucial—to everyone. On Sunday afternoon, the wind freshened up to twenty knots, but the forecasters' word, confirmed and relayed by the Royal Navy observers flying overhead, expected good visibility and, for the foreseeable days, a relatively calm sea. The wind dropped again and the members of the operation wondered cautiously whether safety had truly set in. After twelve hours that indeed seemed to be the case; after twenty-four they began to believe it. Dancy and Carlsen took alternating watches from the bow of **Flying Enterprise,** which was reported as "making three point five knots." Other news stories described Carlsen as "feeling like a million." Commander Leslie O'Brien on **Willard Keith** looked in two directions at once when he told the Associated Press, "Captain Carlsen is jubilant and desires to remain on board in case the tow parts."

Monday's press kept the interest revved. According to **The New York Times,** when **John W. Weeks** arrived in Plymouth on Sunday, "the ship's band blared out a series of marches." Commander Thompson "stepped onto the torpedo deck to address newspaper and radio correspondents and camera men assembled on the dock," where he told them that, in his opinion, **Flying Enterprise** had a "75% chance of making it."

The newspaper went on to report from London that "Captain Carlsen's parents are expected here later today by air. A hotel has placed a suite at their disposal and will invite Captain Carlsen and Mr. Dancy to stay there." When the parents landed, "Mrs. Carlsen, who received a bouquet in Denmark's national colors—red and white—was surrounded by newspaper men and photographers at London Airport. 'How terrific and terrifying all this is,' she said."

Meanwhile, down in Kent, Mr. and Mrs. Stanley Dancy were reported to have held a

"Sunday luncheon party" in their flat above the post office and village shop.

"Asked if they would go to Falmouth to meet their son, Mr. Dancy said, 'We cannot, I am afraid. There's the business.' "

33.

IF CARLSEN AND DANCY HADN'T BEEN aboard, **Turmoil** would frequently have had to send back a crew detail to inspect the towline as it emerged from **Flying Enterprise.** Vigilance needs to remain constant at both ends of a tow; towing has as many variables as the sea has moods. In this case, given the weight and condition of the freighter, Captain Parker had extended his precautions—literally. He had played the steel cable out to over two thousand feet, more than twice a typical towline, because he had peculiar difficulties to address.

A swell under **Flying Enterprise** could have swung the ship at the end of this backward umbilicus—and did, along a side-to-side arc of up to a thousand feet. This called for the **Turmoil** crew to switch the towline repeatedly, port to starboard to port again, as they saw the freighter, pushed forward by the sea, drift up almost in line with them. Or a bow wave hitting **Turmoil** could have ripped like a spring tide back to the freighter and caused her to lurch and stagger. And a rogue wave coming through from anywhere out in those badlands would take both vessels down together.

Also, **Flying Enterprise** lay more or less on her side—the pendulum gauge in Carlsen's cabin showed her, when steady, listing now at between fifty-five and sixty degrees. Not only did this aggravate the risk of taking on more water, it meant that the ship, not being upright, had no bow with which to cut the seas. And worst of all, the ship had been fractured. Were Parker to tow her too vigorously, the fissures might spread wider. **Turmoil** had the horsepower to tow the freighter twice as fast— even faster in a flat sea—but did not dare to do so. Any further strain on the rope might give an extra opening to the sea.

It had been a weekend of high drama, but now it seemed that the Atlantic had given in, had allowed Carlsen his victory. In every merchant marine establishment, at every workbench and desk, on every school playground, a strong but cautious jubilation set in. Everybody wanted to share in this success, especially fellow seamen. Other ships traveling anywhere near the convoy's pathway veered by to rubberneck, and they sent messages of congratulation and praise. Carlsen never heard most of them, but **Willard Keith,** who swept the area with radar and kept all shipping at a safe distance, picked up some and passed them on. **Turmoil** overheard them on her own wave bands. The land stations along Ireland's and England's south coasts also put out detailed alerts to steer clear of the convoy's path—as if any seafarer in the North Atlantic hadn't already known that **Flying Enterprise** had been taken in tow. Broadcasters led every bulletin with mile-by-mile news of progress.

This story had a shape to it that gave news desks great relish; they could cover this in a way that they had only dreamed about. The reporters set out to reach deeper and deeper into the middle of the event while it was taking place—something that had proved difficult to do during the war, with the continuing and increasing obstacle of military censorship. On Monday and Tuesday, the press went out again, and their chartered boats kept pace with the convoy; their hired pilots flew over the procession of ships; they even suggested dropping in on **Flying Enterprise,** if they could, by helicopter—because, by now, every single detail of Carlsen, Dancy, and Parker made news.

Commander O'Brien, on **Willard Keith,** attempted a preemptive strike: he took to releasing daily bulletins through the public relations arm of the U.S. Navy headquarters in London. For example, he announced that he had, on Sunday, sent across—among other things— vegetable soup. His bulletin included the detail that Carlsen and Dancy had mistaken it for coffee, and had added cream and sugar—"but they enjoyed it anyway"; Commander O'Brien evidently understood the press.

As is so often the case, the men of the moment, however, wanted nothing to do with the news. In the food parcel, **Willard Keith** had included a bunch of newspapers with all their blaring headlines; Carlsen and Dancy registered discomfort and embarrassment at seeing their exploit so fulsomely discussed. Nevertheless, Carlsen, who had seen the national concern voiced for him in the Danish press, gave a fifteen-minute interview to Danish radio in which he confirmed his good spirits and his optimism and conveyed his gratitude to people for taking such an interest. He came across as calm, dedicated, and focused now on the next phase of the job: bringing in his ship.

Many of the reporters came back early from the sea. On Monday afternoon the Associated Press serviced the world with a description of the convoy as seen from the air: "Some 750 yards behind the **Turmoil** came the wallowing lopsided hulk of the **Enterprise,** with its stubborn skipper waving happily at a small parade of planes and ships which passed to cheer him on."

Delete the word "happily"—and perhaps the word "skipper." Dancy, out on deck, saw a tug called **Englishman** get safely close behind **Flying Enterprise**'s stern; being a tug, she literally knew the ropes. Eager to reward the tug captain by giving his clients, the bunch of photographers aboard, a good picture, Dancy clambered up and held himself out from the rail—a dramatic picture. The newspapers used it abundantly. When he came back in, Carlsen ripped into him. He told Dancy that he didn't like the stunt; that he thought it "unwise"; that he believed that Dancy had taken an unnecessary risk, because those rails "had not been built" to take Dancy's weight; and he "advised" Dancy not to do anything like it again.

OTHER THAN THIS flash of reproof, the odd couple had settled in easily. Much of the discomfort Carlsen endured when alone had now been eased. Changes of clothing created the first breakthrough; a second came with the steady level of supply from **Willard Keith.** Now Carlsen had a better diet, including steak from Commander O'Brien's chefs. Even better, the destroyer had sent over grease to lubricate the cable. And, perhaps best of all, the navy had sent heavy work gloves.

The two men observed a routine laid down by Carlsen. They took watch, checking the tow; they made their frequent "excursions"; Carlsen observed his two-hourly radio stints, and they rested at the same time, chatting about, among other things, similar pastimes. Dancy spoke of his knitting, and Carlsen, trained to sew sails, had gone on to macramé and specialized in making belts for his wife and daughters.

They spent their downtime in the adapted radio shack. The room's dimensions came to not much more than nine feet by seven feet. An L-shaped section accommodated the metal radio cabinets all along one wall and, in front of them, at sitting height, the operators' desks. The two men lived in the cramped area remaining, Carlsen on the piles atop the leather bunk and Dancy on the floor mattresses as far away from the door as he could get. Above his head dangled two green curtains. Ordinarily they covered a porthole, so that the radio officer would not have his dials whited out in the glare of sunshine. Now these curtains hung down vertically from, as it were, the ceiling.

Looking outward, the men could see into the corridor that led to the rest of the bridge—to the captain's quarters, the wheelhouse, and then to the world. Just outside the door dropped a tight metal staircase to the level below. At the foot of this staircase, the ocean washed over the ship.

No lights, no heating, no dryness or warmth, no certainties; the two sat there, opening the newest U.S. Navy food package or chatting by candlelight. On the sea, **Turmoil** chugged on and Dan Parker had eyes for nothing but the ocean ahead and the tow behind, and ears for nothing but potentially lethal sounds, such as the cracking **thud!** of a cable snapping or the sudden whine of a rising wind.

And he had words for nothing but the commands that needed to be astute enough to control this especially awkward casualty. When the press contacted him during the tow, he refused all invitations to be interviewed; he turned down all questions as to his optimism; he ignored all requests to comment on the progress of the tow. He did send one message, however.

He radioed ahead to the mayor of **Turmoil**'s home port: "I will endeavor to deliver **Flying Enterprise** safely to Falmouth."

34.

CARLSEN AND DANCY SCARCELY DIS-cussed the ship or her condition. They needed to focus on what lay ahead. On Thursday night, they had each, on their separate vessels, started work immediately after **Turmoil** had arrived. Friday brought a day of frustrations and "Dancy's Leap," as the newspapers in England now called it. Saturday established the tow, settled it down, and began the journey. Sunday became a day of rest—good food, the newspapers, and placid clouds in the sky. By nightfall on Sunday they had a distance of about 250 miles to go. That meant approximately seventy more hours together; by Monday night the **Daily News** was reporting that they had 170 miles to go and were "still being towed well."

· · ·

FOR ALL THIS PROGRESS, if George Brown, the conscientious chief engineer, had remained on board the freighter, his anxiety levels would have been climbing. Brown knew that a fracture had taken place in one of the internal pipes leading from the large freshwater tanks beneath the holds. He had reached down and tasted that water when it started to pour over his feet during the worst hell in the engine room. By now, Brown would have been making calculations along these lines: What is the rate of that freshwater leak—how much water is now slopping about down below? And to what degree is the momentum of the tow through the waves exerting pressure on the fracture in the plates? Just because the sides seemed originally to have taken no more than hairline fractures did not mean that water could not seep in. En route, under tow, the sea was surely pressing those thin cracks a little farther open. Therefore, the ship was, without a doubt, subject to new, twin pressures: from the gradual loss of internal control over her water tanks and from the determination of the Atlantic to squeeze into the holds through the cracks in the metals. Brown would have agreed that Carlsen had on his hands a race against time. Even without any adverse weather, the ship might have a problem winning this race. In one last hour of one last day, she might simply take on one last ounce too many of the weight of water. And sink.

Carlsen, who knew his ship like he knew his hands, never raised anything like these concerns with Kenneth Dancy, with Captain Parker, or with any of the four standby captains, Olsen, Donahue, Thompson, or O'Brien—but he must have been sharply alert to them. And Dancy did know that Carlsen checked the inclinometer in the wheelhouse every time he went to make radio contact. No: as far as Carlsen displayed to the world, he had secured his ship under tow and he intended to bring her in.

Monday passed by, and as Carlsen and Dancy pursued the ship's routine, they dealt with all their chores, which now included the reporters and photographers on the boats and planes. By nightfall, they felt easier and more confident. And again, all day on Tuesday, as they checked and checked, the freighter continued her long, sagging swing from side to side, with the hawser submerged from just behind **Turmoil** to just before she swung up onto **Flying Enterprise.**

Seen from the air, it appeared routine. The slight wakes showed nothing more abnormal than a towing operation moving slowly, with other vessels tagging along. Up ahead steamed the tug. The listing ship had settled down and seemed accustomed to the tow; her stern in the air, she moved at an angle in the water, not quite broadside-on, but very definitely not head-on.

SUCH A STEADY pace should have calmed everybody—but it seemed to have the reverse effect. Our hearts, which had settled down again in the good news of Saturday, Sunday, Monday, and Tuesday, actually climbed back up into our throats as we followed every moment of this enthralling journey and knew that it neared success. In our Tipperary village, people dropped by the school to ask my parents, the local authorities on everything, whether "Carlsen would make it." We looked at the Mercator's Projection map on the schoolroom wall as my father plotted, in ink erasable on the oilcloth surface, the course on which **Turmoil** was towing **Flying Enterprise.** She had been southwest of us when she foundered, when the passengers and crew were saved. Then she drifted, and when Captain Parker got to him, Carlsen lay due south. The tow began to take him southeast of us, and brought him nearer— by Tuesday he had come within a hundred miles of the Irish coast, south of Waterford Harbor. The school prayers now included everyone out there in the slow, steady parade of ships.

I remember rain flogging our windows. I remember the comforting fire in the school hearth. I remember the relief that Carlsen was not, at this moment, enduring any of the bad weather that we were having, that the winds and the waves had begun to leave him alone. I remember the almost unbearable concern that he should be safe. I remember the marveling and the relief at Dancy's Leap.

That same day, a French schoolgirl, one year older than I, Dominique Boutinaud, went to the Danish embassy in Paris. Dominique had been chosen to represent ten thousand French schoolchildren whom Denmark had sheltered in World War II. The message read, "Captain, what you are doing is wonderful, but be careful. Jump into the sea quickly if you see that the ship is going to capsize. Even if you come back to port alone, the whole world will applaud you. It is the greatest sea story we have ever heard. The ten thousand French children who went to Denmark shout 'Bravo!' and send you their kisses. See you soon. Long live Captain Carlsen."

. . .

CORNWALL, ENGLAND'S southwesternmost county, has two coasts. The north coast looks out at the Celtic Sea, and the south coast looks down into the English Channel; the snout of Land's End noses into the Western Approaches. On Monday afternoon and Tuesday morning, January 7 and 8, although a wind had freshened and a swell had begun to roll, yachtsmen and other seafarers came down from Cornwall, from the north coast and the south coast and from the toe of the county, to catch a glimpse of the convoy. Everybody listened to the radio bulletins, and by now other ships had joined in. Heading elsewhere but going through the Channel anyway, every one of those skippers wished to add a little shepherding of his own to a brave colleague.

How any ship could have survived such a long listing in that position amazed the men with binoculars. Sometimes when she rolled, they could see up the nostril of her funnel, and she was swinging her hips from side to side, sashaying like a slow dancer, instead of moving forward with economy.

The town of Falmouth pulsed with excitement. From **Willard Keith,** Commander

O'Brien warned Carlsen and Dancy that the mayor and council had planned a reception committee, which would likely prove massive; for a start, over four hundred journalists from fifteen countries had already billeted themselves. The police said they expected thousands of people to pour in from everywhere, just to welcome home the seafarers.

They put out the flags in Falmouth on Tuesday. Little triangles of red, white, and blue bunting ran in dancing strings all along Customs House Quay, in front of the Chain Locker pub, where Dancy had slept the night before he'd joined the tug—Dancy, the new young hero, who had, as we all now believed, leapt across a giant's gap of ocean to help a fellow mariner. The home port would celebrate the success of its local vessel, **Turmoil.** A Falmouth company would land a fine contract repairing this now world-famous cargo ship. Rumors flew that the kings of England and Denmark wanted to meet Carlsen and Dancy, that great dinners and luncheons were being planned in London in their honor. An emissary from the Court of Denmark would come down to Falmouth and pin a medal on Carlsen—whose parents had already left London and would be standing on the quayside when their son came home from the sea.

On Tuesday afternoon, the convoy drew close to the Scilly Isles, the ancient land of Lyonesse, where the "three Queens with crowns of gold" took the dead King Arthur in a barge "dark as a funeral scarf from stem to stern." Scarcely a household along that coast had not listened out for a weather forecast that day; every follower of Carlsen's fate had been looking at the sky. On the ships in the convoy, the crews had been looking at it, too, and with rather more edge because the weather forecasts had started to sound uncomfortable. Since late on Tuesday morning, the waters had been climbing a little higher over **Flying Enterprise,** making tow supervision more and more difficult. And now a storm might come after them.

Close to five o'clock, the storm did come in; it had been threatening for hours. Captain Parker discussed with Carlsen what they should do. Should he heave to? Let **Flying Enterprise** choose her own direction at the end of the towrope? And adjust gently ahead of her, without taking up the slack on the line? The last thing they wanted was the sea snapping that hawser; and if it proved too taut, the waves would cut it like a thread. He and Carlsen debated. They concurred on sitting it out; general reports said that the storm would move on.

It did—and when the weather calmed, after dark, Parker took up the tow again and resumed the steady pace for Falmouth. But—by now able to "hear" the ship acutely, neither Carlsen nor Dancy felt at all easy. The fallow period had done her no good; she had lost for those few hours the momentum that had been keeping her up. She rolled in greater anxiety than ever, she dipped farther down, she pitched harder, and it seemed to Carlsen—as he reported to Commander O'Brien—that she now rode lower in the water.

And the sea, it transpired, hadn't relented much. The weather came back in again, and the swell climbed on the wind. Not long after the tow resumed, Carlsen and Dancy heard a tremendous **bang!** just beneath where they lay down to sleep. They went out, in the dark, in the spray. The sea had ripped apart the gripes and davits on the port lifeboat, the one Carlsen hadn't dared launch. For an hour or so, the useless boat hammered and smashed against the side of the ship within a loud earshot of the radio shack, and then the sea cut it loose.

WEDNESDAY, JANUARY 9, 1952, began unusually early for the two men on **Flying Enterprise**—at half past one in the morning.

A siren blasted right beside them, which meant that **Turmoil** rode near, which meant that she had come right back to the freighter, which meant that the tow had gone. Waves more than ten feet high had snapped the hawser, and Parker had come back close to tell them. Carlsen and he agreed not to attempt anything in the night, and Carlsen went back to sleep. By his calculations they were less than fifty miles from the mouth of the Fal. On **Willard Keith,** Commander O'Brien monitored everything. His frequent signals revealed the shared anxieties. "Weather still worsening—Captain Carlsen reports Enterprise lower in the water and seas quote playing heck unquote with ship," he noted, adding, "Force 7 winds and boiling seas into exposed port beam."

Wednesday's dawn broke, gray as mourning. Carlsen and Dancy went forward and inspected the damage to their end of the tow. They found a metal shambles, a miniature scrapyard. The cotter pin that closed the mouth of the shackle was supposed to work on a quick-release mechanism if excess pressure came on. But too many things had attacked it, on a deck where so much flew loose, and the quick release had not released quickly enough when the sea closed her jaws on the tow. The cable had torn away from the bollard, leaving a loose end, a frayed and nasty length of hawser that lay there twitching like a half-dead giant eel; the necktie had been ripped away just below the knot. Before another cable and shackle could be wound around the bollard, the short stretch of the old hawser must be cut from the neck of the bitt and all debris and damaged equipment cleared from its feeders, its chocks.

In driving winds, with the waves lambasting the bow of the ship, Carlsen went to work on the loose cable end with a hacksaw. Now Death took another crack at him. He and Dancy prepared to take turns sawing; they squatted by the bollard, their backs to the weather, trying merely to see what they were doing in the spray. Ten men heaving buckets of freezing water on them nonstop from a foot away wouldn't have caused as much stress or drenching.

Carlsen sawed and sawed; he made some progress and handed the hacksaw to Dancy. At that moment, a wave bigger and more vicious than the others, forty feet tall, the leader of the gang, blasted in over the bow rail and hit Carlsen from behind. He lost his grip on the top of the bollard and went flying.

Dancy saw it happening, saw Carlsen go— and then he got hit by the edge of the same wave. He spun backward, half stunned, and dropped the hacksaw. When he recovered his composure, he couldn't see the skipper and started to move, hoping to help. Then, through his daze, he spotted Carlsen again—several yards away, wheeling and sprawling down the sloped deck, being sluiced fast toward the sea. The wave had swilled him lengthways and then, when it found a clear space, washed him down the sharp slope to the port rail.

Carlsen's body hit the upright stanchion and swung around under the lower spars of the rail, where he stuck for a moment. The waves tried to push him through the gap, to wash him off the deck. They got him into the ocean, free of the ship, but he hauled himself back, dragging and swimming against the tide pouring down over his head from the decks.

Just ahead, Carlsen saw a spar that had partially snapped off one of the masts. In desperation, he reached up and grabbed it. He held on and waited until the billow and its aftermath had poured through. Perhaps he knew of the fabled hiatus after every seventh wave of the sea; in the lull that came, he got himself to rights. He clambered back aboard his ship and made his way over to Dancy—whose own call had been close—and they found a relatively sheltered nook in which to draw breath. Both men knew that they would fix no tow that morning, not with those waves attacking them. They headed back to the radio shack to recover and sat there in the half darkness, soaked, dismayed by the sea, somewhat traumatized but still determined. Outside, they could hear the wind—this weather was not letting up.

In midafternoon, Carlsen got on the radio. Were a new tow to be attempted, they must do it soon; they had no more than an hour of daylight left. Parker wondered whether they could try—as they had done before—to use a loop rather than a shackle. He even offered to have his men attempt to heave it over, no matter how heavy, and Dancy and Carlsen could simply noose it around the bitts. Carlsen ruled it out; he ruled out any chance of getting a line in as far as the bow bollards and argued for the stern.

Willard Keith came through again and gave no good news of the weather forecast. By now, Commander O'Brien's signals had begun to sound like a Greek chorus. He told of the damaged shackle: "Capt. Carlsen had to cut it away with a hacksaw." He recounted the misadventures: "Carlsen and Dancy managed to cut it loose while water and spray broke over them occasionally knocking them down." He kept the world's spirits up: "The task now is for **Tur-**

moil to pass eye of towing wire with new shackle to **Enterprise** after which Carlsen and Dancy must connect this shackle to the main shackle already on board." And he mentioned options: "Alternate plan is to pass loop at end of towing wire to stern which is dryer and now more accessible than bow."

Parker agreed with Carlsen: try for the stern; she's higher and dryer there. Once again, at great risk, he moved **Turmoil** closer alongside **Flying Enterprise,** almost to keep pace with Carlsen and Dancy as they made their way aft. Within seconds Parker and the **Turmoil** crew could see that neither man on the freighter had a chance of getting to that fantail, not with that sea and that gale and on those decks. Dodging the sacks of naphthalene and all the other debris sliding around the decks, the two men turned back.

That evening, Carlsen, who simply did not want to give up, advanced a new scheme. He suggested to Parker and O'Brien that if any kind of a lull came by the next morning, he would drop a bow anchor. (He hadn't decided between the lower port or the higher starboard bow.) Couldn't **Turmoil** then fire a rocket across to **Willard Keith,** which would pass a cable behind Carlsen's anchor chain? And with the destroyer and the tug acting as the two forward points of a triangle, couldn't they tow **Flying Enterprise** the rest of the way, with the anchor chain caught on this cable? After all, they had come so near to port.

Carlsen never considered how he would lower his anchor; he did not know how much of the deck equipment was damaged. He simply assumed that he, by himself if he had to, could release and drop an anchor chain. Dan Parker radioed back, "Best thing we can do is wait for daylight and come in and try to reconnect. Try and get some rest if you can." Carlsen's plan never came to fruition; none of those decks could easily be traversed anymore.

He and Dancy prepared to get whatever sleep they could. Both men, cold, wet, exhausted, had extensive bruises. Carlsen had shredded and grazed skin on many parts of his body, and the rawness of his skinned feet was exacerbated by the salt in the water. As they lay wrapped in blankets, on their sea-drenched mattresses, the waves teemed in beneath them, flooding over the port side, and **Flying Enterprise** settled lower and lower in the water.

And yet she drifted on. If she drifted much farther, the land would soon bring a measure of shelter, even without a tow. When the line had parted, she had kept going for some time, as she would have done, on the same course, on her own momentum. Even when **Turmoil** lay hove to, **Flying Enterprise** still kept going forward; she had come several miles nearer to Falmouth after the parting of the cable, and she continued to drift gently toward haven. Falmouth lay less than fifty miles away.

LOW-LYING CLOUDS make aircraft noise louder. That Wednesday afternoon, the engines echoed over the stalled convoy, because the world had heard of the parted towline. The airborne reporters began to gather and down they came, down through the cloud ceiling, and circled the halted parade. Now, at last, perhaps Carlsen would give up; now, at last, the Atlantic would win. Carlsen had saved forty-nine people so far—could he save a fiftieth, Dancy? And save himself? Carlsen's wife and his two daughters said that they "prayed and simply prayed."

In the town that awaited **Flying Enterprise,** the same storm that left the freighter gasping tore down all their flags. On Wednesday morning, while Carlsen and Dancy were being swilled around the decks of the ship, the people of Falmouth came out and put up the flags again. On Wednesday night, the storm once more ripped away the little red, white, and blue pennants. And on Thursday morning, the people of Falmouth put them up once more.

35.

OVERNIGHT, ON **TURMOIL** AND **WILlard Keith,** anxiety reached a new height, even among such stoic and experienced men. Not a word had come from **Flying Enterprise.** In his situation report, at eight o'clock on Thursday morning, in which he described the sea as "very rough," Commander O'Brien observed that he had heard "nothing from Captain Carlsen" since the previous evening. The weather had again come across the Western Approaches like a mad bandit. By nine o'clock in the morning the BBC was calling it "gale force."

AT NINE O'CLOCK New York time that morning, a different gale began to blow across Carlsen's fate—on Lafayette Street, in lower

Manhattan. Today, Lafayette Hall, No. 80 on the street (which edges Chinatown), belongs to New York University as a residence, housing over a thousand students. On the morning of January 10, 1952, a large room in this building filled up with people, who sat at tables set in a square. They had come there by law in order "to inquire into the circumstances surrounding the cracking and listing of the S.S. FLYING ENTERPRISE on 27 and 28 December respectively."

At the head of the table sat Captain Lewis H. Shackelford of the United States Coast Guard, flanked by Commander Alf S. Lie and the recorder of the inquiry, Lieutenant Commander Clinton J. Maguire, both also of the USCG. They had already received the Rotterdam information gathered by their Antwerp colleague Lieutenant Commander William Sayer. This inquiry would scrutinize what had happened, would scrutinize Carlsen. To the world he had become a hero—but had his peers, with their expert knowledge, detected flaws in his performance, misjudgments for which he might deserve censure? For example, had the economics of hiring dock labor in Hamburg caused a hurried stowage? The men running the inquiry had no brief to do anything other than find out what had gone wrong and make recommendations to prevent recurrences.

Lieutenant Commander Maguire read aloud the reach of its authority, including the standard wording, "whether any act of misconduct, inattention to duty, negligence or willful violation of the law on the part of any licensed or certificated man contributed to the casualty, so that appropriate proceedings against the license or certificate of such person may be recommended and taken."

The hearing certainly had the power to find Carlsen—or anyone on board, or the shipping line—negligent. A damning conclusion could cost Carlsen, as the most visible involved party, his master's ticket, his career, his place, his means of supporting his family. As they sat down to open the inquiry, the officials and all who came to give evidence to it—all people of the sea—knew this. They also knew that the cable between **Turmoil** and **Flying Enterprise** had parted the previous day, that the weather in the Atlantic boded ill, that the ship's condition had not improved, and that she was once again out of control.

Most of Carlsen's crew showed up to give evidence about their skipper. They had docked from **General A. W. Greely** that week—and

on the dockside they'd seen familiar faces waiting in high anxiety. In Rotterdam, the Müllers,
Elsa, Leanne, and Lothar, had heard that one
passenger, a middle-aged man, had died in the
jump from **Flying Enterprise.** They didn't
know his name; they received no other details.
As they flew to New York, they had no idea
whether the man who had died was the
beloved head of their family. For days they had
been staying in a Brooklyn hotel, a few blocks
away from the Carlsens' temporary residence
in Hans Isbrandtsen's sister's house; like the
Carlsens, all they could do was pray.

As **Greely** docked, the Müllers waited and
watched. Down the gangway came some crew
members they recognized . . . and then came
some more crew members . . . and then—Curt
Müller! He looked a little battered; he had hurt
his arm in the rescue and broken two ribs—yet
he managed to catch his twelve-year-old son,
Lothar, who jumped into his arms.

ON LAFAYETTE STREET, the Coast Guard
inquiry called John Edward Drake, the first assistant engineer. Answering Lieutenant Commander Maguire's questions, he took them on
the voyage: through the early, foggy reaches up
to the morning of the crack, and the ship's

pitching, pounding, and rolling. Given the preliminaries, the settling down, the establishment of the necessary formalities, Drake's evidence could not have begun until close to ten o'clock—three o'clock in the afternoon on the coast of England.

WHILE DRAKE AND everyone else in the Coast Guard inquiry room had been sleeping, waking up, and preparing for the day, the fates of Carlsen and Dancy were being defined. They had survived the night. Carlsen had decided to make no radio contact until he had sufficient daylight to give him some visibility on board—he also had a worry about battery strength. When daylight came, he and Parker conferred. **Turmoil** stood off by not more than a few hundred yards, as she had done all night, and the two captains, with Commander O'Brien across the conversation, debated whether a new towline could work—if they could get it aboard. Dancy had earlier braved the lower decks via the internal ladders, and he came back to report that water now poured almost at will through most of the doors and portholes.

Parker gave the opinion that perhaps a towline might not work in that weather; Commander O'Brien asked Carlsen whether he and Dancy might consider coming off now; Carlsen doubted whether "the cause is lost yet." O'Brien feared, though he never raised the fear with Carlsen, that the dying freighter he was looking at across the waves could trap Carlsen and Dancy as she went down.

When Carlsen finished the radio conference, he turned to ask Dancy where, in his opinion, they might most safely leave the ship. They had limited opportunities for surveillance; the weather made the decks unattainable. Not only that but the floor of their "suite" in the radio shack now lay under six inches of water.

In time for the twelve o'clock radio call, they climbed up to Carlsen's cabin, where he now had to clamber onto the bulkhead to get across to his radio. From there, the two men rigged a rope out to the starboard rail; the ship had keeled so far over on her side that the original escape route, the radio shack door to the outside world, lay under the sea.

During the noon radio contact, Commander O'Brien told Carlsen that RAF Culdrose in Cornwall was preparing a rescue helicopter. Onshore relay stations and lifeboat posts eavesdropped on these conversations, and from Penzance the lifeboat **Satellite** set out. As did the Falmouth lifeboat. Carlsen and Dancy "sat" like acrobats in the two easy chairs in Carlsen's cabin and again discussed the best, the safest, the easiest ways of escape.

Other boats in the area around the halted convoy still carried reporters and cameramen, whose roles had turned somber. **Flying Enterprise** was going down—there was no longer any doubt about it; the men with the lenses had now gathered to see not so much the death of the bull but whether the matador would live. Not that they felt all that safe themselves; the newsreel men had to strap themselves to deck fittings in order to get any steadiness of focus.

At two o'clock, Dancy hauled himself up on the rope, looked out, and reported back to Carlsen that the ship was "almost on her beam-ends." Carlsen had to see for himself. After a long moment he dropped down again and said to Dancy, "She won't last."

He called in for his radio conference and told Commander O'Brien and Captain Parker to let the helicopter come from RAF Culdrose. Above their heads, the spray began to come in through Carlsen's door. In New York, John Drake had just begun to give evidence at 80 Lafayette Street.

. . .

WHEN A SHIP begins to go down, the sea fills
with shocking debris. Spars float, deck cargo
bobs in the water, a massive flotsam is born.
Any of that can kill a man. On the afternoon
that Carlsen effected his rescue of passengers
and crew, nothing much had broken off his
ship—the sea had a mercifully clean surface.
After agreeing to the helicopter, Carlsen and
Dancy climbed up on deck again and clung to
the starboard rail, the highest point on the
freighter, easy for a helicopter winchman to
reach.

At the starboard rail, the two men stood
looking at the sea, the rain, the carnage, the
ship. At one moment, she lurched up several
degrees, as she had been doing since the day
she listed—and she went down again. This
time, though, she showed no signs of wanting
to get back up. The surface of the decks became indistinguishable from the surface of the
sea, and everywhere they looked, Carlsen and
Dancy could see the final true signs of a ship's
sinking: the beginnings of the deep and dangerous swirl and, above all, the debris.

They could see the naphthalene bobbing on
the waves—a smack on the side of the head
from one of those sacks and a man's gone.
Scraps and shrouds from the masts, wires from

aerials—one of those could sever a limb if whipped the wrong way. Or any of Carlsen's (brand-new) tarpaulins might rip from the hatch coamings and become a winding-sheet. And the port lifeboat must be hammering about somewhere on the water—**Willard Keith** had not yet had time to machine-gun it to make it sink.

Carlsen went back down the rope to his cabin and got to the radio—where Parker told him that the helicopter wasn't coming. At RAF Culdrose, Lieutenant Commander Suthers had tried and tried, but had been forced back by the appalling weather—which, after all, had been afflicting these seas now for more than two weeks. Commander O'Brien had monitored Suthers on radar, had seen him within seven minutes of **Flying Enterprise,** had seen him turn back. Carlsen and Dancy now discussed dropping into the sea from a point at the starboard rail.

Commander O'Brien came through to confirm that the helicopter wasn't coming, that the gale had proved too strong. As he began to suggest to Carlsen that at last they must get off the ship, Carlsen heard the first explosion. He said to Dancy, "Time to go."

Up on deck, behind them, they heard a second, louder explosion. When they looked back, they saw the wheelhouse door detonated outward. Then they heard another and another—the pressure building up inside the ship was blowing the watertight doors and the hatches that had long been battened down tight. The two men headed toward the funnel, which now lay as horizontal as a diving board.

IN THE VILLAGE, I heard it that evening, on the radio beneath the brocade cloth—the crackle, the ships' call signs, the commentary from the radio operators at the scene. At eight minutes past three, **Willard Keith** said, "**Flying Enterprise** is going down. Making attempts to rescue them now." A minute later, **Turmoil** said, "We have just received news that the weather is too bad for the helicopter. She can't make it and is returning to base. It's up to us to take them off now." Three minutes on, **Willard Keith** said, "Plenty of ships standing by to take Carlsen and Dancy off." By now an extra lifeboat had joined the flotilla, and a wide semicircle of watchers, tugs, freight ships, and chartered tenders stood in the ocean. Any one of them would have moved in for those two men.

At sixteen minutes past three, **Willard Keith** said, "**Flying Enterprise** still afloat. Captain

Carlsen and Dancy standing on starboard side of deck." (Signals at sea mean to be as austere as telegrams, yet on almost every occasion, Commander O'Brien spends an extra word by referring to him as "Captain" Carlsen.) At eighteen minutes past three, the tug **Englishman** said, "**Flying Enterprise** appears to be sinking. Rescue craft close in. **Turmoil** throws rope ladder over side."

Two minutes later, **Willard Keith** said, "**Flying Enterprise** now taking water down stack" and **Englishman** added, "Stack dips under and comes up." At three twenty-one, **Willard Keith** asked **Turmoil,** "Do you want Dancy to go back to **Turmoil** when picked up?" **Turmoil** replied, "We don't care where he goes as long as he is safe."

In the gloom of the winter afternoon, Carlsen and Dancy, barefoot and wearing life vests, reached the foot of the funnel. They climbed up carefully, in their one-hand-on-the-ground monkey walk. From **Turmoil,** Parker watched, anxious as a parent. He knew the problems associated with a sinking ship, and he knew that these problems could extend to him. The vortex from a ship as big as this would run so wide and so deep that he might have no chance—however nimble his tug—of getting to Carlsen and Dancy before they got sucked down into the spin. He also knew that they knew; he had confidence in Dancy's intelligence, and supreme confidence in Carlsen's experience and common sense.

Dancy sat down on the funnel's lip. **Turmoil** said to her sister tug, **Dexterous,** "Dancy and Carlsen are preparing to jump from the funnel. Stand by." (Touchingly, **Turmoil** had put its own boy's name first.) **Willard Keith** and **Turmoil** fired blue flares to bring light to the sea.

The mouth of the funnel touched the water. By using it as their escape route, the two men, as the passengers and crew had done, had elected to go off on the listing port side—without question the place where the sea had offered the most danger; but the drop on the other side was even more dangerous.

At twenty-three minutes past three, **Englishman** reported, "Terrific heave to port and great mass of debris from **Enterprise** deck." The ship was belching. Carlsen and Dancy crouched near the top of the funnel. In theory, they had no more than a foot or two to jump. Carlsen suggested to Dancy that they jump together. Dancy said no, that the captain must be the last to leave the ship. Carlsen agreed; he said that the tip of the funnel wasn't, in any case, wide enough for both of them. They hunched there in silence. Dancy turned back

to Carlsen and said, "Shall we go now, Cap'n?"
Carlsen nodded.

Dancy mistimed his jump. He meant to go
on the crest of a wave, but instead he hit a
trough, dropped twenty-five feet—and went
under the surface. He came back up and began
swimming fiercely in order to take himself away
from the swirl beginning at **Flying Enterprise**'s
edges, a swirl that was pushing him back
toward the freighter. On **Turmoil,** Captain
Parker edged closer than any seaman, including
himself, would have advised him to. **Flying Enterprise** was shooting off violent spouts of water like jets—he could get hit by one of those.
And oil had begun to pour upward through the
cracks in **Flying Enterprise**'s metals. Some of
the flares ignited the oil, and little blue fires
blazed on the ship and on the sea.

When Dancy got sufficiently clear to feel
safe, he looked back at the ship and saw
Carlsen still crouched on the funnel. Dancy
yelled to him. Carlsen stayed; the sea had
reached his knees. Dancy yelled again—
"Come on!"—and Carlsen jumped. He disappeared, came up, and swam to Dancy. **Willard
Keith** relayed, "Carlsen and Dancy have
jumped from the funnel."

Carlsen reached Dancy; they joined hands

briefly in the water and then swam toward **Tur-moil,** where the crew threw out two white life rings. Carlsen got his head through the first, settled it under his arms, and allowed himself to be hauled through the waves to **Turmoil.** Then Dancy did the same. At three twenty-nine, **Englishman** radioed, "One man seen climbing out of water, up rope ladder onto deck of **Turmoil.** . . . Second man climbs up."

Carlsen got aboard with a forest of hands helping him. When Dancy came up, Dan Parker embraced him (although Englishmen, famously, are not given to emotional display). Carlsen told Dancy, "I wish I had ten mates like you." The **Turmoil** crew applauded them—but reported that the two men had barely enough strength to walk from the deck to the captain's quarters. At thirty-two minutes past three, **Turmoil** said, "We have got both off **Enterprise.**" **Willard Keith** radioed back, "Congratulations."

IN NEW YORK, John Drake's evidence became increasingly technical. He and Commander Lie discussed the number of revolutions in the main engines, the difficulty the crew had keeping water in the boiler; they talked about sounding pipes and watertight bulkheads. As they spoke, all these fixtures and fittings were blowing apart in the North Atlantic. The chairman joined in and inquired about pumping, about water in the engine room, and about leaving the engine room—about leaving the ship after the port lifeboat proved unusable.

"At that time," Shackelford asked, "it wasn't feasible to use the main deck for leaving the vessel?"

Drake replied, "It would have been all right for the crew to go off from there, but we had to get the passengers off, and they wouldn't move; some of them were even tying themselves to the ship."

Directly after that, the inquiry paused. It is not the purpose of time zones to generate deep and powerful emotion; more typically they engender irritation. On January 10, 1952, the five-hour time-zone difference between the Atlantic facades of Europe and the United States produced a moment that still leaps off a page, even though the page is simply, almost elementarily typed, and the powerful moment appears in brackets.

It appears on page 18 of the Coast Guard inquiry proceedings, third paragraph down. Captain Shackelford and John Drake have been discussing **Flying Enterprise**'s steering gear. In the middle of the page appears this small note:

[Off the record. At this time an announcement was made by the Chairman of the Board that both lives were saved aboard Flying Enterprise.]

36.

THE SAVED MEN BELOW TOOK MUGS of tea and rum, and changed into dry clothes. Carlsen fell asleep. **Turmoil** and **Willard Keith** watched over **Flying Enterprise.** The sea now had her. Waves stove in the hatches and, because of her internal bleeding, water poured like a river from her smokestack.

At three thirty-nine, **Turmoil** radioed, "**Flying Enterprise** still afloat. Going down stern first." Captain Parker went below and personally awakened Carlsen. At a quarter to four, **Englishman** radioed, "Carlsen stands on **Turmoil**'s deck to watch death struggle of his ship." Dancy, almost paralyzed with exhaustion, found himself unable to move. The sun was still setting, not that it had made much contribution in that gray, overcast sea.

Flying Enterprise went stern first, her bow rising fifteen feet into the air. **Turmoil** said, "Starboard bow just showing above the waves. She is very brave. Keeps going down and coming up." Two minutes later, **Willard Keith** said, "**Enterprise** now about ninety per cent under water." At eight minutes past four, **Englishman's** radio said, "Bow of ship points almost straight into air and ship stands poised there"—and, two minutes later, at ten minutes past four, "All gone."

When **Flying Enterprise** finally disappeared under the waves, when all that could be seen on the surface of the sea was the sad scum of debris, every ship nearby—**Turmoil, Willard Keith, Englishman, Dexterous, Abeille 25,** and all the other support ships who had followed the tow like shepherds, all the lifeboats, and the charters with the newsreel cameramen, and the merchants who had joined in just in case a helping hand was needed—they all sounded their horns, their hooters, their sirens, like whales at a funeral. Carlsen, on deck, watching her go down, said nothing and looked at nobody. In New York later that day, a bell tolled slowly, in accordance with tradition, as Hans Isbrandtsen held a press conference to announce the sinking of his ship. He was in tears.

MARINERS ALL OVER the world have a strong gift of acknowledgment. They name their vessels after wives or lovers or places in the heart. Walk any port anywhere and the names of the craft at the dock abundantly prove that seafaring is also a matter of emotion. The superstitions, as my grandfather told me, confirm this: never change a ship's name; never sail on a Friday.

In the port of Amsterdam, where, as everybody knows, there's a sailor who sings "of the dreams that he brings from the wide open seas," I spent part of one Christmas Day nearly thirty years ago, drinking with able seamen from Cork, a city forty miles from my birthplace. One of them sang the Jacques Brel song because his pals told him that he had a voice like John Denver, who had recorded it. He hadn't—his voice sounded not nearly so muscular or pure—and by then I knew that I, too, had had too much to drink.

I left the bar and set out on a long walk to clear my head. Amsterdam has quiet powers to enchant, especially when the streets widen out

from the narrow, tall houses of the Herren-
gracht, each residence built slim to keep down
property taxes. Away from the poshness of this
"Gentleman's Canal," I wound north, past the
curtained windows and closed shops of the almost silent city.

The air of the North Sea knifed down into
my lungs and, already too revved up, I resisted
the stalls that sold Amsterdam's instant herring
with little accompanying cups of Dutch gin.
Beyond the salaried houses, farther and farther
up into the smaller streets where people on
wages live, the safer harbors open up, and in
one marina I came across moored rows of the
pontoon-like pleasure craft they use on the
Zuider Zee. Tied amiably together rested two
of these blue boats, keeping each other company until the tourists came back in the spring.
They had, for me, electrifying names—one
was called **The Captain Carlsen,** the other,
The Kenneth Dancy. Mariners on Europe's
northern seaboard had found their own small
way of commemorating an extraordinary and
poignant event, involving a ship that had
changed her name from **Cape Kumukaki** to
Flying Enterprise and had sailed on a Friday.

37.

THE SHIP OFFICIALLY WENT DOWN AT eleven minutes past four, one minute before the official time for sunset on that day in that latitude. All vessels left the area, and nearly four hours later, at eight o'clock that night, **Turmoil** reached Falmouth, in seas that still heaved, amid winds that still blew a gale. She docked a little way out, closely followed by **Willard Keith.** The authorities had asked for privacy; certain formalities had to be observed. Eastward, along the coast, the United States maintained a consulate at Southampton, principally to cater the transatlantic liners; now the consul, Mr. Ragland, boarded **Turmoil** to begin the paperwork. Carlsen had papers to sign—principally a "Note of Protest."

For legal and insurance reasons, he had to go before a notary as soon as possible and swear a statement as to what had happened on **Flying Enterprise**—how the ship, her cargo, and the possessions of her passengers and crew had been damaged or lost by circumstances beyond his control. Isbrandtsen had sent over his own brother-in-law, Carl Hogstedt, who also boarded **Turmoil.** As they shook hands, Carlsen worried to Hogstedt as to what H.I. would say about the loss of the ship.

Immediately, Hogstedt began to work with Carlsen on the statement that would form the basis of the Note of Protest. Carlsen was also notified that the United States Coast Guard would interview him in London—in the person of Captain E. H. Thiele, who now appeared aboard the tug.

The press chartered boats. Having **Turmoil** stay out of the port wasn't going to confound them. As they drew alongside, their flashbulbs pierced the dark again and again; they hoped to find one of the heroes on deck. They got no satisfaction; the **Turmoil** crew told them that all interviews and appearances would have to wait until the morning. Kenneth Dancy's brother, still a schoolboy, was allowed aboard—as was a man with a hat and a bag who said that the two survivors had to be checked medically. For privacy, Carlsen and Dancy were taken to Parker's cabin, where the door was shut and locked. From his bag, the "doctor" took out a camera and flashbulbs. His picture of the pair, the first since they jumped from **Flying Enterprise,** appeared around the world—he was a freelance photographer who had trumped all his rivals.

Early next morning, the people of Falmouth began to line the quays. Many of them had been doing so for days, in rain and wind, aching for a glimpse of **Flying Enterprise,** even though they knew she was many miles out—but if they could have grown magic, science-fiction eyes, they would have drawn her ashore. The loss of the ship, and the obvious danger through which the two men had come, intensified the town's warmth.

Captain Thiele, as part of his official duties, accompanied the party from **Turmoil** to the official reception. Carlsen no longer owned a cap. Dancy had stowed all his gear aboard **Turmoil** when he signed on, and he lent Carlsen his work beret. The two men, surrounded by relatives, local dignitaries, and American and Danish officials, finally stepped ashore. Carlsen, the center of attraction, called to his side Dancy, Captain Parker, and Commander O'Brien.

During the morning, the crowd had grown and grown, as though all of Falmouth's twenty thousand residents had turned out. It had been a week and a day since **Turmoil** had sailed from this port to help the listing freighter.

Carlsen's mother handed him a bouquet of red and white flowers. Falmouth's mayor, Mr. T. L. Morris, made the expected speech. Compliments fell like petals from all sides—including a message from the officers and men at COMNAVEASTLANT, who had been monitoring Carlsen's every word by means of the U.S. Navy vessels that had stood by. Captain Thiele also presented a cablegram, which had been sent on Tuesday, three days ago, when all had looked so promising.

With the specific instructions that it be delivered to Carlsen by hand, Vice Admiral Merlin O'Neill (whom President Truman had two years earlier appointed commandant of the U.S. Coast Guard) had written, "It is with great pleasure that I personally and on behalf of the U.S. Coast Guard, commend you for courageous and meritorious performance of duty."

The cable went on to point out how, "with your vessel without power and with a 60 to 80 degree list you directed the removal of passengers and crew and then at great peril to yourself you elected to remain on board your disabled vessel and bring her into port. Your devotion to duty under such trying and dangerous circumstances is in keeping with the best traditions of the sea."

Other honors included a telegram from the

king of Denmark, which said, "By your devotion to duty and heroic conduct you have cast glory over your old fatherland and over Danish seamanship. I regret for you that it was not possible for you to bring in **Flying Enterprise.** You really deserved it."

Notwithstanding all this praise, when his turn came to speak, Carlsen publicly apologized. He stood in front of a bank of microphones on the quayside, his parents standing directly behind him, and expressed "deep regret" for having failed to bring in his ship. He took full responsibility; he barely acknowledged that the elements had been stacked against him. The next day, the newspapers would say that he looked tired but composed, and they reported that "at the first let-up in the bestowal of honors, Captain Carlsen had a ten-minute telephone conversation with his wife in the United States."

Mayor Morris and the teams of visiting dignitaries pressed forward to the town hall. A press conference began immediately, which gave Carlsen a foretaste of the rest of his life. This is how it opened:

Q. Could you tell us, please, what was absolutely the worst moment of the whole trip?

A. It was the moment that the **Flying
Enterprise** disappeared beneath
the sea.
Q. That really hurt you, Captain, did it?
A. It hurt quite a lot.

Describing why he had decided to stay on
board, he said, "[I] came to the conclusion that
I could manage to bring the **Enterprise** into
port. I could see she would stay afloat for quite
some time and I felt it was my duty to my
owners and all those people to ensure the safety
of the cargo so that it could be given a chance
to be utilized to the fullest extent." Within moments, he hailed Dancy not simply as "a
helping hand" but someone who also "was a
companion in my loneliness, somebody to
boost me."

When not manipulated and controlled, press
conferences take on a delicious life of their
own; all kinds of questions may surface. Carlsen was asked how long he and Dancy spent in
the water before climbing aboard **Turmoil:**
"Nine minutes." What personal possessions
did he manage to salvage? His wristwatch, but
it was now full of water. Were the pictures of
his wife and children any inspiration to him?
"Definitely." What did he and Dancy talk
about?

"We carried on a conversation like two ordinary people."

"About the sea mostly? About past experiences?"

"No. About this press business. To be quite frank we were both scared of it."

Carlsen was asked if he was "a religious man. Did you pray?" He answered, "I'm not exactly a heathen." He took questions as to whether the ship would be raised from the seabed—he didn't think so, since she lay in "about forty fathoms." And he knew nothing of "a line of washing" said to have been seen aboard the ship, as though at the height of the gale he had been attending to a little laundry.

The inevitable question of motive arose: was it true that he stood to gain significantly had **Flying Enterprise** been salvaged? Carlsen said, "It is absolutely not true. The master of a ship cannot in any circumstances claim salvage. I most strongly want to impress on everybody present here that the thought of commercial or financial advantage has never entered into my mind at all."

SO BEGAN CARLSEN'S telling of his own story. He gave long answers where it seemed as though the questions warranted seriousness;

his shorter answers never lacked courtesy. Whereas his entire career had given him the grounding and experience that had stood him in such good stead in a crisis at sea, nothing in his life had prepared him for this.

For a start, even though he understood the huge press interest, he thought it excessive for an event in which a seaman, as he repeated over and over, had only been trying to do his duty. And he had no idea that he might not be believed when he said that he, a ship's master, merely intended to bring the ship home and that he had no thought of gaining financially.

Nor, he insisted—against an undertow of astonishment in the huge room—would he take any commercial advantage of any kind; not from newspapers or magazines, not from advertisers or sponsors, not from book or movie agents. He would not exploit this event.

At the end of the questions, the room stood and applauded. The next day, Saturday, January 12, **The New York Times,** in an uncommon editorial move, published a transcript of the entire press conference. The following week, under the headline THE HERO RECITES HIS OWN SAGA, **Life** magazine reported, "He seemed as tired as a man can be. His knees were stiff and his fingers were callused from crawling along a slanted, pitching deck for most of two weeks. He was obviously uncomfortable in his unfitted new suit and unfamiliar situation. But Captain Henrik Kurt Carlsen was still the man in command, though his ship had gone down—and what he commanded more with each passing day was the admiration of a world which had found a hero."

THAT NIGHT, Carlsen stayed in the same hotel as his parents, a little distance outside the town of Falmouth, in Nansidwell. On Saturday, he finished swearing the Note of Protest: "Before me, Jocelyn Vivian Ratcliffe of Falmouth in the County of Cornwall, NOTARY PUBLIC came and personally appeared HENRIK KURT CARLSEN." The note blames "a cyclonic storm of hurricane force, crippling the said ship by mountainous seas of at least 60 feet in height."

Carlsen must have been tired. Mr. Meticulous himself, he made an error in the note by giving December 28 as the day on which he was "compelled to disembark the passengers"; in fact, it had happened on December 29. With the first legalities completed, he knew what lay ahead. The Coast Guard board of inquiry had opened in New York, and now he had to consider a preliminary contribution to that process by way of an interview in London.

Nothing in that legal arena contained any certainty. As it now stood, his colleagues in the merchant marine and his superiors who made the law of the sea had the right to view him as a master who had lost his ship. And as the world—and Agnes Carlsen—knew, a master who loses his ship does not get another. Had he done enough? That would be the Coast Guard's judgment. For the moment, he caught up on his sleep.

CAPTAIN THIELE OF the U.S. Coast Guard "returned to London 0700, 12 January, mission completed." He brought with him the smooth, or legal, log of **Flying Enterprise,** which Carlsen had wrapped in plastic and secured next to his skin before he'd jumped off the ship. Thiele would be the first questioner of this very public seaman who could, in theory, lose his captain's license.

At four o'clock on Monday afternoon, Carlsen appeared in Captain Thiele's office, accompanied by Isbrandtsen's London shipping agent and "Mr. Gordon, counsel for Captain Carlsen," to give his first official testimony.

State your name, occupation, and home address. What license do you hold? When was that license last renewed? Do you still have that license or was it lost in the ship? ("I managed to save my license, Sir," Carlsen replied.) How many years have you been licensed as a master? From the general details of Carlsen and the ship, he gradually funneled in to the particulars of the last voyage.

The sixteenth question at last released Carlsen to talk: "Now, will you tell in your own words the events which occurred between the time the ship departed Hamburg and when it was abandoned?"

Here is the first sentence of his answer; he and Captain Thiele had already identified the fact that Carlsen had **Flying Enterprise** heave to on December 26: "On this particular afternoon that I hove the ship to, realizing that I had a lot of old passengers aboard the ship, and a lot of unboxed automobiles, I thought it would be very wise to heave the ship to in good time as I had heard the weather forecast—it was indicating a gale—and I did so in that particular afternoon and I did stay hove to on the course of about 260° and running the ship approximately two points to the wind."

This is not so much a written document as a nonstop flow of words from a man whose story has been bottled up inside him, who is driven by the natural need to tell it and the dutiful need to report as he saw it—part of his legal duty as a master. The issues that Carlsen regarded as paramount appear very early: "I did not pull the alarm bell because I did not want to create any unnecessary panic" and "There was no disorder and no disobedience and everybody acted in true seamanlike manner."

Carlsen paid tribute by name to the "two officers and two men" who had volunteered to stay and then gave the reason for not accepting their offer: "That were the 3rd Assistant Engineer Cosaro and the 4th Engineer Johnson; and AB Higgenbotham and Ordinary seaman La Buda—and knowing the condition of the ship, I could not possibly accept the responsibility for their lives aboard; as I knew that if the storm would last or worsen then—then the ship would definitely founder and I, therefore, simply ordered them to leave the ship which they did quietly and in good faith with all the others."

For two hours, Carlsen took Captain Thiele carefully and in detail through the major phases in the events aboard **Flying Enterprise** on December 27, 28, and 29. With a pencil he traced on Captain Thiele's plan of the ship the location and the length of the crack, saying, "approximately maybe here is where we made the bulwark of bags to hold back the seas."

He paid tribute to his Black Gang: "The engineers worked almost like slaves in order to recover the plant and they went down there until the absolutely bitter end, and it was inhuman to work down there." Then he broadened the praise: "I can honestly say, Sir, that none of the crew or officers failed to carry out their duties; they were extremely well-behaved and calm." And he narrowed it—he singled out George Brown, the chief engineer, and David Greene, the radio officer, who was "taking a terrific beating because he was there at all times and right on the duty and right on the job and he worked under extremely difficult conditions because he actually had more or less to support over half his weight with one hand while he worked the telegraph key with the other."

As a preliminary to a greater and deeper investigation, Carlsen's London appearance sounded more than an overture. It provided extensive basic information and a clear picture of the foundering events, with a full sense of cause and effect. Both the interrogating officer and the respondent spelled out all the headlines and filled in many details. The U.S. Coast Guard, through Captain Thiele's questioning, had now sketched a clear map of the events as described by the most central person involved; and Carlsen had received an impression of the areas in which the New York inquiry would shine its light brightest.

The last exchange between the interrogating officer and Carlsen ran as follows and contained a startling revelation:

(I.O.) That's fine, Captain. I appreciate your coming here and giving this story and I think it will help to clarify the situation.

(Carlsen) Thank you, Captain, and if this is possible, may I use this opportunity through your Service to relay my thanks to all those people that limited the disaster to a very slight loss of life— it has disturbed me very much to find out about this one passenger but I did not know about it before I landed.

Nobody in the entire and intense chain of events had told Carlsen the fate of Mr. Bunjakowski—who had just been buried in Cassville, New Jersey, thirty-five miles from Carlsen's home.

. . .

CARLSEN WENT TO dinner that night in the Grosvenor House, where the menu had smoked salmon with "H'Ors d'Ouevres des Gourmets" and tournedos with "pommes parisiennes"; the same pommes showed up on the menu the following day at lunch with caviar and "faisan souvaroff." He accepted with modesty all the praise heaped upon him by the Danish community in London. At the request of King Frederik the Ninth, the Danish ambassador in London conferred on him the Knighthood of the Order of the Dannebrog. Once again, in his replying speech, Carlsen made the plea that the fuss levels should come down; he had merely been doing his job.

FROM THE MOMENT he'd arrived at Paddington Station, on the train from Cornwall, he had been mobbed. The police threw cordons around him, but everywhere he went, people besieged him, asking for his autograph, giving him flowers, and seeking—as with all heroes—to touch him. Carlsen's own wish extended no farther than an urgent desire to get home to his wife and daughters.

38.

FOR DELIVERIES AROUND THE VIL-
lage, Stanley Dancy had a motorbike with a
sidecar. In this contraption, his famous son
rode home. All the population of Hook Green
turned out, estimated by one source as num-
bering ninety-nine. As the newspapers reported
the following day, the temporary mate of the
tug **Turmoil** walked into the house and "cheer-
ily" asked, "What's for tea, Mum?" Thereafter,
he accepted the huge interest in his great adventure with the same modesty as Carlsen did, and
to this day Mr. Dancy remains a little bewil-
dered by the size of the world's interest.

Long after the event, at Hans Isbrandtsen's
invitation, Mr. Dancy wrote a recollection in
Albatross. "My Six Days with Carlsen" creates
two abiding impressions: of the chaos they had
to endure and of the character of Carlsen. It
begins with his first "eerie" sight of the casualty
that **Turmoil** had come to collect:

There on that expanse of windswept
sea, the huge waves lit from time to time

by the moon when it came from behind the clouds, was the black hulk of the **Flying Enterprise,** lying on its side. The ship was in darkness, not a light showing. As dawn began to break, the ship started to take shape for me. Seen at night she was nothing more than a huge shadowy specter. Now I could pick out her masts and her yellow funnel and the name of her line—ISBRANDTSEN—in bold white letters on her side.

(As **Albatross** was Isbrandtsen's house journal, the name of the shipping line naturally appeared in large type.)

Mr. Dancy insists that his involvement happened accidentally, that he did no more than anyone else might do. But here he is; I am sitting in front of a man who was once set large in the public—and my boyhood—imagination, and I want to hear exactly what happened during that afternoon of lowering clouds and furious seas.

"I think we worked all day," he says.

"Just throwing line after line over?"

"Yeah."

"Were you at that stage, when you were throwing the line—were you practically touching the **Enterprise?**"

"Reasonably close."

In one final maneuver, he says, Captain Parker came right up behind the freighter and with his stern—which his winch faced— nudged **Flying Enterprise**'s stern, from which she was meant to be towed. Parker can't have meant to touch the freighter, Dancy figures; it would have been too high a risk. Together, the two ships made a total length of over six hundred feet, a thick metal spar to be swung here and there by the Atlantic.

"And that was just the moment," Dancy recalls, "that, yeah, I ran from the bridge, across the deck of the **Turmoil,** and sprang up onto the **Flying Enterprise.** And then wanted to spring back, of course"—he laughs—"but that was no good. It was too late to get back because the two had parted again."

He tells this with big beaming smiles.

"Why or how did you take that decision?" I ask.

"I have no idea. I just went. I didn't think about any decisions."

"But you knew that if you could get on board—you could get a line fastened?"

"That was the idea, of course, yes. And"— Mr. Dancy laughs again—"I couldn't shout to somebody else to do it."

"Did anybody know you were doing it?"

"Not beforehand, no. I didn't know myself."

And still the airy refusal to see this as anything spectacular—to cross from one heaving ship to one stricken ship, just above the tongues of enormous waves, in the freezing cold North Atlantic.

"Were you afraid at all?" I have to ask. "Frightened?"

"Immediately. Yes. In the first place I had no life jacket on and—"

"Why had you no life jacket?"

"Well—because I hadn't prepared myself for such a thing to do."

The **Turmoil** crew knew that Dancy faced no picnic. From the moment he landed, he came under pressure. In **Albatross,** he described how Carlsen taught him "how to get along the deck." Dancy wrote that he was "reminded of doing gym in my school days, when one of the exercises was, 'On the hands down!' That was the posture you had to get into and then move forward, hand over hand."

From the moment he hit the ship, he was stricken with fear, and he was candid enough to air it in **Albatross.** "We entered the housing," he wrote, "and at once a wave of claustrophobia came over me. I got the most awful hemmed-in feeling. I found myself starting to panic."

All the days that Mr. Dancy stayed on board **Flying Enterprise,** he suffered, in varying degrees, from that panic. He tended toward claustrophobia anyway—and for anyone under that pressure, the circumstances of the wrecked ship added up to a kind of torture. He fought to bring most of it under control; but sometimes he had no chance.

He was different from Carlsen; he had a less disciplinarian, less forceful nature. Who is braver, the fearless man or the fearful? Before Dancy jumped across from the tug, he knew to some degree what was facing him aboard the foundering ship. After he had settled aboard, it got steadily worse.

On one of their "excursions," they needed supplies that had been locked into an awkwardly inaccessible cupboard. When they got the door open, Carlsen ordered his temporary mate to search the deep, slanting darkness. Dancy held back. Carlsen picked up on the hesitation and asked, "Claustrophobia, Mr. Dancy?"

"Yes, sir."

"Get over your claustrophobia."

Dancy fetched the supplies.

. . .

WHEN THEY CAME ashore and faced the world's press, neither Carlsen nor Dancy discussed the concept of **fear.** They came from a culture that never referred to it. Never admit to anything weak. Above all, never admit to fear. Thus were boys raised. And thus we all made our ways into a working life with no means of addressing "ordinary" fear: fear of showing ignorance, fear of being humiliated socially, fear of not being strong enough to do physical work. Accordingly, entire generations of men grew up with a great and pervasive handicap: fear coursing through the veins and no idea how to manage it.

Flying Enterprise brought this issue close to the surface. When the event began, I probably could not have been more impressionable. So vividly was it reported that I was able to reach beyond my own small world, enter this distant story, and imagine what it was like for a grown man to feel—perhaps—a version of the same fear that I knew. The **Flying Enterprise** incident not only stayed in my mind, it strengthened and became a reference point. The more I found out about the stresses on those two men, the more I wondered how afraid they had been. In time, and with thought, their example helped to make fear a manageable part of my

life. Other men climb mountains, dive the sea
to address their general sense of fear; I reached
for this listing freighter and the men who
fought for it. It didn't matter that they never
said, "Oh, we were so afraid, we were terrified";
it had become perfectly obvious that nobody
could go through their experiences and not feel
afraid.

And now Mr. Dancy confirmed for me that
indeed he'd felt fear. He did not belabor the
point; nor did he have to. No matter how
much fear he had felt, he had pursued duty,
and he had accepted a responsibility.

KENNETH DANCY'S INVOLVEMENT with
Flying Enterprise never quite went away. The
Carlsens and the Dancys became good friends
(contrary to a myth that the two men never
saw each other again), and Mr. Dancy appeared from time to time in documentaries
and in print, where he often sought to correct
mistaken impressions.

In any and all of his discourses about the
event, he never failed to pay tribute to Carlsen.
Directly after their safe homecoming, he described Carlsen as "truly a very great seaman
and a very great man." In **Albatross,** he wondered aloud "what manner of man was this 37-

year-old Danish-American. A man of terrific strength of character, there was no doubt about that. Shorter than my five feet ten, he had a physique as strong as his will. Few other men could have taken this thing on alone and gone through with it as he had done. I felt proud to serve under him, even if it was at a 60-degree slant."

In April 1952, Reuters news agency carried a report that Kenneth Dancy had quit the sea for a desk job as an "assistant district secretary for the Navigators and Engineer Officers Union." The report added, "Like Captain Carlsen, he turned down a fortune from newspapers and manufacturers who sought to capitalize on his experiences." He later went back to sea and in due course fetched up with an electronics corporation in Holland, part of whose industry attends to the development of marine navigational equipment.

There is about Kenneth Dancy something of a slightly older world, when men stood up if a lady came into the room. Part of a marine officer's training included courtesy, even if only absorbed by example and osmosis, and this sense of dutiful behavior still hangs about him.

He also typifies a certain strain of Englishman much written about in the past, though rarely discussed today. Such men were trained that to express too much—or too vociferously—was "poor form," a violation of longstanding codes. In that breed and generation, to foist one's feelings on someone else—even to discuss one's emotions—constituted a serious breach of some unspoken code, the famous English "stiff upper lip."

And yet, strong emotions feel not too far away when Mr. Dancy speaks of Carlsen and those astounding days. One of the crewmen from **Flying Enterprise** told reporters in New York that being aboard the ship when she was listing felt like "sitting on the wall at home." In Dancy's Leap, the twenty-seven-year-old young man risked, at the least, that unease. And he knew that he also faced genuine danger. He knew what it was going to be like when he crossed over to help Carlsen; he knew that he suffered from claustrophobia. And he knew that he would not easily or lightly—or perhaps ever—get off that ship.

39.

CARLSEN HAD DIFFICULTY GETTING home. After he took off from London, he landed in Shannon Airport; the Pan American Clipper threatened some engine difficulty, and Carlsen had to stay all night. I could have met him; we lived fifty miles or so from Shannon. He even met the mayor of Limerick, a man well known to my grandfather. I never knew this until Carlsen had flown on to New York; he had arrived too late for our news bulletins.

He had a searingly long day of it—his flight next had a scheduled stop in Gander, New-foundland, but as Gander proved fogbound, he was diverted to Moncton, New Brunswick. Once again he had to meet and greet local dig-nitaries. Carlsen didn't complain, and on the last, long leg of the journey, he slept.

By the time he arrived in Idlewild, all the elaborate plans of a day had been scotched; guards of honor had been stood down, the crowds had gone home. All day too, Agnes, So-nia, and Karen had waited in the same room as the press. Dozens of reporters and cameramen kept plying them with questions. Eventually eleven-year-old Sonia jumped on the table and yelled at them to show a little respect; they did.

The plane touched down at two minutes past one on the morning of Thursday, January 17. All the other passengers disembarked, and customs officials boarded. A few minutes later, Agnes went on board; Carlsen never disclosed, nor would she, what they said to each other.

When they appeared together in the door of the aircraft, Carlsen almost reeled back from the blaze of lights and flashlights. A welcome platform decked in yellow flags had been set up on the tarmac and, wearing a merchant marine captain's uniform, he made his way there to meet his daughters and his employer, Hans Isbrandtsen. Within minutes his arms and those of his wife and children were filled with flowers.

To nobody's surprise, Carlsen looked exhausted. All through his ordeal and homecoming, however, he behaved with a sense of Isbrandtsen's image, as though he had been briefed on the shipping line's public relations. Initially, it had entailed going out on those terrible decks and waving to the photographers in the aircraft above, or on the chartered boats lurching nearby. Now it meant speaking to the microphones after a journey that had taken close to twenty-four hours.

"I cannot express my feeling for this tremendous welcome. Thank you. Thank all of you," he said. Then he continued, as he had done in Falmouth, answering patiently.

"How do you feel?"

"A little older."

"How does it feel to be back with your family?"

"That just can't be described."

The Carlsen family spent that night in Isbrandtsen's Brooklyn home.

THEY HAD TICKER TAPE ready for Carlsen; they had postponed using it for twenty-four hours because of the delays in his journey home. Ten hours after his arrival, exactly one week and one hour after his ship went down, he would embark upon the parade of his life. The newspapers published the plans in some detail: starting at the Battery, Carlsen would lead his crewmen up Broadway. Along the route he would, of course, pass 26 Broadway, the office of Isbrandtsen Lines. When he reached City Hall, he would be greeted by the mayor of New York, Vincent Impellitteri, at the rail of a temporary edifice that the city had built for the occasion—a model of **Flying Enterprise**'s stern.

Before that could happen, the men who worked the Port of New York had to have their say in honoring their colleague. Shortly before eleven o'clock, forty motorcycle outriders led a cavalcade of cars—local politicians and officials, as well as the Isbrandtsens—escorting the Carlsen family from Brooklyn Heights to the pier at Sixty-ninth Street, on the Bay Ridge shore.

There, **Sauk,** a Coast Guard harbor cutter, cast off at ten minutes past eleven and headed upstream for the Battery. Every ferry boat, every tug, every freighter, every liner, every vessel that had a throat made a noise that morning—they hooted, they blasted their sirens, they wailed, sometimes for more than a minute at a time. Other boats joined in behind **Sauk** under the low-lying clouds and the threat of rain.

Carlsen stood with his family and **Sauk**'s captain, Chief Boatswain William Burton, and identified the landmarks that every cargo ship-master knew. Helicopters flew overhead and, as he neared the place where he would step ashore for the parade, New York Harbor's fire tenders weighed in with their greatest tribute. They shot jet spouts of red, white, and blue water so high into the sky that they formed curtains of spray as they fell.

When the Carlsens disembarked, they walked to the point where the parade would begin. Many of the **Flying Enterprise** crew waited there; they wanted to walk up Broadway behind their "Old Man." Not all of them had been unequivocally supportive of him in their testimony at the Coast Guard inquiry; nevertheless the exchanges this morning had a friendliness, informality, and backslapping delight that Carlsen would never have permitted on board.

In less than a minute, it became frantic—the crowd broke the crush barriers and began to engulf Carlsen. The police stepped in, and soon they had perched him in the traditional open-topped car. As he rode up Broadway, behind a marching white-booted military honor guard, the rain began to come down. So did the confetti and the rice from the financial offices on Wall Street, and the famous ticker tape from the machines that in those days sent miles and miles of financial information across the world.

When the city operatives gathered it all up later, they said that the weight of paper—their means of judging it—was consistent with a crowd of four hundred thousand people, among the biggest ticker-tape welcomes ever recorded, as big as General MacArthur's welcome home from the Pacific he had "delivered" after World War II.

Agnes Carlsen wore a new hat. On Karen's green coat, somebody had pinned a lapel button saying, WELCOME HOME, CAPTAIN CARLSEN. Sonia Carlsen Fedak recalls of the day that she had never put on ladies' stockings before, that until then she had worn only the hose of a schoolgirl, and that this was the day when a part of her grew up—and how uncomfortable she found it.

She may be expressing a metaphor for her father's unease. Carlsen had too much self-control and too much courtesy to let his discomfort show, to come across as a churl. The words heaped upon him could have amounted to a vast burden—and did.

For instance, Mayor Impellitteri said that Carlsen had enkindled in everyone "a renewed faith in the all-pervading strength and dignity of man for which, with abiding trust in the Almighty, the lies and hates and the ignorance of the world are no match; even as the mighty sea, though it sent your ship down, could not conquer your indomitable will." They gave him the New York City Medal of Honor.

The final public event of the day took place at the Advertising Club. An ironic venue: since he had come ashore at Falmouth, Carlsen had resisted—quite openly—all offers to capitalize upon the fame that had reached him. Both he and Kenneth Dancy said over and over that they did not wish to commercialize or exploit what had happened to them.

During lunch, a man from Pennsylvania tried to have Carlsen presented with an inscribed gold watch. Carlsen, smelling a publicity stunt, recoiled. And accurately so: the papers were later given the man's name, plus the words of the inscription. Yet even in the rejection, Carlsen got compromised—because the fact that he would not accept it was publicly relayed to the people at lunch as further proof of his modesty, humility, and therefore great character. And it got worse. In the limousine on the way from City Hall to lunch, he had told the mayor that he didn't feel entitled to all the applause. "I failed to bring my ship back to port," he said. At lunch the mayor told everyone of Carlsen's remark, noting, "Doesn't that sum up the type of man he is?" With the rain pouring down, the family got back to Woodbridge at four o'clock in the afternoon. Children—and reporters—had been watching for them, and neighbors emerged, with flowers, handshakes, and smiles. Inside, unopened gifts lay beneath the Christmas tree. For some hours, visitors came and went, but slowly the evening settled down and the family ate dinner. Carlsen had at last reached home. But he still had to face the Coast Guard inquiry.

40.

BY THE TIME HE APPEARED AT LAFAY-ette Hall on the following Tuesday, January 22, twenty-two members of Carlsen's crew had given evidence. Only two more people would testify after him: John Crowder, the second assistant engineer; and the photographer Leonore Von Klenau. Captain Thiele had written his report based on Carlsen's London interview (it was numbered "1-52"), and Captain Shackelford and his two fellow inquirers had it in their possession; the transcript of Carlsen's actual testimony in London did not follow for some time. Captain Thiele made no specific recommendations. Nor was he expected to, in view of the fact that the New York board of investigation had been convened—but he did give opinions. These opinions also lay before

Captain Shackelford, as did the transcripts from the previous interviews.

AFTER THE MOMENT on the first day when the inquiry chairman had announced that Carlsen and Dancy had been saved, the inquirers had returned to the issue of the crack in the metals. In their questioning of John Drake, they showed their direction: the members of the board wanted as much technical information as they could get. Bilges, pumps, suction discharges, hydraulic pressures—they clearly intended to assemble a comprehensive picture of how the ship had been working and how she had then been affected by the crack and the subsequent listing. They asked Drake no questions about Carlsen and only one general question about the "performance of duty by the crew." Drake made positive comments.

Richard Cosaro came next, and he gave more vivid evidence. He covered Carlsen's refusal both to have volunteers stay and to get off the ship himself. They touched briefly on the death of Mr. Bunjakowski, principally to establish whether he had died in the sea or after he had been picked up. Cosaro also described his own departure in the final lifeboat, onto which they tried to entice Carlsen.

By the end of the first day, when the third witness, the chief mate, Frank Bartak, had given his evidence, it was clear that the inquirers had chosen to pursue two lines of thought. They wanted to establish how gravely the fracture (Bartak called it "snake-like") had affected the ship's possibilities; and they wanted to ascertain whether the cargo had been incompetently stowed. Had it ultimately caused the ship's doom, both by placing undue pressure where the ship had cracked and by shifting under the force of heavy seas? Some of the exchanges had a sharp edge, as though the inquirer found Bartak inclined to slide away. They asked whether Carlsen had been kept informed about the stowage.

Bartak said, "Yes; not with the minor details—wherever I thought anything would affect him—where we drew the line I don't know. I wouldn't do anything that would embarrass him later on." Upon that they pressed harder, asking whether he had gone below to see whether cargo had shifted, whether he and Carlsen had had any discussions about the listing, whether Carlsen had expressed any opinions. He hadn't, according to Bartak. Before they released the chief mate, they showed further irritation; when they received yet another answer that irked them, they said, "If you don't know, say so."

So had ended Day One of the inquiry. As they adjourned after hours of discussing him publicly in New York, Carlsen was at that moment resting aboard **Turmoil** in Falmouth.

NOTHING MUCH CHANGED over the next four sitting days. The board went through witnesses swiftly: four the next day, then seven, then six. A pattern had been established: the fracture, the listing, the issuing of life vests, the "abandon ship" events, and the behavior of personnel. Officers took the stand longest and received the most detailed questioning. The inquirers expected less of the lower ranks, especially where language skills had limits— **Flying Enterprise**'s crew had a United Nations touch to it.

A picture began to materialize of the loading, the stowage, the dunnage, the shoring; of the waves, the weather, the fractures, the list. A few witnesses wished to distance themselves— they said they knew little because they were asleep or never heard anything or nobody told them a thing or they didn't recall. Some took a more robust line, such as Janssens, the boatswain, with his criticisms of the loading—but he also emerged as the only person who heard Carlsen say, "Get the children and women first." Ordinary Seaman Samuel Miller, a steward, from Michigan, took a strong line too; he said he had asked more than once "why the ship didn't turn around" and head for Falmouth the morning she cracked, and he complained that the captain seemed to be taking orders from the office in New York. Able Seaman Clark Hall, who had wanted to send a message to his wife in Germany, made the same complaint.

A schedule of the time spent questioning witnesses shows that they devoted the longest time to the captain and his first mate, followed by the two most senior engineers. They may have taken marginally more time with John Drake than they did with his chief, George Brown—but Drake happened to be the first witness, and the inquiry had not quite warmed up. In some cases, they questioned people for not more than a few minutes. Of all the witnesses, George Brown creates the strongest impression: the most conscientious, the most anxious, the most willing to respond to anything the board might put to him—until, of course, Carlsen appears. Throughout Brown's testimony (given within earshot of the bands, bells, and whistles that, as he spoke, led Carlsen up Broadway), a desperation comes across—the desperation of disappointment that he couldn't have done more, that his men had worked so hard and had come away with so little.

Like Kenneth Dancy, he too had known the danger, and he too had taken it on with a simple bravery. "I mean," he said, "the conditions were so bad down there, why nobody got hurt, I don't know. The heat was terrific. In fact, had she gone down that day [when she listed], I am sure none of us would ever know it, because we were too exhausted to ever make the top of the engine room."

AFTER BROWN CAME Carlsen. He looked rested; he had had time to think. As he had done in London, he faced some preliminary questions to establish who he was and where he lived and how long he had been going to sea. When the deeper questions began, he again answered at length, although his first answer was somewhat shorter than the first answer he had given in London. And once again, he gave the same clear history from the port of Hamburg to the wastelands of the North Atlantic.

They asked him to identify some documents: the ship's smooth log, which he had preserved, and some telegrams that he had authored or received. He then revealed that "while the **Golden Eagle** was standing by, I prepared a complete set of records, having accounts and draws, slop chest accounts and most of the officers' licenses which I took out of frames and put them in a watertight container and lashed them to two life jackets." By arrangement with "the Master of the **Golden Eagle**," Carlsen tossed them into the sea toward the standby ship. "He did see them, but he failed to get them and now they're lost."

He also complained of a loss that he had suffered. "The ship's bridge log book, the ship's register and other documents I considered pertinent I had taken in my little hand bag and tied to a life preserver"; but he lost them because he had to get off via the funnel to avoid "the ship's backwash."

After two or three long answers, Carlsen surrendered himself to the rhythm of the inquiry.

Q. Was the ship taking any seas during that time?
A. Yes, she was taking very heavy seas.
Q. She was taking green seas?
A. Yes.

Meaning that **Flying Enterprise** was taking the full force of the sea; "green" water is water that has not softened into spray.

Unlike certain members of his crew, Carlsen not only responded without any trace of evasion but testified vividly. Of the moment when she listed under the second great wave, for instance, he said, "It was just like it whacked everything out of the water, like one terrific blow that crippled the ship instantly almost."

Away from the physical details of the vessel and her pressures, Carlsen the shipmaster appears once or twice, in answers that reveal the stern nature that so often provoked crewmen. The inquiry raised with him the names of two seamen: "Captain, do you know anything of an injury [a broken leg] to the man named Miterko?"

Carlsen said he had observed the man, told him to "sit tight, sit quiet because I realized that he would need all his strength the next day for the rescue, and then he told me he had been injured. He did not appear very much injured."

Carlsen cranked up his ire a little and concluded, "In fact, I saw him later on get up and move around just as brisk as the others."

Then they asked him about "the physical

condition of the wiper Cordero a day or two prior to the casualty."

Carlsen said, "Wiper Cordero had from the time that man signed on in New York until the time the man came to Antwerp, he never did a day's work. He got sick the first day out. He claimed he had a sore stomach, something like that."

The indignation feels palpable. Carlsen, having diagnosed mild appendicitis, had had Cordero hospitalized in Antwerp. The doctors wanted to operate, but Cordero objected and asked to go back to the ship. Carlsen refused to accept him; the American consul insisted—and Carlsen demanded a written order before he would comply. Thus emerged the Carlsen who ran a tight ship, whom one witness said he had once wanted to "punch in the nose."

The tone of the inquiry toward Carlsen showed firmness within respect. None of the three board members held back, yet none of their questions took a pejorative line. They queried directly and in detail; they established Carlsen's view of the facts; and they took care to remind themselves and everyone else of the inquiry's scope and limits. This became particularly evident toward the end of Carlsen's evidence.

Several lawyers were in attendance on and

off during the inquiry. One said he represented all the cargo interests; another appeared for underwriters and insurers in London; a third said he was "the attorney for several of the passengers and crew." As Carlsen's testimony was coming to an end they began to ask for an opportunity to question him.

After much debate, the chairman, Captain Shackelford, denied them. He said that nothing in the board's investigation "would cause the shipowners or owners of cargo to suffer any penalty." Likewise, the passengers had no relevance "unless it can be demonstrated that they caused or contributed to the casualty." Nor did the inquiry have a concern with civil liability.

When he heard these exchanges, Carlsen must have known that he had weathered the inquiry, that he had come through with his master's license intact. He would have felt greater comfort had he known Captain Thiele's opinion, forwarded from London: "There appears to be no evidence of negligence on the part of any of the ship's company which contributed to the loss of the vessel or the death of one passenger."

One last moment clinched it. Even though it would be some weeks before the inquiry published its conclusions, Carlsen knew without question that he remained a shipmaster when the chairman closed the day with these words: "I [would] like to state at this time, so far as we know, there will not be any further proceedings of this Board and I would like also to thank the captain for appearing here. I realize what he went through out there in the North Atlantic Ocean and I would like to say I sincerely hope, Captain, that you never have to do it again. Go back to sea with my best wishes."

41.

IN FEBRUARY, WHEN THE COAST GUARD inquiry board published its "Findings of Fact, Opinions & Recommendations," it made three main points. The third one suggested that "the method of stowage of pig iron" as executed aboard **Flying Enterprise** be considered a potential hazard. The second singled out ten members of the Black Gang to be "highly recommended for their action in attempting to restore power to the vessel." The leading observation, however, employed significant language: "Since the Master, Henrik Kurt Carlsen, has been cited for his outstanding performance in connection with the casualty by both government and civic organizations, no recommendations in this respect appear appropriate."

You can read this statement two ways. The board is saying either "Carlsen needs no praise from us—the world knows how much he has done" or "Although we have reservations about some of the things that happened on his watch, this man has become a hero and far be it from us to pull him down." If the inquirers had come down more firmly on either a positive or a negative side, the future of the Carlsen legend might well have turned out differently. We need heroes, but once we have them, we take two further and paradoxical steps: we generate extra mythology about them, and we set out to pull them down.

In pursuing Carlsen down the years, I found that these two opposing forces had addressed him: he rose to the status of legend, and skeptics sought to tarnish him. In the process fact and myth merged, time after time. Some things remain unclear to this day.

To begin with, in the heat of the moment, many day-to-day facts got muddled. These touched on or grew into or added to the legend. For example, there's the matter of Carlsen's personal flag. The newspapers reported that as she crossed New York harbor to reach the ticker-tape parade, the cutter **Sauk** flew Carlsen's own flag, the black-and-gold pennant that bears his name beside a lightning flash. People who knew Carlsen believed that Hans Isbrandtsen had the flag created to hail Carlsen's exploit with **Flying Enterprise.** The countering story says that the flag had flown on Carlsen's ships since 1948, when he became an Isbrandtsen Line captain. A third faction insists that the Isbrandtsen Line office flew the Carlsen flag all through the **Flying Enterprise** saga. But if he habitually flew the flag on his own ship, why did it not fly on **Flying Enterprise**? And how did it come to be in the Isbrandtsen Line headquarters?

Another part of the lore was that thousands of New Yorkers held candlelight vigils on the sidewalks of Wall Street outside the offices of the Isbrandtsen Line. Jakob Isbrandtsen recalls no such vigils. He does, however, remember how the public attempted to contribute. "Tell him to come off that boat," insisted innumerable telephone callers—often in the middle of the night. Others wanted to charter vessels and "go out there and shift that pig iron and the boat will right itself."

In one of the more interesting demonstrations of how fact amplified into legend, two sources told me "without fear of contradiction" that CBS had hooked up with Carlsen on his radio on the listing ship and connected him to his wife every night so that they could speak, and so that each could comfort the other. It never happened—but Agnes did hear his voice. Through one of the U.S. Navy destroyers, Carlsen arranged to make a wire recording of a message to his family, which was then played to them on their home telephone.

It seems likely that the myth had also harvested word of a later system—when Carlsen had his friend Ben Stevenson patch him through to the family home. But that didn't begin until years after the **Flying Enterprise** accident—and probably gained color along the way from the fact that Sonia Carlsen had her own shortwave license. To this day her call sign is KN2IVT; her sister Karen's was KN2JAT— in each case the "N" represents "novice."

Another myth: during the height of the event, the Carlsens had to leave their home because American appliances companies, hoping for endorsements, had showered the family with gifts. Refrigerators, vacuum cleaners, and washing machines were supposed to have descended on them. It never happened. They left because the pressure of the reporters had become too great for them and their neighbors.

In any case, nobody—not the family, not the

appliances companies, not Carlsen himself—
knew how it was going to turn out. In part,
Hans Isbrandtsen took them from Woodbridge and concealed them because he had
enough knowledge of the sea and of his own
ships to have calculated Carlsen's odds. He
might have had to break to them the news of a
tragedy, in which event they would truly have
needed privacy.

Here's another "certain" fact, this time about
the rescue operation: "A lone young seaman,"
many people told me, "from the only ship that
bothered to help Carlsen, single-handedly
launched a rowboat and took everybody off
safely, in waves of frightening height." From
the outset, I knew that some of this story failed
to stand up, because I had heard on our big
glowing radio the voice of "**Willard Keith**
calling, **Willard Keith** calling," with the magic
echo of the ether's static. The myth, of course,
had its foundation in Robert Husband's feats
of seamanship. Remarkable though they
were, he could not—and would not—have attempted it single-handedly. As to the "only
ship": Carlsen never lacked ships to shepherd
him, or to stand by until the sea resolved his
future.

The world—at least my part of it—also
knew without a shadow of a doubt that

Carlsen threw his cap into the sea from the deck of **Turmoil** as **Flying Enterprise** sank. Not so: documentary footage shows him and others removing their berets like mourners as the ship sinks. No seaman loses a cap easily. And out of that myth arose another myth: that the skinflint Hans Isbrandtsen made Carlsen pay for a new cap when he came back, because he had lost the old one. Not true either; in fact, the lore in the Isbrandtsen camp, confirmed by Jakob Isbrandtsen, tells a more attractive story.

When merchant shipping went under sail, captains came back with account books for every port to which they had tramped. Once everything had been tallied and agreed, the captain, by tradition, asked his owner to buy him a new cap, because the voyage had been so long that the old cap had weathered poorly. Carlsen, in his first contact with Isbrandtsen—he had by now reached his Falmouth hotel—observed the tradition.

When Isbrandtsen telephoned, Carlsen apologized to "Mr. H.I." for having "lost your ship." Isbrandtsen steamed past the apology and instead told Carlsen to lose the beret—he had already seen it in the photographs of Carlsen coming ashore and didn't like it. That was when Carlsen said, "Will you buy me a new cap?"

In ·there resided yet another myth, this one half-true. The myth says that Isbrandtsen telephoned the hospital in Falmouth looking for Carlsen. The examining doctor was interrupted and asked whether Carlsen seemed fit enough to come to the telephone. At the Falmouth end, Carlsen was heard to say, "I apologize, Mr. H.I., that I lost your ship," and at the New York end, Isbrandtsen was heard to say, "Never mind, I've got another ship being built for you." In fact, Isbrandtsen telephoned Carlsen's hotel, not a hospital; Carlsen did apologize, but nobody recalls Isbrandtsen replying with an offer of a ship, even though he soon put a vessel called **Flying Enterprise II** in place with Carlsen in command.

Some of the mythology lingered near the sunken ship. Truth: dismayed at Dancy's lack of a life vest when he landed on **Flying Enterprise,** Carlsen offered his new mate his own life jacket—and then they found the child's one, which Dancy wore overnight and which they replaced the following day with a full adult life vest. This article eventually made its way to the bar of the Chain Locker in Falmouth, where it hung for many years under a sign, "Captain Carlsen's life jacket." That was a myth: Kenneth Dancy saw it on television and, from a distinguishing rent in the fabric, recognized it as the life vest he'd acquired on **Flying Enterprise.**

Another myth: when Carlsen received a new ship from Isbrandtsen, **Flying Enterprise II,** the entire crew that he had rescued signed on, and he sailed, as a first voyage, on a commemorative mission over the spot where the first **Flying Enterprise** went down. Truth: Isbrandtsen did give him a new ship, and it was indeed called **Flying Enterprise II.** And a substantial number of the rescued crew did sign up—but not all forty; the figure was closer to twenty. As to sailing over the site of the famous sinking, that was not specifically done, not on any kind of pilgrimage. But every time Carlsen came or went through the En-glish Channel he could scarcely avoid the spot.

ONE ISSUE, HOWEVER, entered the most powerful world of all mythmaking, that world where truth and myth simply will not part from each other. The question of why Carlsen stayed aboard so determinedly became and remained the central issue in the **Flying Enterprise** saga. Many "reasons" surfaced—surmises, guesses, wild speculation. One suggested that he had stayed aboard because he could not swim. Wrong: he swam and dove excellently and had done so since boyhood.

Another put forward the notion that Carlsen feared Isbrandtsen, feared losing his job, and therefore obeyed a repeated mandate from New York to stay aboard. Carlsen did not fear Isbrandtsen; they both understood that at sea the captain ultimately takes responsibility. As to telling Carlsen to stay on board, all of Isbrandtsen's signals came to Carlsen via the relays of, initially, **Southland** and then **Greely** and her navy successors. At no stage in the signals—which the naval captains would have been obliged to report to the U.S. Coast Guard—did Isbrandtsen do other than urge Carlsen to think of his own safety.

At the time of the incident the most common theory said that Carlsen stood to profit were he to bring the ship to shore and recover the cargo. Over the months, this idea endured, and Carlsen responded to it with increasing asperity. He pointed out, over and over, that a master may not profit from the salvage of his own ship. Ah, they said, but Isbrandtsen paid his captains a bonus—as did many ship owners—according to the value of the cargo, and this was an especially valuable cargo, even if it had not been declared as such.

Isbrandtsen captains did profit from their voyages; they earned a kind of commission that depended upon how much cargo they had succeeded in acquiring. In no case would it have been enough to keep Carlsen aboard in such perilous circumstances, however, given the sense of responsibility he felt toward his family. Nor would he have ever permitted Dancy or any other seaman to take such chances. Furthermore, having the zealous patriotism of the immigrant, he would never have allowed U.S. taxpayer dollars to be spent on the navy ships standing by just so he could gain financially. Not only that, Isbrandtsen had insurance on **Flying Enterprise** to the tune of, in 1952 values, $3.41 million—and within days of the ship's sinking, the insurance companies in New York began to pay out handsomely and very publicly.

However, the theory persisted. Immediately following the ship's sinking, it flourished with enough strength for people to raise it over and over. And it began to sharpen into a new and more specific focus on what was said to be **Flying Enterprise**'s "secret cargo," of which there were supposed to be two kinds. First it was alleged that she carried nuclear munitions freight, the property of the U.S. government. The theorists pointed to the fact that the U.S.

Navy gave Carlsen a substantial commitment: **Greely, Weeks,** and **Willard Keith** came to his side. Second, **Willard Keith** even accompanied him to Falmouth. Therefore, he must have been carrying something of importance to some bureau in Washington.

As we know, **Flying Enterprise** did load a freight of zirconium. Chemistry students know of zirconium from the periodic table; it's a white powder whose name derives from an Arab word meaning "similar to gold." Zirconium does have an application in atomic energy, in nuclear reactors. In 1951, the United States government had started the **Nautilus** nuclear submarine program. Therefore, said the theorists, Carlsen received the shepherding protection of the U.S. Navy because he carried on board zirconium for **Nautilus.** (Moscow, stoking the fires of the Cold War, said he carried rockets.)

In addition, the "secret cargo" theory said that **Flying Enterprise** also carried a great deal of cash, in registered and unregistered packets. Since the unregistered mail would not be covered in its potentially massive value by any insurer, Isbrandtsen (according to the theorists) told Carlsen, "Do all you can." Or else Carlsen himself knew about that cargo and decided that it was best to stay aboard.

The "secret cargo" allegation grew to become the most powerful and persistent of all **Flying Enterprise** conspiracy theories. Eighteen months after the ship sank, it received an injection of support from an unexpected source—a source that gave no direct evidence for the nuclear fuel factor but did support the cash theory. In the summer of 1953, an Italian salvage company out of Genoa called La Società di Ricuperti Marittime di Genova, acronymed Sorima, dove the wreck from a salvage vessel named **Rostro.** Much was made of the fact that the Sorima personnel told no one what they were doing or why.

But the nature of their work on such salvage operations made Sorima secretive; that was their stock-in-trade. A trading policy of telling no secrets to anyone, ever, brought them a lot of work in an arena where secrets mean cash. When it emerged that Sorima was diving the wreck of **Flying Enterprise,** eyebrows flew up; this had meaning. Much was next made of the length of time that the Sorima divers spent in the area: two and a half months. People made the calculations. They offset the cost of the salvage operation against the known, declared value of the cargo; it looked like a lot of work for a small reward.

Then came the bonanza. Sorima did recover,

and declare, and allow to be photographed substantial quantities of cash. Now the skeptics said, See! **That** was why Carlsen stayed aboard. The notes, stacks of them, in different currencies, were seen drying out in the back rooms of a Belgian bank. In addition, a report averred that when Sorima eventually came back to shore (in Belgium), the dive ship was met by gray-suited American men in official-looking cars. They solemnly carried from the dockside impressive metal box-chests, which they spirited away to Washington. This was, of course, the nuclear fuel—game, set, and match to the conspiracy theorists. But if such government agents did appear and did wish to collect something that had come from the wreck, would such activity not have been classified? And if it was that important and secret a cargo, would it have been loaded for transit in full view of dockside passersby? And did Carlsen know about the cash? He said that all he knew about it was the possibility—because his cargo manifest said that he was carrying tons of registered mail.

One by one, the conspiracy theories tend to buckle under pressure. First of all, the idea that the U.S. Navy had a security motive for standing by Carlsen falls down. Any vessel of whatever nationality or commission, whether national navy, merchant marine, sporting, or leisure, goes to sea with a specific obligation, not merely an understanding, to come to the aid of a distressed vessel, if it can. If a ship does go to help another vessel and incurs extra-heavy costs—such as penalties for late delivery of cargo or, in **Flying Enterprise**'s case, U.S. Navy ships standing by for days—the ship's proprietors can recover those costs. Depending on the policies, insurers will pay; national governments make provisions for such a contingency; and ship owners long ago established appropriate funds into which they pay internationally. In short, **Flying Enterprise** did not need to carry a politically sensitive freight to receive assistance from other ships.

As to the boxes of nuclear fuel, theorists have backed up their arguments by pointing out that many of the signals during the **Flying Enterprise** incident were copied to the Central Intelligence Agency. This proves less easy to counter—except for the fact that the CIA is probably copied in on more communications than any other organization in the world, and was especially so in the first four years of its life.

Of all the "secret cargo" theories, I most like the unregistered—rather than the registered—packets. When reporters asked Sorima who was paying for this dive, Sorima referred all inquiries to lawyers in London and New York. One clear answer did emerge—from an Antwerp office of a London firm. And these men were not lawyers; they were loss adjusters and valuers. Their reply cannot be called "expansive"; they called the Sorima dive "a normal professional operation of the firm on behalf of companies that insured certain packages sent by mail from the continent to the U.S." They did not suggest that the packages were registered.

That's as much as any lawyer anywhere, in Britain, Europe, or the United States, has ever said about the Sorima dive. Their clients, in all possibility, needed such protection. If German, Swiss, Belgian, or Dutch bankers had put mail packets aboard in the cargo marked "general," and had not sent them by registered mail, they had a reason. The bankers would not have wanted their details to come to light if the contents of those packets dodged international currency regulations or ignored essential insurance declarations.

But they would equally have wanted the contents back. Those packets could have contained millions in currencies, bearer bonds, stock certificates, or any of the international

"paper" used to convey value in financial trans-
actions. Also, there would have been something of a race to get to all this paper—cash or
bonds—before the sea mulched it.

THERE IS, HOWEVER, yet another possibility regarding the unregistered packets. Here I
am indeed tempted to believe that **Flying Enterprise** could have been carrying a "secret
cargo." What freight could have been so valuable that any length of salvage dive would have
been worth it? And a comprehensive dive, not
a gentle scuba operation—a full-blooded, flat-
out dive with explosives and diving canisters so
the divers could trawl the wreck in detail and
spend week after week on the seabed? And
what would have been portable enough to
bring to the surface, and what would have survived the worst depredations of the deep Atlantic and her nibbling creatures?

On her outward voyage, before turning
around in Hamburg, **Flying Enterprise** called
into three European ports, Antwerp, Rotterdam, and Bremen; and she picked up cargo in
each. For what do Antwerp and Rotterdam
have a traditional fame—going back into history and still valid? What kind of cargo could

have been packed in relatively small, even very small, packets?

International diamond traders and jewel merchants of all kinds send their goods through the mail—often unmarked, often unregistered. If registered, such packages will frequently carry only a nominal value. This keeps attention away from the actual value of the contents and obviates vast insurance costs. Yet a small packet innocuously presented and perhaps addressed to a jeweler's private address could easily carry gems worth several million dollars.

Just one such packet, no bigger than this book, would have made the Sorima dive well worth the money. All Sorima had to do was hoist the cargo up in toto, take it away to a workshop on land, and extricate the gems. It is perfectly feasible—if completely uncheckable, then and now—that **Flying Enterprise** was carrying a diverse private cargo from precious stone traders in Antwerp and Rotterdam to the jewelers of New York. If so, nothing more than customary, normal practice would have been taking place—they would have been doing what they always did, sending packages of jewels through the mail.

Would Isbrandtsen have known? Perhaps—

and it would not have fazed him, unless he had been told in such a way that required him to take out extra insurance for which, as Jakob Isbrandtsen says tartly, they would have been charging extra freight fees. And there was no record that anything unusual by way of extra fees had been charged or asked for or invoiced in relation to **Flying Enterprise**'s last voyage.

Could Isbrandtsen have known about such gems on board without telling anyone and receiving some sort of compensation from the gem trade? Certainly—and it would have been completely in keeping with the type of buccaneer he had always been. He pushed every envelope that contained a contract, he fought for extra points on every deal, and he had such grave reservations about lawmakers and—as he saw it—the biased shapes of the laws they made, that smuggling, to give this possibility its accurate name, would not have bothered him too much. Nor would he have been alone in the freight shipping industry.

But, his son insists, on this occasion he certainly did not know. He and his captain knew officially about the registered mail that went to the strong room—for which he charged extra fees. And Isbrandtsen himself declared no further interest, financial or emotional, in **Flying**

Enterprise after she reached the bottom of the sea.

As for Carlsen, could he have known about jewels in his cargo? Possibly—but almost certainly not. He would likely have fought so hard with Isbrandtsen over the legal risks to himself as the ship's master that H.I. would have chosen not to tell him. Nor would Carlsen have consented to anything that jeopardized him or his master's ticket or the straightforward execution of his duty.

At the same time, he surely had enough knowledge of "off-manifest" cargo to wonder. He did make some early attempts to scotch the story; he pointed out that if he had known there was U.S. currency aboard he might have tried to get that to one of the U.S. Navy ships—a naive idea: given the condition of his decks, what can his holds have looked like? More acceptably, he said that had he known of "treasure" aboard, he'd have "gone crazy." Meaning—and completely in keeping with the kind of man he was—that he would have fought tooth and nail with Isbrandtsen for not having told him and then found a way of making Isbrandtsen cover the freight with insurance.

. . .

CARLSEN COULD NOT shake off the "secret cargo" story. In the year or so after **Flying Enterprise** sank, he managed to control the rumors with his forthright denials. Then, at the end of the Sorima dive, came the new blast of publicity when Sorima's hirers decided to make their selective announcement of the salvage finds. All the newspapers carried the photographs of the piles of banknotes.

This heated up the story. For the next year or so, in port after port, when **Flying Enterprise II** appeared as an arrival on local shipping lists, reporters waited to beard Carlsen. He resolutely denied any knowledge of anything unusual. All he had ever known about a possible cargo of cash or other valuables came from the fact that registered packets had been stowed in the strong room.

The implications of the story became serious. Carlsen's repeated protestations of modesty began to look threadbare. Now the public had gotten the impression that he knew his ship was carrying much more valuable cargo than the manifest showed and that he had stayed on board because he stood to profit financially—and secretly. If this was true, it virtually made him a privateer—and a tax evader, a cutter of corners, a hypocrite. It also played into a general unwillingness to accept or believe that any man would go to such extraordinary lengths against such insuperable odds merely because he was doing his job.

Carlsen decided to clear his name. Sorima belonged to a well-known Genovese family, the Quaglias, and when **Flying Enterprise II** tramped into Genoa, Carlsen sought an audience with the head of the Quaglia family. He also made sure that the local and international media knew this meeting was taking place, and they showed up in force. Carlsen asked Signore Giovanni Quaglia to make a statement specifying where such valuables as he had found aboard the wreck had been located.

Quaglia released a statement that included one new and crucial detail—a detail vital to Carlsen. Carlsen had always claimed that he knew—and could only know—of possible valuables in the strong room because they had been declared as such; they were registered mail. Now Signore Quaglia made clear that they had found the currencies and valuables **not** in the strong room but elsewhere in Hold 3.

This satisfied Carlsen. How could he possibly have known what might be in cargo marked "general" and sealed before it came aboard? Or in unregistered sacks of mail? It was to Carlsen's evident satisfaction that the world could now see he wasn't concealing anything; as far as he was concerned, he had laid the ghost of that particular accusation to rest. What Carlsen did not know was that someone had taken the strong room from the wreck.

42.

THE HIGGLEDY-PIGGLEDY VILLAGE OF Salcombe, in the south of England, has a horseshoe bay thronged with moored boats, their masts dipping like bowing guests. Two and a half hours and thirty-eight miles out from this point on the Devon coast, **Flying Enterprise** lies in 280 feet of water, at the edge of the Western Approaches, where she first encountered the storm that would, days later, crack her and turn her over. She's at latitude 49°40' north and 04°15' west, south of the great and famous port of Plymouth, and it's 205 feet to the top of the wreck; she lies on her port side, as she had done during the last two weeks of her life.

On a late-summer morning, under a lemon sun and fluffs of cloud, I descend the tidy hills of this resort village to join **Skin-Deep,** a boat

that is taking some of the top scuba divers in
the world out to the wreck. The boat has been
specially built for diver crews; Ian Taylor, the
captain, in his thirties, dives commercially—
meaning he joins construction crews who
build the legs of bridges or work pile drivers
under the water.

Having imaged **Flying Enterprise** on the
echo finder, when directly above her **Skin-
Deep** will drop the "shot," a grapnel weighing
ten pounds, to hook into the ship's seabed tan-
gle. The divers will follow the line down until
their frogmen feet land on the sand of the
ocean bed beside the hulk. Five divers will
work in three units: a man skilled in these waters who will act as a scout and guide, followed
by two teams of two.

The scout, Leigh Bishop, has the compelling
nature of all men who are driven, who test
their limits. A fireman by day, he dives wrecks
lest firefighting prove dull. This ship, he says,
has a hold on his heart. Too young to remember its long drama, he learned of it through the
folk legends about Carlsen and Dancy, things
that he overheard or encountered somewhere.

The other four divers are filming this dive
for the **Deepsea Detectives** series on the History Channel. The teams are John Chatterton
with Carl Spencer, and Richie Kohler with the

youngest of them, Evan Kovacs, who, as team captain, has the greatest responsibilities; he has to ensure that everything works: the cameras, the equipment, the air tanks, the coordination of the dive.

Chatterton and Kohler are superstars of scuba diving, the star players in the best-selling book **Shadow Divers.** Brawny men, with immense mental as well as physical muscle, they became famous when they braved several levels of danger to find a German submarine sunk off the U.S. coast in World War II. Today's dive may be easier—the U-boat's history included the deaths of divers trying to find her. Nevertheless, the tension on the boat heightens as the men suit up on the deck. It takes them each over an hour to dress for the deep, spreading out diving suits, scrutinizing and checking gauges, assembling tanks and rebreathing equipment, and testing valves, from which little bursts of compressed air escape, sounding like exhaled hisses of anxiety.

The camaraderie essential among all men who enter danger and depend upon one another has already been much in evidence; banter runs high, as among sportsmen. Now the chat dies down and the focus tightens—and tightens. Faces take on withdrawn expressions, concentration intensifies; nobody speaks to the divers unless the diver speaks first; and they handle their own equipment with a savage exclusivity.

This sea journey has not been totally comfortable. Making sixteen knots in a thirty-five-foot catamaran, we have been not a little roughened up by a swell. But we have seen no waves more than a few feet high—small animals, so to speak. I keep thinking about Carlsen's waves: twenty, thirty, forty feet high as he was preparing for that astounding rescue, and the two waves of more than sixty feet which put him out of commission.

Through these waters **Turmoil** headed out to Carlsen; back through these waters she came again with Carlsen and Dancy aboard exhausted. When Carlsen got on deck, as the crew of **Turmoil** pressed around him, one young seaman, tongue-tied and near tears with excitement, shook Carlsen's hand. In the way of all people compelled to speak in such circumstances but unable to find the appropriate words, the boy asked, "Did you get wet, sir?"

WE ARRIVE OVER the wreck. As we rock to a halt, a lightning storm breaks out, and the flashes spear the sea. Thunder cracks directly above our heads; the lightning strikes harder and closer, slivers of magnesium light touching the ocean; with all that metal strapped to their bodies, the safest place for the divers is underneath the sea.

Ian Taylor drops the dive shot; its marker, a great red, pink, and orange bulb, sits like a toy on the water. The first three men are suited up and ready, and they begin the last ritual of the mask. Water is poured into the eye pieces, and finally the divers are assembled. No one else in the party of eleven will speak of anxiety, yet it lines every face—except those of the divers, where I take the furrows and frowns for concentration rather than concern.

The young boat crewman opens the little gateway to the hydraulic platform astern. Leigh Bishop, who knows more about the wreck of **Flying Enterprise** than anyone, steps backward into the sea. Next we see his head proceeding to the bright buoy where he will pick up the shot line to guide himself down. He reaches the Day-Glo bulb out on the sea, fifty yards or so from our hove-to boat. His black rubber head pauses briefly beside it, and then he's gone.

Soon, the first of the two teams is ready. Evan Kovacs and Richie Kohler climb down into the water, one immediately after the other, and both black heads follow the path Leigh

Bishop took. Briefly we see the red of their suits, the yellow of their tanks, they reach the Day-Glo bulb, and they're gone too. Within minutes, John Chatterton and Carl Spencer follow. The captain of the boat, Ian Taylor, in reply to an anxious question from me, says that if anything is to go wrong, this is the most likely moment, when everything is as yet unknown.

Soon the four men reach the wreck. On a submerged microphone line we can hear their voices, but not easily make out what they're saying. We can, however, judge the great excitement; this wreck entered diving imagination a long time ago.

They traverse the wreck, avoiding the innumerable pitfalls of such a dive. **Flying Enterprise** had more than her fair share of loose artifacts when she went down; in the intervening fifty years the sea will have loosened a great deal more. By now, of course, no trace will remain of Carlsen's temporary bed, or Dancy's mattresses on the claustrophobic floor, or the candles with which they made tea, or the small shortwave radio on which Carlsen spoke to the world.

Farther down, the divers may have more luck. Pig iron doesn't melt in the salt of the sea; there may even be some trace of the Volkswagen cars or the steel pipes that were loaded with them. No point in checking whether the cargo had indeed shifted—nor will there be a trace of the softer goods, the animal hair, the grass seed, the gherkins in brine; they will have dissolved long ago. And as to the vans of furniture and musical instruments, and the tons of birdcages, the sea will have shunted some of that freight a mile away by now, and perhaps even farther.

Nevertheless, as this is the closest I have ever come to the physical presence of **Flying Enterprise,** anything they find down there will have the greatest interest for me. Our boat heaves on the mild swell; so does my stomach, and I barely escape the indignity of seasickness.

THEY STAYED BELOW longer than any of us had expected. Our skipper, Ian Taylor, waiting in the wheelhouse of **Skin-Deep,** evinced some concern—which escalated dramatically when he saw a speck on the horizon. He raced to his binoculars and established that a large container ship had come into view. Not good news for those underwater; propellers send out great waves, and a diver can expect at least a severe headache if a big ship crosses the sea above his patch.

Skin-Deep had raised a dive flag, blue and white, advising all ships to steer clear and respect the divers. It's hard to say whether the ship veered away—it may have seen us so far in advance that it changed course without our knowing it. It still came close enough for us to determine the nature of its cargo. On every available inch of deck space it carried large containers of Chiquita bananas. We also clearly identified the shipping line: Maersk, owned by cousins of Hans Isbrandtsen, with whom he once went into business.

The divers surfaced. None of them came up near the shot buoy, which had long since become disengaged from the wreck. Each diver had carried in his equipment a tall conical balloon, a high narrow elf's hat made of Day-Glo plastic. It tied to a device on his belt that looked like a fishing reel. If too far from the shot line or unable to find it, a diver releases the balloon called an MSB, a marker surface buoy, which then unspools the line from the reel and rises to the surface. When it appears, it rises so prominently above the waves that any boat can see it from a long way off. Soon, the diver should appear beside it—he guides himself up along his own line.

Four hours after the men went into the water, we saw the Day-Glo elves appear, one by one, all within an impressively close distance to the boat. Some rose no more than a few yards away. And one by one, each man made his way, with his MSB, to the metal diving platform at the stern, which had been lowered a few feet into the water. They had spent more than forty minutes down there and more than three hours on their slow ascent.

When they came on deck, everyone wished to help them, but nobody touched them; they seemed too remote, too enclosed. Each man found his place on the benches where he had kitted out before the dive and sat there, slowly divesting his gear. Rarely have I seen men look so exhausted. As they took off their equipment piece by piece and came back into the world above the sea, their common sense in winding down seemed finally almost the most impressive thing about them.

They said that they had seen the wreck clearly enough, although Leigh Bishop said he had had better light down there on other occasions. "Some days," he said, "it can be as bright as the Mediterranean." Not that day—but they saw enough to establish some essential facts.

There is nothing left, they said, on **Flying Enterprise.** The cupboard is totally bare. Nothing—not a knife or a spoon remains; it has been completely cleaned out. They found evidence of a great fissure just forward of the ship's buildings, the famous crack that Carlsen had stuffed with cement. And they also found evidence that someone had gone down there and blown apart sections of the wreck with explosives—and taken the strong room.

Were someone to raise her, there would be almost nothing to see of **Flying Enterprise**— just the same old barnacled rusting hulk as you'd find if you went diving on **General A. W. Greely,** on **Golden Eagle,** on **John W. Weeks,** on **Willard Keith,** all long since scuttled or sunk for target practice by the U.S. Navy.

43.

No pig iron, or grass seed, or Stradivarius violins; no bales of silk, barrels of port, and casks of brandy; no carved elephants of ebony with tusks of real ivory; no tobacco for my grandfather—the wreck of **Flying Enterprise** contained none of the poet Masefield's "diamonds, emeralds, amethysts, topazes, cinnamon, and gold moidores."

Masefield, however, still had a part to play.

As its editors prepared to make Carlsen "Man of the Year 1952," **Life** magazine quoted a Masefield poem in tribute: "The Old Man said, 'I mean to hang on / Till her canvas busts or her sticks are gone.' " Carlsen, as the editors at **Life** understood, had become the stuff of ballads. In time, ballad makers did celebrate him, as did country-and-western songwriters—and "Cap'n Carlsen of de Flyin' Enter-Prize" caught the imagination of men who write calypso and balladeers who could rhyme **compromise** with **Enterprise.**

ON RARE OCCASIONS, an event in the larger world enters the mind of a child and makes a lifelong and intimate home there. The deeper, the more arresting the remembrance and the more compelling the story, the more unshakably it will take root. Which essentially describes the cause and creation of this book: an engrossing incident declaimed across the world's headlines grabbed the imagination of a nine-year-old boy living in a remote country village and stayed forever.

When a story insists on being told, the storyteller cannot resist it. Carlsen and his **Flying Enterprise** seemed an obvious choice anyway, given all its narrative ingredients—but it always hinted that it had something else in it, something above and beyond the hero and adventure factors. I set out to list the possibilities: a boy's need for heroes; a struggle against great odds; our general powerlessness against the savagery of the elements; the romance of the ocean and the men who go down to the sea in ships; persistent bravery overcoming fear; being part of the universal response to an extraordinary tale—all the obvious reasons gleam.

It had the advantage, too, of relatively clean edges. Whereas our own life stories are messy and ill defined and we make them up day by day, **Flying Enterprise** had a beginning, a middle, and an end. And a future; as if to ensure that the story would not fade, all the "secret cargo" questions came up. Almost wonderfully, the thrilling incident matured into a mystery. When we thought the story had ended, a new story began, with stashes of money and government agents on the quayside and—maybe—diamonds.

Significantly, though, I also lived in—was born into—a ballad tradition. My other grandfather, gone a long time before my birth, had been a ballad maker, attacking landlords, praising the dead, eulogizing parish sportsmen and patriots. My mother's father, with his old freighters and sailors who stuck knives into their cork legs, and his glistening language, had even spoken like a man in a ballad.

Carlsen became for a time a local hero to us; his name, his voice, came into our living room every night, and we said prayers for him and gave thanks that he had been saved. So the news story that became personal grew heroic— perfect foundations for a ballad, for a legend.

Yet it had to be greater even than that to have struck so deeply. As a first level of thought, I came to believe that Carlsen had also drawn me into an adult male world, a real one, harder and more direct than, say, **Treasure Island**—because it was actually happening. In real life, my father talked incessantly of it, reminded us that it was taking place not much more than a hundred miles away.

My father became one of the motive forces for my interest. Obviously it had caught his imagination too, sufficiently for him to break his house rules and share the excitement with his children. As I came to get a better view of the austere, frightening Edward Joseph Delaney and his many hidden bewilderments over which he seemed to have little control, I came to understand what a huge gesture such a sharing must have been for him. Anger has always been the emotion by which I best recalled him, anger and sarcasm and aloofness.

But he showed another dimension when Carlsen came ashore and said over and over that he was only doing his job. My father made him a household lesson; he said that Carlsen, by his example, was teaching us things that grown-ups should know. The Danish sea captain and his exploits became, in effect, a schoolbook.

In the family I came last of eight, almost in some ways an only child. My siblings' cliques and claques had long been formed; not much more than eighteen months on average separated them from each other—while almost four years separated me from my nearest superior. The usual rivalries abounded and prevailed; the tensions of all large families became the rocks around which we navigated day by day. The riptide, however, swirled around my father.

He had many benign and wonderful qualities, chief among them a love for my mother that I can still perceive every time my mind visits them. He had a sharp and high intelligence and an elegant writing style. He had the rare gift of keeping friendships in good repair over many, many years.

Those who feared him—as I did—never got over their terror. And those who liked him loved him; he had laugh crinkles around his eyes and a raconteur's gift. Every movement of his life uttered responsibility and conscientiousness. His place in the parish, among the farmers and their hired hands, contributed to the running of their lives in a sound and practical way; he filled in their forms, applied for their agricultural grants. When he alone had a car, he drove birthing mothers to the hospital, bereaved relatives to the distant houses of their families or to train stations. His hip pocket acted as banker to the local blacksmith; he acted as presiding officer in elections, making sure with a dry, paradoxical wit that as few people as possible voted as often as possible.

And, paradox again, he delighted in words. I have one or two of his books, in which I often find little penciled notes of his soft humor in the margins: "You can't cure a ham with a hammer" and "In his castle slowly dying the Norman baron lay / While outside his serfs were crying 'Shorter hours and better pay' "—he had obviously been working on some ballad or parody relating to a labor chant of the time.

My father also had impeccable taste in poetry. Wordsworth enthralled him, and Coleridge; it was said that he could, for a wager, recite all of "The Rime of the Ancient Mariner" and make fewer than five mistakes. He loved Dryden, and Walter Savage Landor, and Alexander Pope, and I once heard him, for the sheer pleasure of enchanting my mother, speak all of Thomas Gray's "Elegy Written in a Country Churchyard." I was studying it in school at the time and had—as required— freshly memorized it; his rendition seemed flawless.

His clothes, their texture, their sensations, remain with me vividly. I recall a blue shirt made by Viyella, which specialized in soft wool textures, and the color seemed the same as his eyes. He wore a red paisley tie with it, and a tweed suit whose vast jacket I often fingered as it hung in his closet. The shoes also seemed huge to a small boy, with their brogue punchings and their eternal polish.

He had a shoe habit. My father polished his shoes every night of his life—and then came a time when he insisted on my nightly polishing of my own shoes. Over and over he gave them back to me, dissatisfied with the result, and I learned how not to polish over existing mud but to scrape it off, and only then try to shine the leather. Many years later, when my sanity was being challenged by the bombing, shooting, rioting, or kidnapping events that I found myself reporting, this footwear routine, which I inherited, saved me from myself and from my poor decisions and stabilized me, one day at a time.

His early days contained many difficulties. Of these, I knew little during his lifetime, and in the long years since his death I have only patchily assembled some of his story. For example, only when I visited a small graveyard out under the unique cloud formations of south Tipperary did I discover that he had had—unknown to me—a sibling, a child called Sarah, who'd died in 1916, at the age of five. He was twenty-two that year and I must believe that the bereavement permanently scarred him. It would in part account for the way in which his delight in small children began to fade when they reached five or six years old.

Nor had I known that when his own father died, my father was only fourteen. He was the oldest of nine children, which probably means that he never had a chance to finish living out his own childhood. His next phase remains shadowy; from what I can gather he won a position in the local elementary school as a "monitor," effectively a teaching assistant. At the same time, or later, he took local jobs with farmers or publicans or merchants to supplement his mother's tiny widow's pension. Eventually, he won a scholarship to teachers' college, graduated, and found the teaching position that eventually brought him to the village in which I grew up. And from that quiet base he became a well-known writer and newspaper columnist of his day, whose books of essays became nationally popular.

Even then his troubles had not ceased. In his late twenties, he had gone to Dublin, where he earned a good bachelor's and, in time, master's degree (in the wide discipline known as "Arts"). While he was away, local guerrillas mounted a bloody and successful ambush in our village against the British soldiers traveling between nearby garrisons.

In the army's reprisals that night, my father's house, the teacher's residence, was burned to the ground. Typically, many years later, when my father interviewed the same guerrillas to create a record of the event, he made scant mention of his own loss. Nor did he recount to any of his children his observations of the events he witnessed in the war of independence, which lasted from 1916 to 1922—and in which he had never participated. Likewise, he never spoke of the subsequent civil war. In fact, he rarely spoke to us of anything.

For all these reasons and many more, and

above all on account of his presence, his sheer personal force, my father exercised absolute power in the household. He must have had a true despotic streak: nothing influenced him, nothing impressed him, and he could generate more brain-melting fear than a gun barrel. This did not form a useful or vicarious fear, as did Cops and Robbers, Cowboys and Indians, Jim Hawkins and Long John Silver; Dracula or Frankenstein; such fears brought a corresponding comfort in their unreality. To this day, if I hear a footstep anything like my father's, I start in alarm as to a gunshot. Neighbors' children in the home parish have told me the terror they felt at his footfall in the church behind them.

Therefore, on account of all I had measured about my father, fear included, I had to figure that if he admired—and used as a text—a suddenly famous Danish sea captain who stood no higher than five feet six or seven inches tall, there had to be reasons beyond the obvious.

I can see some of them. A ballad maker's son would thrill to the feats of a hero. Also, my father had his own storms, and who is to say they were not, in their way, as savage as the tempests that almost devoured Carlsen? Duty also rode high in him, as did modesty; easy for him to identify with Carlsen's deflection of praise— for merely doing his job. Add the firmness of

Carlsen's bearing: my father cultivated a forbidding appearance. Even at the age of nine, I picked that up. The difference, though, seems to have been that this sea captain would not have to terrify me to make me behave well. And, as a bonus, my father so evidently admired him that my appreciation of the man would surely impress my father. The fact that it was constitutionally impossible for me to impress him did not dawn on me for years.

But at least I understand—and enjoy—my father's interest in Carlsen, and I relish its overlapping with mine. A teacher, perhaps even more than a politician, likes to watch history being made. So does a writer, especially a reporter. My father believed that Carlsen's name would endure; I wanted it to, because this sailor went straight into the long canon of marine greats, a line that stretches back to Homer, to Jason, to Odysseus. And, after all, they had all been celebrated by local poets.

The overlaps continue. Carlsen's shipmasterly aloofness from his crew also strikes a chord. By the time I reached the age of eight, my father couldn't bear to have a conversation with me; my arrival in a room often made him leave. I can also equate Carlsen's desire to bring in his ship with my father's anxiety to keep his school, to educate those in his professional and personal care, even if he did so with, it seemed, emotional cordite. And if he lost his school—what would he do, what would we do?

In the end of it all, when I tried to separate myself from my father (and failed), I understood that he suspected—perhaps even detected—something else about Carlsen, something with which he could identify from his own spirit and that I never thought about until it was told to my face by Carlsen's daughters. My father, for all his faults, admired a certain kind of character supremely—and occasionally judged accurately; Carlsen, too, had a wife to whom he was devoted, a wife who repeatedly said, "He did it for me."

44.

HANS ISBRANDTSEN DIED IN MAY 1953, on Wake Island in the North Pacific. On his way back from Japan, he had stopped on Wake, where he had business interests. In the heat, he dropped to the ground and died shortly afterward. He was sixty-two; until the end his spirit remained huge—the doctor who pronounced him dead could not believe he had survived moments, much less hours, after a coronary attack so large.

Two years later, Captain Dan Parker fell from the bridge of **Turmoil** as she went through the Strait of Dover. By the time they got to a dock, he had died. Although he recognized that he had been compelled by the sea, he had never formed an affection for it and had always been afraid of it. He never wanted the sea to be his grave; the men who served under him knew that he wanted his life to end ashore, with, as he said, "an organ pealing slow music—and flowers."

Captain Carlsen also died ashore. At the age of seventy-five, he suffered a cardiac arrest at a quarter past midnight on the morning of Saturday, October 7, 1989. He had been suffering from Parkinson's disease, which had gradually reduced him physically. Finally, it impaired his powers of recall too—but on at least one occasion, despite an otherwise total departure from the world of his memory, he jolted back. When somebody admired a model of **Flying Enterprise** in his room, he became lucid and for some moments even seemed prepared to talk about it.

Which had not been the case in his daily life, where he'd always wished that the story would simply go away. When he first came back, Isbrandtsen's office, after an initial and sincere welcome that lasted less than an hour, gave him the boon of a no-nonsense atmosphere. Hans Isbrandtsen, even though he had worried for Carlsen's safety, shared his skipper's view that a job was being done, that a ship had to be brought home—and to a certain extent he shared Carlsen's bewilderment and irritation at the ongoing hullabaloo. He also grasped, though, the publicity and marine-commerce value of Carlsen's image.

In London, on his way to see Captain Thiele and the Danish ambassador, Carlsen had been invited by Lloyd's, the great marine underwriters, to ring an honored bell. The Dutch named a lifeboat after him; Carlsen launched it. But he rarely gave interviews—except to radio ham magazines or people with merchant marine connections.

From Morocco to Maine, almost every land in the world that had a shoreline awarded him medals. Belgium bestowed the Maritime Medal for Merit; from France came the Merchant Marine Order of Merit. Honored among his own, he was hailed by the National Federation of Shipping, representing American ship owners; and by the Veteran Wireless Operators Association, which gave him the Marconi Memorial Outstanding Service Award. Add

the American Institute of Marine Underwriters
and the American Legion membership medal;
he also received the U.S. Merchant Marine
Distinguished Service Medal and the American
Bureau of Shipping Gold Valor Medal.

For a time, Carlsen went along with the
rock-star status. Graciously, he accepted the
honors with which he became festooned, and
graciously he recognized the awarders' need to
laud him. He smiled during the receptions
they created for him, including a great parade
in Woodbridge, where the town council
named a park for him. (Residents continued to
celebrate him in Woodbridge, with a great
banquet in 1985.) On they came with their
awards, and on they came with their ribbons,
and on they came with their citations. Carlsen
could have been on the road seven days a week
around the world, smiling, pinning medals to
his lapels, still saying, "I was only doing my
job." Instead, he went back to the sea.

Even there, his fame pursued him. Jakob Isbrandtsen told me that they could have sold
the twelve-berth allocation for passengers on
Flying Enterprise II many times over, on account of all the people who wanted to sail with
Carlsen and who seemed to care little as to destination. "Most of the inquiries," Mr. Isbrandt-

sen added, "just happened to come from ladies."

In foreign ports, reporters and local politicians scanned shipping lists for his impending arrival, and an official welcome often followed. For as many years as he lived, people wished to meet Carlsen, talk to him, shake his hand, peer into his face, looking for the ocean's scars.

Outwardly, Carlsen seemed to take all this in his stride. As ever, he exuded the impeccable manners and gallantry of the traditional officer, and when decorated, he repeated the standard demurral that he spoke at his great welcome in New York: "I am no more than a humble sea captain." He said it when the U.S. Senate honored him on Capitol Hill; he said it on every subsequent occasion on which he was required to speak. Carlsen being Carlsen, that was exactly what he meant to say—because that was how he wished the world to view him.

The world took a different view. Carlsen's deeds and his justification of them continued to call wide attention to moral obligation. **Flying Enterprise** had caused the world to discuss a man's responsibility to his employers and to his own profession and to duty. Politicians praised him for their own purposes; my father was not the only teacher to cite Carlsen as a role model; Oxford University announced that it "has chosen the story of Capt. Kurt Carlsen and the **Flying Enterprise** as a subject for undergraduate poets"—entrants would compete for the distinguished Newdigate Prize.

Those around him, however—his wife, his daughters, his friends—knew very well that the subject of **Flying Enterprise** brought Carlsen acute discomfort. His internal feelings on the matter differed widely from the world's perception, but he had too much grace to deny the public the hero that it had created. (Sonia Carlsen Fedak has said to me, "Why would I ask him questions about it? I didn't want to hurt his feelings.") Nevertheless Carlsen rebelled—a little—against the world's praise. The family got an invitation to appear on **The Ed Sullivan Show;** Carlsen declined. The sponsors offered him a Buick if he would appear; Carlsen went down to his local car salesroom that same day and bought a new Oldsmobile. Private schools in New Jersey sought his children; Sonia and Karen stayed where they were.

It became noticeable that Carlsen never raised the story of **Flying Enterprise** unless and until someone else did. As time went on, this diffidence escalated—for two reasons. On one level, he could not understand why people got so excited about a man carrying out his duty; on another level, he felt deep personal shame.

He knew that the fraternity of sea captains judged him by its—and his—own harsh standards, because he knew that he would have felt the same had the calamity occurred to one of his colleagues rather than to himself, especially if he saw them "grandstanding" after the ship went down. By his own measure, he was now the rarity that no seaman ever wants to become: a captain who had lost a ship. Effort had not been enough; the ship had not come into port.

Too shrewd not to read between the lines of the Coast Guard inquiry's summary, he remained too honest not to be stung by it privately. He never failed to defend his decisions on stowage and on his actions after the fracture; he believed that he had done the right things. Similarly, he believed in his decision to stay aboard—to him, the very notion of leaving his ship afloat on the sea and her then being taken on successfully by some other passing ship or predatory tug would have been a disgrace. Much worse would his life have been if he had left her while she had a remote chance of being saved—and the temptation had not been small. And he believed, until the very last moment, that he'd had a chance of making it to some sort of safety.

So on and on he went, swallowing his embarrassment at the many laudatory greetings, welcomes, and honors. Carlsen understood the goodwill behind them, and the general need to be associated with someone who is perceived as having done something heroic. But in this, too, he saw a kind of duty—although no matter what anyone said to him or about him, they could never make him feel heroic.

Kenneth Dancy understood this—and shared in it. His eyes never flickered, he didn't shift his feet, and he showed none of the usual human flinches of falsehood as he said, "No, we weren't heroes. We were two men trying to do a difficult job. Yes, the circumstances were bad, but what were we to do? Carlsen was trying to save his ship and I was a mate on the tug that was trying to help him save his ship. That's all there is to it."

Which is, of course, not the case; there are matters of character and there are matters of behavior and both men shine through on both counts. Neither exhibited the trait of boastfulness. A storm threw them together and they behaved—at the very least—according to their training: as two merchant seamen in trouble at sea.

Unless he fooled everybody, which I utterly doubt, Carlsen never pulled a cynical shrug; he felt nothing but regret over the fate of his ship. When, on rare occasions, he unbuttoned, he told inquirers that, after all, the ship had been his home. It had died under him, he said. He had presided over a dead ship. He had wanted to bring it back to life.

IN THE FINAL perception of him, Carlsen stood at the bridge of two generations, between those who felt hero worship for this stainless mariner, and those who asked the cynical question "What's in it for him?" On the one hand, the world had permitted him to become a hero as it used to have heroes; on the other hand, it began to smear him, as it would later tarnish everybody in the public eye. Yet no matter what Carlsen heard, good or bad, he never turned cynical about what he had been through.

The true reason for the lack of cynicism had, naturally, something to do with Carlsen's own nature. But something more than duty to his employer, something that canceled all cynicism drove Carlsen—something extra in his motivation that adds a deeper luster to his name and deeds.

45.

THE SAILOR'S WIFE WAITED FOR HER husband to come home. She also had to endure a tempest—a whirlwind of publicity that blew, scouring and cold, through every crevice of her life. Camera lenses peered in her windows. Her children had to be taken out of school to evade the reporters and photographers at the playground.

Every newsreel every night ran footage of the life that she had thought would always be private. In its coverage and feverishness, its stress and excitability, this was—for her, at any rate—the world's first truly invasive media event, and she was lit as brightly as any star.

Even in the moment of triumph, she had no hiding place. **The New York Times** wrote, "At City Hall, where Mrs. Carlsen straightened the red ribbon after the Mayor had hung it around her husband's neck, her tear-filled eyes and trembling lips betrayed her and for a moment she seemed on the verge of faintness." For a woman of her temperament, this exposure equaled a private Force 12.

As well as the invasion of privacy, her husband's sudden prominence had another painful twist, one that only another woman of her background could understand. All across the universe, people of whom she had never heard, and whom she would never meet, other wives, mothers, and daughters, reached out to her. They crocheted samplers for her; their children painted pictures and scribbled poems. The letters and packages arrived by the thousands, so many that they had to be piled into barrels.

As she herself came of a tradition where hospitality has to be answered, all of this pitched her into a one-sided relationship where, to her pain, she could never repay these kindnesses. Her ordinary social pride, key to her knowledge of who she was and what she came from, was subjected to fierce and unprepared-for pressure.

Her distress, she told me, became great. Yet whatever the natural anxiety, from which she suffered intensely, and whatever the fear for her husband's well-being and survival, she also had to keep face. She knew she had to turn away all the "How does it feel to be married to a hero?" questions with the calm answer "My husband is only doing his duty" when it was her inner voice that asked the most critical questions: "Is he all right? Will he drown?"

Daily she had to cope with the images of her husband being hammered by the Atlantic, dramatic pictures of Carlsen clinging to the lurching "old ship." The head of her family had been reduced to a tiny and threatened figure. Each of the three Carlsens at home had to think, in Sonia's and Karen's words, "How can he hold on? That deck is wet. That deck is cold. That deck is icy. How in the world can he hold on to that railing and grab that size rope?" They added, "I didn't understand how he could do it."

They knew about the beer and pound cake, they knew he was sleeping on the walls because the ship is listing. They knew that, as they said to me, "the waves could come in that door any minute."

The family operated out of a deep religious faith. In April 1958, six years after Carlsen came home from his accident, the **Reno Evening Gazette** published an inspirational column called "Lenten Guideposts" with, as guest contributor, Agnes Carlsen. Writing under the subheading "Storm Lashed Prayer," she described how, after a neighbor had alerted her, she had turned on the radio to hear that her husband's ship had a cracked hull and was being battered in the Atlantic by waves fifty feet high. In the newspaper, she described much of what she later told me in conversation, when she emphasized how many "friends telephoned to say that they were praying for us. It seemed the whole world was joining us in prayer."

During our telephone conversations, Mrs. Carlsen often broke off from the steady path of inquiry we seemed to be following to say, "I never had any doubt that he would be safe." She did so again when I went to see her in Michigan.

In one interview, when again I raised the issue of Carlsen's decision to stay aboard come what may, I asked did she think it had necessarily taken her and the children into sufficient account? He might, after all, have drowned, leaving his family bereft.

It seems never to have occurred to her. The Reno newspaper piece concludes with a description of Carlsen coming home to Woodbridge, after the ticker-tape parade and the cheering crowds.

"We all sat down. It was our Christmas. Kurt looked up and saw the tears in my eyes.

" 'There's no need,' he said. 'We're together now.' "

In response to my question, "What was he saying beneath the surface of that remark? What did he mean by 'There's no need'?" Agnes said, as she would repeat many times,

"He did it for me, he stayed on board for me." In the **Reno Evening Gazette** she concluded that her husband's strength was "always there" when he needed it.

Both of her daughters later gave me a different interpretation of "He did it for me." By itself, their revelation offers perhaps the most powerful reason of all for the insistence in his actions. It supersedes Carlsen's duty to his ship, to his tradition, and to his owner. It even rises above his simple statement, "They gave me a ship to bring out and they told me to bring it back." And yet it is tied to all of those things.

IN 1944, AGNES, always timid, went into a severe emotional hiatus and entered Smith-town Mental Hospital, Long Island. She was diagnosed as suffering a severe nervous break-down; she had even torn out her own hair. A number of factors had contributed to her distress. Carlsen was at war, working convoys; the newspapers carried daily reports of sinking ships; Agnes still had difficulty speaking English. Above all, as Karen had recently been born, she was suffering from something so little understood at the time that it hadn't yet been named: postpartum depression.

With the father absent at sea and the mother

too frail to look after the children, the hospital began to make arrangements for the care of the baby and Sonia, not yet five. Carlsen got shore leave. He collected Sonia from an aunt in Brooklyn and took her to the hospital. The mother did not recognize Sonia and asked Carlsen, "Who is this little girl?"

As Sonia Carlsen tells it, her father, speaking to her in Danish in one of the hospital corridors, explained to her that he had to go back to sea and that she and her baby sister would have to go into an orphanage, that she, too, would have to be looked after by other people, that there was nobody to whom he could "give" her, because her aunt had to go back to her work.

Anita Trygsland, also Danish, who owned a beauty parlor on Long Island, was at the hospital that day as a volunteer worker. Mrs. Trygsland overheard Carlsen explaining the difficult matters to Sonia; she watched the painful conversation between father and child and eavesdropped further. Then she intervened: she offered to take Sonia and Karen into her home that same day.

The Carlsen children lived with the Trygsland family for seven months, until Agnes recovered; Mrs. Trygsland became part of the recovery pattern, visiting Agnes every day and easing her back into normal life.

After this, however, Carlsen understood that should Agnes fall ill again, he could lose both children to institutions; Sonia had probably been no more than a conversation away from an orphanage. This fact haunted him. He would not have been the first seaman to whom this had happened, and he found many ways of watching over Agnes, of supporting her, even when away at sea. She often traveled with him, as did the children, and he set up the radio contacts for the specific purpose of keeping in the closest possible touch.

He also knew that as a ship's master, he could exercise some control over his times at sea, were another crisis to develop. Therefore, although to a limited extent, he could maintain an influence over his family's destiny more than an ordinary seaman would be able to.

However, were he to lose his ship, especially through any perceived carelessness, neglect, or unskilled misadventure, he would not get another—and thus he would lose all control over the time he could spend ashore. He would lose his license; he would lose his power; he would lose his place in his life. Agnes knew this too; that lay beneath her repeated comment to me that "a master who loses his ship loses his cap." By demonstrating to his owner that he was prepared to fight without limit for any ship under his command, Carlsen took steps to prevent Isbrandtsen from being able to dismiss him. To Carlsen's good fortune, the world stopped to observe what he was doing, and all chance of his not getting another ship evaporated—Isbrandtsen, whatever he thought of Carlsen's great effort, would never go against that tide of public approval—and Carlsen did not lose his symbolic "cap."

EPILOGUE

ON THE NORTH ATLANTIC THAT winter, **Flying Enterprise** became a powerful moment in the life of the times. One man died in the waves; several others reached into themselves and found resources they never knew they possessed—and never afterward forgot. More than one man emerged from the incident with great and deserved status.

Other matters triumphed: tradition, duty, responsibility, human nature. Not just the ancient tradition that says that aboard ship the word **master** is what it means (after all, it derives from words that, centuries ago, meant **powerful** and **upright,** as in **mast**); more than the honorable tradition that the captain will be the last to leave his ship. And not just duty in the narrow sense of doing what is asked by one's employers: but duty in the sense of my father's lecture, meaning "du tout," giving everything: George Brown in his engine room; Robert Lumpkins, the cook, who tried to ease Mrs. Dannheiser's worries and who put Lothar

Müller's safety above his own; Cyril Francis, who almost drowned trying to save a woman whom nobody else wanted to help. Kenneth Dancy sat facing me in his house in Holland and said, "We weren't heroes"—as if his impulsive action and his conduct in the environment he willingly took on thereafter were commonplace. He may call it a "step"; the world thought it gigantic.

Human nature came best out of it—on all sides, in spontaneous bravery, in expressions of support, in goodwill. Few people behaved badly; many behaved superlatively. And a man still in his thirties went far beyond the call of duty to protect a frail wife and mother.

Carlsen's accusers said he should have turned back when the ship cracked. He believed that he had done the right thing. None of his official interrogators disagreed. And: he saved all his passengers except one, while all around him ships were splitting in half and seamen were dying in the waves. A great number of shipmasters in the North Atlantic during those days would have given a great deal to have accomplished a fraction of what Carlsen achieved.

They said his cargo shifted because he had stowed it less than perfectly. But the Coast

Guard inquiry found that the method of stowing the pig iron conformed with port practice at that time—and Carlsen himself said, with no hint of defiance, that he would have stowed it in the same way again. At the end of it all, his motives, however intensely they were questioned, now seem to me as visible as he meant them to be—even if they do have modifying shades. He may, for instance, have had an eye to Isbrandtsen's protection, especially if H.I. wasn't paying enough money in dock labor, as a result of which they had had to hasten the stowing of the pig iron. And it's possible that he suspected the European gem traders of loading him up with stuff and that the zirconium had stayed off the manifest because of classification.

But it wouldn't have mattered; Carlsen would have stayed on that ship if she had been carrying a cargo of sludge. If he had left her lying there on her side, the world—and his boss—would have seen only a captain abandoning a ship. That remained his primary motive: not to leave her for anyone else to pick up.

Usually at the end of a search, at the resolving of a compulsion, a hollow must surely form around the heart. As the adrenaline drains away, an unease could so easily spread. But in tracing Carlsen, I found that something began to counter the natural fatigue of investigating a legend: the comfort that lies in observing generations.

I now believe that I latched onto this story for very specific reasons, unknown to me then and only slowly coming to light as the tale began to tell itself. Carlsen offered me another idea of a father. Significantly, one of the questions that I seem to have asked most frequently is "What was he like at home?" By all accounts—and this came from beyond his family too—he was a soft and loving father, as delightful with his family as he was hard at sea. He had a warmth that I never saw in my own father.

Therefore, and with complete if unexpressed logic, I began to wonder what kind of father he might have been to me. I wondered it at the time, and now I believe I know. This is not the same as saying that I wanted a hero for a father, as small boys do; this is a search for another way of being fathered, by a man who was hard but not hurtful, who was direct but not terrifying, who also understood duty and responsibility but didn't need to make them frightening.

Nor do I believe that I pursued a fantasy about a man who could have been a perfect father. It feels more the case that, first of all, I admired this man because my father admired him too, and thus I could win approval. Second—and this was in adulthood—if my father saw so much in Carlsen, whom I never found wanting when I went looking for him, then my father had better qualities than I have allowed him. He did, after all, enable me, one way and another, to come out into the world with the curiosity to search for such a marvelous tale to tell.

Over and over, I have regretted not meeting Captain Carlsen. Unlike the sailor with the cork leg, the imagination does not feel the better for it. I believe I would have found the man I have written about. What was it everybody said about him? "What you saw was what you got." Which, it seems, was a lot.

AND CARLSEN'S EFFECT goes on, in other lives, outside of me and the village of my mind. This story began with my grandfather and intensified on account of my father, both of whom, like me, have never been seamen. Looking forward, Captain Carlsen's grandchildren build school projects about their grandfather. When I called or met seamen of the period, a number of them said, with some pride and always intense interest, "I sailed with Captain Carlsen."

The "small house with a garden" in New Jersey that Carlsen bought for Agnes at the suggestion of her doctors on Long Island still stands. Agnes sold it in 1992 to Juan Maldonado, a Hispanic immigrant. Mr. Maldonado had been searching for a good school district; his two young children had shown immense promise.

In the real estate transaction, Mr. Maldonado came up short by ten thousand dollars. He told the Realtor, who suggested he tell Agnes—who was accompanied by Karen, herself a Realtor. Agnes waived the burden of the ten thousand dollars and helped Mr. Maldonado find a way of financing the house. She said her husband would have done the same.

On the street outside the house with the garden, whose neat, wooden kin I have seen in the shadows of Hamlet's castle in Denmark, Mr. Maldonado tells me with tears in his eyes that his two children—whose intelligence he had carefully outlined to Mrs. Carlsen—have scored unprecedentedly high grades in each of their schools. Both will go to distinguished schools, Harvard and Boston College. Mr. Maldonado gives credit for this to "the example of the immigrants who lived in this house before us"—i.e., the Carlsens.

A few moments earlier, I had asked him, on his own doorstep, "Do you know who lived here?"

Mr. Maldonado said, "Yes. A hero."

ACKNOWLEDGMENTS

IN THE YEARS SINCE 1952, SURPRIS-
ingly little work has appeared discussing Kurt
Carlsen and S.S. **Flying Enterprise**. There
have been a handful of radio and television seg-
ments and documentaries, some chapters in
books, an interview-based article in **The New
Yorker,** and occasional pieces in seafaring or
amateur radio journals. In the absence of a
substantial bibliography, therefore, and since
many of these secondary sources seemed so often to conflict with one another, the piecing
together of this narrative had to come from as
many primary records as possible: eyewitness
narrative, personal experience, sworn testimony, contemporary record.

A good deal of the detail was originally assembled by means of conversation, but here I
have difficulty in paying due thanks—because
this story was for a long time no more than an
informal and private search into my own past.
Thus, in forty years or so, I have spoken to
more people than I can recall, had more infor-

mal discussions than I later—or ever—did formally, asked questions of passing strangers, received vivid information from people I would never see again. If I could remember everyone I met who recalled **Flying Enterprise,** or who offered a thought on this astounding and famous incident, I should be pleased beyond measure to thank them one at a time.

I now thank them collectively. They included seafarers in Irish and Danish towns—in fact all along Europe's northwestern coasts; ocean and meteorological scientists; officers and crew from the merchant marine; men who worked tugs and towropes; journalists, policemen, and clergy in various towns and cities, some of whom attempted to track down survivors for me; veterans' associations; heritage and museum groups in Europe and the United States; and professional seamen and hobby sailors who sailed with Captain Carlsen and who said so proudly. They all helped to shape the story. And, individually and cumulatively, they often gave me a stronger flavor of the sea, of the merchant marine, and of **Flying Enterprise** and its skipper that more formal sources would (rightly) have eschewed.

Of the others who have addressed this subject, I hope I have been sensible enough to take guidance from them, especially in the chronology of events. Particularly, I wish to acknowledge James Dugan's **American Viking** (Harper & Row, New York, 1963). Mr. Dugan's biography of Hans Isbrandtsen remains as energetic and informative a profile as has ever been written about the world of commercial shipping. His four chapters on the **Flying Enterprise** saga adorn a book already crammed with valuable and enjoyable material. And since he also undertook a sea voyage with Carlsen, his insights into the man permeate his book.

In **Alone Through the Dark Sea** (George Braziller, New York, 1962), Thomas Whiteside persuaded Captain Carlsen to speak of his great event. The resulting article, with Carlsen's unprecedented comments on his famous experiences, shines a bright light on a man troubled by his own feat.

Of the people to whom I can directly express gratitude, I must begin with Sonia Carlsen Fedak and her husband, Robert Fedak; with Karen Carlsen Mueller; and—though it is regrettably too late to do anything except record my appreciation—with Agnes Carlsen, who passed away in October 2005, at the age of ninety-four. This family, who had had good reason to distrust the media, showed me extensive kind and open supportiveness and did not flinch at the most intrusive of questions. In their uncalculating candor, they keep their flame alive in the best way possible—by forthright response.

Next, I wish to thank Kenneth Dancy, the onetime mate of the tug **Turmoil**. Though understandably reluctant to have this long-ago event revisited yet again, he permitted me to intrude upon his home and his time, proved generous with fact and detail, and allowed me to tape record him at length. The inflections of his voice, when repeatedly listened to long after our interview, sometimes enlightened me as much as his actual words.

Jakob Isbrandtsen gave me long and generous hours of his time and access to such records as he still possesses; he also offered refreshing redirection on different aspects of how the story and its characters had been perceived. Ben Stevenson supplied valuable and objective perceptions of Carlsen and his family.

My assistant in the early reaches, Michael Clyne, searched deep and long for survivors and veterans; in the course of his enquiries he uncovered valuable tangential information, always an author's joy. Bill Cronin of the New York Port Authority opened up, in two telephone conversations, not merely lines but rivers of research, as did Frank Breynard. Robert Schnare at the Naval War College in

Newport, Rhode Island, and his reference librarian colleague, Alice Juda, steered me through a difficult and crucial thicket regarding U.S.S. **General A. W. Greely** and directed me to possible sources of information about the unsung heroes of that ship. From sources that I had long been gathering and from the BBC archives, Simon Elmes of the BBC produced a gripping commemorative documentary; in the process, he helped to sharpen my focus.

Leanne Müller Smith of Sandy, Utah, relived willingly the events of the shipwreck and rescue; her energy of recollection embodied the insight of the true eyewitness. Sonia Rimback gave me pertinent detail about the connection between her mother, Mrs. Trygsland, and the Carlsen family. The incomparable Leigh Bishop provided an insider's view of the wrecked ship on the ocean floor, as did John Chatterton, Richard Kohler, and Evan Kovacs. I am especially grateful to them all for permitting me to watch them at work. Juan Maldonado, who now owns the Carlsen family home, graciously allowed me to invade his privacy.

My special thanks go to the television producer/director for the History Channel, Jonathan Robinson, who, while creating his own reconstruction of the story, read the manuscript in progress, challenged many assumptions, and raised different interpretations of sworn evidence. He also shared detailed research with me, including his files of sworn testimonies from the National Archive in Washington—whose librarians I must also thank for enquiries answered with unfailing courtesy down the years. Kirk Wolfinger and Dana Rae Warren of Lone Wolf Productions in Portland, Maine, facilitated my observations of the last resting place of **Flying Enterprise,** and I render special thanks to Mika Lentz for her generosity.

The staffs of the following institutions helped in large and small ways: the New York Public Library; the British Library, especially its newspaper division at Colindale; the Naval Dockyards in Plymouth; the Plymouth Public Library; Jordan's Salvage Yard, Portsmouth; Captain George Hogg of the National Maritime Museum, Falmouth, Cornwall; the voluntary complement of U.S.S. **John W. Brown** in Baltimore.

I also wish to express gratitude to the Library of the Merchant Marine Academy at King's Point, Long Island; Greenwich Maritime Institute; the National Library in Dublin; the London Meteorological Office; the Irish Meteorological Service; the National Oceanic and

ACKNOWLEDGMENTS   *457*

Atmospheric Administration (NOAA)—all of these offices gave me unfettered access, and some gave me innumerable and patient explanations of weather patterns, marine phenomena, and other—sometimes unrelated—matters. Unnamed and numerous members of the United States Coast Guard always proved willing to answer a question from a stranger; inquiries that to them may have seemed commonplace were to me vital. As to the merchant marine, in one simple encounter, Captain Charles Weeks, who may know more about freight ships than any man alive, summarized Captain Carlsen for me.

Rich Remsberg provided a wealth of illustrations—many of his **Flying Enterprise** photographs stimulated ideas that appeared in the text. Dinah Molloy directed me toward an aspect of the event's deeper effects that I might otherwise have missed. Kaja Gam gave me valuable pointers to the Danish character and the ongoing status of Captain Carlsen in his home country; Ethan Enzer proved crucially helpful at a moment that made a great difference to my searching; Jean Gallo and Jeff Memoli helped through understanding.

If I have overlooked contributions, then those errors and omissions, along with any others that arise from this text, are mine alone and I ask forgiveness and offer only the lame excuse of an eye too close to the subject matter to permit a wider view. But I do want to pay tribute to the passengers and crew of S.S. **Flying Enterprise;** not only did they brave frightful seas and keep themselves and their fellow travelers alive—they also reconstructed their traumatic experiences for the purposes of the official Coast Guard record.

At Random House, the production supervision of Dennis Ambrose and Benjamin Dreyer gave me the copy editing of Bonnie Thompson; in this, they not only threw an extra safety net under me, but did so in the shared way that makes the technical side of authorship a delight. Nicole Bond, Jacob Bronstein, Sanyu Dillon, Karen Fink, Stephanie Higgs, Matthew Kellogg, London King, Thomas Perry, and Clare Tisne all play on the team led by the remarkable Gina Centrello; she took a direct interest in this story and I am grateful for the sharp interest she has shown this book. Her colleagues, Laura Goldin and Janice Barcena, with Michael Rudell, and Eric Brown at Franklin, Weinrib, Rudell, & Vasallo, steered this work into existence, and I am grateful to them for their patience, ethics, and good humor. And in my own office, David Goodwin, Ben Goodwin, and Lyndon Mosse, all stimulatingly unimpressed, listened patiently and unwearily to theories, ideas, thoughts, possibilities, and endless running commentary.

Finally, my peerless editor at Random House is Daniel Menaker. Of him, the less I say the more I applaud. In the same deeply felt vein of gratitude and admiration, I thank my wife, Diane.

ABOUT THE AUTHOR

FRANK DELANEY was born in Tipperary, Ireland. **Ireland** was his first novel to be published in the United States. Following a career in broadcasting in the United Kingdom, he now lives in New York and Connecticut.